ADMINISTRATIVE COUNTY GOVERNMENT IN SOUTH CAROLINA

THE UNIVERSITY OF NORTH CAROLINA
SOCIAL STUDY SERIES

UNDER THE GENERAL EDITORSHIP OF HOWARD W. ODUM. BOOKS MARKED WITH *
PUBLISHED IN COÖPERATION WITH THE INSTITUTE FOR RESEARCH IN SOCIAL SCIENCE.

The University of North Carolina Press, Chapel Hill, N. C.; The Baker and Taylor Co., New York; Oxford University Press, London; The Maruzen Company, Tokyo; Edward Evans & Sons, Ltd., Shanghai; D. B. Centen's Wetenschappelijke Boekhandel, Amsterdam.

ADMINISTRATIVE COUNTY GOVERNMENT IN SOUTH CAROLINA

BY

COLUMBUS ANDREWS, A.M.

Research Assistant, Institute for Research in Social Science
University of North Carolina

ADDENDUM BY

MARION A. WRIGHT

CONWAY, SOUTH CAROLINA

CHAPEL HILL
THE UNIVERSITY OF NORTH CAROLINA PRESS
1933

FOREWORD

For the past few years it has been the feeling—almost the conviction—of a small but growing group of students and public-spirited citizens that county government in South Carolina was being operated at low levels of economy and efficiency. The official records of the State were persistently revealing unsatisfactory conditions in the organization and administration of county affairs. But nowhere in the State did there exist a body of scientific information and thought on the subject. No one could speak with authority. No one knew the conditions in detail, and the causes. And no one was in defensible position to make suggestions for improvement. Individuals and agencies have all but neglected this phase of the public life of the State.

Therefore, when in 1930 the Institute for Research in Social Science of the University of North Carolina offered to coöperate with the University of South Carolina in a close study of the subject the opportunity was eagerly seized. Beginning in June, 1930, Mr. Andrews spent the remainder of the year in South Carolina making intensive studies in six representative counties, namely: Fairfield, Darlington, Williamsburg, Colleton, Aiken, and Laurens. With the material thus collected together with that contained in official documents of South Carolina and a wide selection of more general works the study was continued for the greater part of 1931. The result is the present volume.

It is of course not claimed that this work represents the last word on county government in South Carolina. However, Mr. Andrews has with rare understanding given its historical development, its present organization and administration, and has in the concluding chapter made distinctly constructive suggestions. He has laid the ground work for improved county affairs.

Not the least important part of this volume is the *addendum*, "Suggested Changes in County Government and County Affairs in South Carolina," by Mr. M. A. Wright, Chairman of the Committee on Government of the South Carolina Council. Mr. Wright's work in this field constitutes a contribution of high order.

It must be here recorded that this study would have in all probability remained in manuscript form but for the interest and generosity of the Contingent Fund Committee of South Carolina, composed of Governor Ibra C. Blackwood, Senator S. M. Ward, and Representative Neville Bennett. It was by a small grant from this committee that publication and distribution has been made possible.

S. M. DERRICK.

University of South Carolina,
Columbia, S. C.,
September 28, 1932.

ACKNOWLEDGMENTS

Interest in county government is rapidly becoming widespread throughout the country. Those who first began to explore the problems of country life found rural government already outworn, as it still is, standing as a barrier to effective civic activity. The growing burden of taxation is forcing the attention of others upon it. But its significance as a factor in the development of rural life is not yet generally understood.

This work is an attempt to contribute somewhat to the growing interest in the subject. It represents some fourteen months of investigation and study, six months of which were spent in making case-method surveys of county governments. It portrays what is believed to be an unique system of county government and makes some suggestions in the light of modern political science for its improvement.

The author is under many obligations to numerous citizens and local and state officials of the State of South Carolina for assistance rendered. Foremost among these is Dr. S. M. Derrick of the University of South Carolina. He is indebted also to Dr. E. C. Branson, University of North Carolina, for constant counsel and guidance while gathering the material and in preparing the manuscript; and to Dr. Paul W. Wager and Miss Henrietta Smedes of the Department of Rural Social Economics, University of North Carolina, for reading the manuscript.

COLUMBUS ANDREWS.

Chapel Hill, N. C.,
August 27, 1931.

TABLE OF CONTENTS

PART I

THE DEVELOPMENT OF COUNTY GOVERNMENT IN THE STATE

CHAPTER

The Origin and Early Settlement of Carolina; The Parish, an Ecclesiastical District; The Care of the Poor; The Parish Becomes an Election District; Road Districts; The Courts, Taxation; Militia and the Patrol System; Schools.

From 1776 to 1868: Counties and County Courts; Districts Replace Counties; Roads and the Care of the Poor; Collection of Taxes; Popular Election of Local Officials; Schools; The Patrol System. The Close of the Ante-bellum Period. New Constitutions: Under the Constitution of 1868; The Name County Restored; Education; Under the Constitution of 1895; The County and Township; Consolidation of Counties; Taxation and Bonded Debt Limits; County Courts; Other Elective County Officials; Education; The Care of the Poor.

PART II

THE COUNTY GOVERNMENT AND ADMINISTRATION

The County Legislative Delegation; The County Board of Commissioners and Subordinate Officials; Officials Subordinate to the County Boards; The Clerk to the County Board; The County Highway Engineer; The Superintendent of the County Chaingang; The Superintendent of the County Poor Home and Farm; The County Attorney; The County Physician. County Finance Officials: The County Auditor; Township and District Boards of Assessors; The County Board of Equalization; The County Treasurer; The Delinquent Tax Collector; The Sinking Fund Commission. County School Officials: The County Superintendent of Schools; The County Board of Education; District Trustees; Other School Officials. Court and Law Enforcement Officials: The Clerk of the Courts of Common Pleas and General Sessions; The Judge of Probate; Magistrates; Constables; Jurors; The Sheriff; Rural Police; Coroner; County Judges and Solicitors. County Election Officials: The Board of Registration; Election Commissioners. County Health, Conservation and Development Officials: County Health Boards and Departments; Game Wardens; Farm and Home Demonstration Agents. Summary.

PART III

CONSTRUCTIVE SUGGESTIONS

ADMINISTRATIVE COUNTY GOVERNMENT IN SOUTH CAROLINA

PART I

THE DEVELOPMENT OF COUNTY GOVERNMENT
IN THE STATE

CHAPTER I

THE COLONIAL PERIOD

The political history of South Carolina began with the settlement on the Ashley River in the year 1670, though the province was not known by that name until a later date. Carolina appears not to have been named for Charles IX of France, as is frequently stated, but by Charles I of England in 1629 in honor of himself.[1] It was originally a vast area including all that territory lying between Virginia on the north and the Spanish possessions on the south and extending west to the Pacific Ocean. With the legal division of the area into North and South Carolina about 1729 and with the establishment of the colony of Georgia, South Carolina became the smallest of the South Atlantic colonies. Its influence, however, is not to be measured by its geographical area.

The earlier colonists were mainly English, who came by way of the Barbadoes and brought with them such modifications of English institutions and customs as Barbadian life had produced. The English and Barbadian influences bound the colony very closely to the islands and also to the mother country. In addition to these there were other influences that have played no little part in giving the state the marked individuality which has characterized it throughout its history. The Atlantic lay between the colony and the mother country; hostile Indians were plentiful in the surrounding territory; until Georgia was settled in 1733, the colony was the outpost against the Spaniards and French, who were frequently threatening to encroach from the south. In the early days access to the other colonies on the mainland was not easy. Thus the colony was forced to depend largely on itself. For about three-quarters of a century its development was centripetal in character, to borrow a phrase from Dr. McCrady,[2] with Charleston as the focal point. This development extended some 60 to 90 miles from the coast. Beyond that was a wilderness and then the up country. From about 1736 Scotch-Irish settlers from the north began

[1] A. S. Salley, Jr., *The Origin of Carolina*, Bulletin No. 8 of the South Carolina Historical Commission, p. 3.
[2] Edward McCrady, *South Carolina under the Proprietary Government*, p. 5.

to locate in this up country. Thus two colonies grew up in the province with a strip of wilderness between them. Since they differed in backgrounds, in racial strains, and in environment, there began to develop that violent antagonism which marked the state's history for so long and which has not yet entirely disappeared. The coastal colony was a planter's colony, which developed largely through urban life. The settlements in the up country did not have the urban influence. The settlers who located in the state consisted mainly of English, French, Germans, Welsh, Scotch-Irish. They were assimilable racially and soon became a homogeneous people. It is notable, however, that the English influence emanating from Charleston was the major factor that moulded the present character of the state.

Due to their peculiar situation, to the racial strains out of which they came, and to the large and increasing number of slaves owned by them, the people of the colony developed a war-like spirit, a strong love of independence, and a sturdy spirit of self-reliance. As a result of these things and also of the centripetal development of the coastal settlements, the people became devoted to a principle which Dr. McCrady has called the autonomy of the state.[3] Devotion to this principle that the state had a right to govern itself without regard to outside influence subsided somewhat for a short period from about 1812 to 1817,[4] and then rose again. A certain aspect of the principle in combination with the aristocratic conception of the state which developed at Charleston has a bearing on the development of local government.

The colony not only manifested a strong determination to govern itself with little regard for influences from without, but also it resisted democratic influences from within. The creation of units with large powers of local control within the colony was doubtless unnecessary in the coastal area which was so closely identified with Charleston until long after the colonial period was over; nor did the influence of the up country definitely take the direction of establishing such units. The up country was concerned primarily with acquiring that voice in the affairs of the province to which it considered itself to be justly entitled. This cleavage between the two sections apparently had little direct effect upon

[3] Ibid., p. 10.
[4] David F. Houston, A Critical Study of Nullification in South Carolina, pp. 6 and 28-30.

the development of local government within the state. But the democratic influence of the up country prepared the state for the sudden creation of counties in 1868 and the delegation of corporate powers to them. Though the establishment of these units was mainly the work of aliens, the units were not greatly diminished in powers when the native whites came into control of the state again. This sudden change, however, was more apparent than real, for it left many of the important details of county government in the hands of the General Assembly. Then the constitution of 1895 increased the power of the General Assembly over the counties somewhat. Thus there remains the anomaly of county government largely centralized in the General Assembly, while at the same time it is as thoroughly decentralized and inefficient as perhaps can be found elsewhere on the continent.

With so much of an approach to the subject, let us now proceed to follow the course of the development of local government through the colonial period.

The inhabited part of the province was divided into the three counties of Craven, Berkeley, and Colleton in 1682, and a fourth was created a little later. These were counties in name only, and the name gave way later to that of district. Then in 1785 it came into general use again for a period of fourteen years; but there was no county government in the state before 1868.

The province of Carolina was granted to the Lords Proprietors by Charles II in 1663. With the maturing of plans for planting colonies in the province, Locke's elaborate scheme for the government of the colony was made. This plan the Lords Proprietors expected to put into operation, but their expectations were never realized. The plan was modified from time to time, but the modifications were never acceptable to the colonists. The only trace of the influence of the Grand Model may be found in the biennial election of the members of the assembly,[5] by which is meant the lower house, for the members of the state senate are chosen by popular vote for terms of four years each.

The government of the colony at first consisted of the governor, the council, and the representatives of the freemen. The council consisted of ten members, five of whom were chosen by the freemen. The freeholders were to elect a parliament of 20 members

[5] David Ramsay, *History of South Carolina*, I, 123.

also. After 1691 the term parliament gave way to that of assembly. The representatives of the freemen were elected at Charleston from the province at large until 1695. At that time the number was increased to 30, ten of whom were to be chosen at a point in Colleton County. This new voting precinct was perhaps not used very long.

For some years the grand council took upon itself the entire administration of affairs, legislative, executive, and judicial. In 1692 the assembly was divided into two houses and the elective element disappeared from the council. Almost from the first there was a continuous struggle between the governor and the council, or that part of it representing the proprietors, on the one hand, and the representatives of the freeholders on the other. This struggle continued with more or less variation in intensity until the Revolution, and it resulted in the acquisition of more and more power by the representatives of the freeholders, or the commons house of assembly, as they came to be called. But the first step taken towards the establishment of local government was in 1706. Parishes had been established by an act in 1704, but the act was not allowed. The act of 1706 dividing the colony into ten parishes was approved.[6]

The Parish, an ecclesiastical district. The parish officers during the colonial period consisted of the rector, churchwardens, vestrymen, sexton, clerk, register of births, marriages, and deaths, and the overseers of the poor. The business of the parish was managed by two churchwardens and the seven vestrymen, though the number of the latter was not uniform throughout the period. These officials were elected annually on Easter Monday in each parish by the members of the English church who were freeholders or taxpayers in the parish. Vacancies occurring in the vestry were filled by special meeting of the parish, while those among the wardens were filled by the vestry. The two bodies held their meetings separately; the wardens met whenever they chose, and the vestry regularly each quarter.

The register was appointed annually by the vestry. He took oaths, kept records of all vestry proceedings and of all births, christenings, marriages, and burials. The clerk kept the parish records and assisted the sexton in caring for the parish church and cemetery. Both of these officials were appointed by the vestry and served during their pleasure.[7]

The rector was an ex-officio member of the vestry, but his duties were principally those of providing for the spiritual welfare of the parish. He was elected by the "major part of the parishioners who are of the religion of the church of England and are settled freeholders within the parish or that contribute to the public taxes,"[8] but a vacancy might be filled by the vestry. The rector received a salary from the province varying from 50 to 100 pounds, and during his official connection with the parish he could make use of the glebe lands, the parish buildings, all the Negroes which belonged to the parish with their increase, and the parish cattle with their increase. He could be removed by the ecclesiastical commission of the province on petition of a majority of the vestrymen and nine freeholders.

When the parishes were first established, they were territorial divisions for church purposes only. The parish was introduced after the establishment of the church of England, which establishment had been secured despite much opposition. In 1698 a maintenance was settled on a minister of the church of England in Charleston, and in 1704 the church of England secured a legal establishment in the province, though it was outnumbered by dissenters. The provincial parliament at one time succeeded in virtually excluding all dissenters from the assembly, and though the measure was later repealed the Episcopalians continued to control the province.[9] When the law was passed dividing the inhabited part of the province into parishes, provision was made also for the erection of churches and chapels.

The care of the poor. From territorial divisions for church purposes the parishes grew gradually into political divisions which took on some of the characteristics of local government. In 1712 the care of the poor was given to the parishes. Before that time the poor had been under the care of a board of five commissioners appointed by the assembly. After that date the vestry of each

---

[7] *Ibid.*, p. 70 ff.

[8] George E. Howard, *An Introduction to Local Constitutional History of the United States,* p. 127 ff.

[9] B. J. Ramage, *Local Government and Free Schools in South Carolina,* Johns Hopkins University Studies, 1st series, XII, 10.

parish appointed annually a board of overseers, composed of two or more members, who with the churchwardens had charge of the parish poor. Aid for the poor was supplied by the parishes and certain societies which had been organized for charitable and educational purposes.[10]

The parish becomes an election district. With few exceptions all elections in the province until 1716 were held in Charleston. In that year an act was passed which provided that writs for the election of members of the assembly should be issued to the churchwardens of each parish, who were authorized to manage the elections.[11] This act, which appears not to have gone into full effect until 1721, two years after the overthrow of the proprietary government, practically made each parish an election district. Elections were held at the parish churches and were to continue for two days. The churchwardens were to enroll the electors. Within seven days after the election they were to give notice at the church door or some other public place in the parish of the result of the election.[12] The parish electoral system, as well as some of the names of the parishes, was borrowed from the Barbadoes.

Road districts. Before 1721, it was necessary, when a new road was to be laid out, for the assembly to pass a special act and to appoint a board of commissioners, usually five, to carry out the provisions of the act. In 1721 a general road law was passed dividing the colony into 33 road districts, and the roads in each were placed under the care of a commission varying in size from three to eleven members, appointed by the assembly at first. In a few cases the road districts were identical with the parishes, but generally the parishes were subdivided into two, three, and even as many as six divisions. Until 1764 the roads in Charleston were under the care of the governor, the council, and five other persons.[13] The work on the roads was sometimes performed by the males of the district; at other times it was done by hired labor and the cost assessed by the commissioners upon the inhabitants benefited.

Other powers were bestowed upon particular parishes by spe-

[10] Whitney, *op. cit.*, pp. 70-72.
[11] John P. Thomas, Jr., *The Formation of Judicial and Political Subdivisions of South Carolina*, p. 9.
[12] McCrady, *op. cit.*, pp. 560-561.
[13] Whitney, *op. cit.*, pp. 72-73.

cial enactment. In 1736 the parish of St. Thomas was authorized to elect a treasurer, an usher, a schoolmaster, and a clerk.[14]

The courts. All judicial business in the province was attended to by the governor and the council until 1682, when a court was established in Charleston. It had been the purpose of the Proprietors to have a chief justice and four associate justices preside over each county court, and appointments were made in accordance with that purpose, but they were unnecessary and from 1698 until 1732 a chief justice alone was appointed. From 1683 to 1698 the sheriff of Berkeley County was both sheriff and chief justice, while appellate jurisdiction was reserved for the governor and the council.[15]

An act passed in 1731 established a court of general sessions of the peace, oyer and terminer, assize, and general jail delivery. This court was to have all the powers, jurisdiction, and authorities possessed by the courts of the King's Bench, assize, oyer and terminer, or any court of general and quarter sessions of the peace of Great Britain. In this court criminals were permitted to have counsel. The court of common pleas was created by an act in 1737. It was to meet four times a year. The two common law courts continued as organized until the Revolution, though in 1772 their jurisdiction was limited to the Charleston district.[16] These two courts and the courts of the justices of the peace for the trial of petty cases served the needs of the province until after 1769.

There were justices of the peace in the colony from the day of the first settlement, and these were appointed by the governor. There were constables also, who were appointed by the court of general sessions after it was established. The parish was the district of the constable and perhaps of the justice also.

In colonial times the justices of the peace were appointed under a general commission issued by the governor and council and held office during his majesty's pleasure. As an example, a new commission dated March 26, 1737, appointed 101 justices for Berkeley County. Included in this number were the members of the council, the members of the assembly residing in the county, the chief justice and the associate justices, various officials, such as the secretary, attorney general, and master in chancery, and a number of other prominent men. Twenty were appointed for Colleton,

[14] Howard, *op. cit.*, pp. 127-128.
[15] W. Roy Smith, *South Carolina as a Royal Province*, p. 120.
[16] *Ibid.*, p. 127 ff.

twenty-four for Craven, thirteen for Granville, and two for New Windsor and the parts adjacent.[17]

The justices could commit trespassers to jail, admit prisoners to bail, give certificates of ownership of horses and the like. They had jurisdiction in petty cases under forty shillings, tried offenders against Sunday laws, and settled claims for damages caused by the erection of dams. They were paid in fees.

In 1690 special courts for the trial of slaves were set up. Any justice of the peace, on complaint being made to him, was authorized to issue a warrant for the arrest of the offending slave. Then he must call in another justice of the same county, and the two of them summoned three freeholders to complete the court. The trial was without jury and the decision final. In case of the execution of a slave as a result of the court's decision, his value was fixed by a board of appraisers and the owner was reimbursed out of the public treasury. A later act provided for a special tax on the slaveholders in the parish out of the proceeds of which to reimburse the owner. After the Stono insurrection in 1739 the old plan of reimbursement was restored.[18]

The constables served writs in small cases, conveyed prisoners to jail, whipped Negroes, summoned jurors, collected several local taxes, and notified the court of general sessions of such wrong actions as came to their notice.

Jury lists were prepared by the chief justice, the coroner, and the treasurer. Freeholders paying two pounds tax were liable to service as petit jurors and those paying five pounds served as grand jurors. After 1721 the captains of the militia companies in the several parishes furnished the lists from which the jurors were drawn.

During colonial days, after the establishment of the circuit courts, the clerks and sheriffs were as a rule appointed by the governor. Until perhaps as late as 1706 the only coroner in the colony was the one at Charleston. After that date there were several in the province. Except for a short period, they were appointed by the governor, and their principal duties were the same as those performed by coroners today.[19]

[17] *Ibid.,* p. 141.
[18] *Ibid.,* p. 143 ff.
[19] Thomas, *op. cit.,* p. 14.

In 1721 an act was passed establishing county or precinct courts of pleas, assize, and jail delivery to the number of five.[20] These courts were modeled after the English courts of quarter sessions. Five judges commissioned by the governor from among the magistrates of the respective counties and precincts were placed over each court. Three constituted a quorum. These courts were to be held four times per year in each county or precinct and had jurisdiction over all criminal cases not extending to life or limb, and over civil cases involving not more than 100 pounds sterling. They constituted the county or precinct authority and attended to a number of administrative duties. They could punish obstinate servants, license taverns, bring suits for legacies left for public purposes, take charge of estates of orphans, inspect the accounts of church-wardens and overseers of the poor, lay out and repair roads, build courthouses and jails, and levy taxes for the same.[21] However, no courthouses were built by them. They dropped out of the system before a great while, since the court at Charleston absorbed the legal business of the province.

Although two attempts to establish district courts had failed, in 1769 an act was passed dividing the province into seven judicial districts and authorizing the holding of courts of general sessions and common pleas twice a year in each. These districts were Charleston, Beaufort, Orangeburg, Georgetown, Camden, Cheraw, and Ninety-Six.[22] These courts were held by the chief justice and his associates, but during most of the colonial period the court held at Charleston was superior to those held in the other districts. There were no district clerks or sheriffs until these courts were created. These officials were appointed by the governor, the latter from three resident freeholders of the respective districts nominated by the judges. Since the parishes did not extend more than ninety miles from the sea coast, local government in the up country may be said to have had its origin in the creation of these districts, four of which were in the up country.

No further developments of consequence in the system of courts appears to have been made during the colonial period. But in 1775 the up country was divided into four large election dis-

[20] Smith, *op. cit.*, p. 145.
[21] *Ibid.*, p. 145 ff.
[22] Thomas, *op. cit.*, p. 15 ff.

tricts, each of which was to have ten representatives in the assembly.

Taxation. Before 1719 taxes were assessed occasionally. In 1686 the taxes were assessed by thirteen freeholders and collected by two tax receivers. Usually, however, tax acts specified inquiries, assessors, and collectors. The first were to take an inventory of taxable property under oath, the second received the reports or returns, and might abate. After 1719 the government was supported entirely by taxes levied upon the settlers, and after 1721 the assessors generally acted as collectors. There was no county tax levied during the colonial period, and there appears to have been no system in the collection of such local taxes as were levied. Each board of commissioners collected its own taxes whenever and as frequently as it pleased. Outside of the city of Charleston the principal local taxes consisted of the road and poor rates.[23]

Militia and the patrol system. In every county there were one or more regiments, and in every parish one or more companies of militia. The larger parishes were divided by the field officers into divisions, each of which furnished one company.

The patrol system was first established by the act of 1704. Under this system a captain and ten men from every militia company formed a patrol to ride from plantation to plantation, to station sentries and guards, and to use every precaution to prevent uprisings. The men forming the patrol were exempt from other military duty during the first years of its operation. In 1734 and again in 1739 the system was strengthened. By the act of 1739 the province was divided into regular patrol districts and the powers of the riders were increased.[24]

Schools. There was nothing that resembled a public school system during the colonial period. The acts of 1710 and 1712 provided for a free school in Charleston, which was supported largely by charitable organizations. Writing, arithmetic, and merchant accounts were taught in it together with the classics.

In 1722 another act was passed establishing seven free schools from time to time. This act empowered the county courts to purchase lands and to build free school houses thereon in each precinct, and to nominate and appoint school masters. The school masters were to receive twenty-five pounds per year to be levied by the

---

[23] Whitney, *op. cit.*, p. 97 ff.   [24] Smith, *op. cit.*, p. 175 ff.

justices of the courts, who were given the same powers as the commissioners of the free school in Charleston.[25] The county or precinct courts did not last long and consequently nothing much was done to establish free schools. The act of 1722 was the general law with regard to free schools until 1811, and there was no state support of schools before that time. At the close of the Revolution there were only eleven free schools in the province, and they were attended by the children of the poor whites only.[26]

During the colonial period the commons house of assembly gradually fought its way to a place of supremacy in the government of the colony. It acquired successively the rights of appointing all public officials paid out of the colonial treasury and of initiating legislation. But when the colonial period came to a close local government had made very little headway. No town in the colony had been incorporated, and aside from the parishes there was little trace of local government. In 1730 some townships were ordered to be laid off. Later some of them became parishes, but otherwise they were mere geographical areas. All the parishes were near the coast. There was no trace of organized local government in the up country, unless the creation of the four judicial districts in 1769 and the four election districts in 1775 may be so considered.

Justices of the peace, who existed from the first settlement, were appointed by the governor. No courts of general jurisdiction were held outside of the city of Charleston until after 1769. The courts established by the act of that year were to be presided over by the justices from Charleston, and the court held at Charleston was superior to that held in the other districts almost to the close of the period. As a rule only members of the assembly were chosen by popular vote, and most of the elections for these officials were held in Charleston until after 1719. Roads were laid out and constructed and repaired under the direction of commissioners appointed by the assembly; the poor outside of the parishes were probably supported by voluntary contributions. There were practically no schools other than private ones. Thus it may well be said, "Until within a few years of the Revolution the will of Charleston, politically speaking, was the will of the province."[27]

[25] McCrady, op. cit., p. 46.
[26] Henry T. Thompson, The Establishment of the Public School System of South Carolina, p. 4 ff.
[27] Smith, op. cit., p. 6.

CHAPTER II

THE PERIOD OF STATEHOOD

From 1776 to 1868. The change from a royal province to an independent state had no perceptible effect on the development of local government. The state's first constitution, adopted in 1776, provided for a lower house of the legislature with large powers. There was to be also a legislative council, or upper house, consisting of thirteen members chosen out of its own membership by the lower house. The two houses were authorized jointly to choose by ballot from among themselves, or from the people of the colony at large, a president of the colony, who was given an absolute veto over measures passed by the legislature. The only officers to be chosen by popular election were the members of the lower house.

The constitution of 1776 was the first of seven which the state has had. It was not submitted to the people for adoption, nor were any of the other six, except that of 1868. The second constitution was adopted in 1778. Article I of this constitution declares that the style of the country hereafter shall be the state of South Carolina. The constitution recommended that representation be reapportioned in proportion to wealth and white population at the end of seven years, and every fourteenth year thereafter, but the recommendation was not observed. Under this constitution the members of the senate were to be elected by popular vote also. Furthermore, it abolished the absolute veto of the president, whose title was changed to that of governor. No veto of any kind was possessed by any governor of the state again until after the War Between the States. Dr. Wallace comments upon this provision of the constitution as follows:

> Thus was illustrated in the highest degree the prevailing American sentiment of confidence in a well-nigh completely unrestrained legislature. The colonial assemblies had waged the fight of liberty against the executive from overseas. We soon learned that legislatures are not therefore infallible, and began to place restrictions on them; but we have not yet apparently realized that the governor is no longer the representative of a distant and would be despotic

potentate, but is our own servant who to serve us adequately must have the handcuffs removed.[1]

The third constitution was adopted in 1790, and under it with some amendments the people of the state lived until 1861. This constitution fixed the capital of the state at Columbia, which was a victory for the up country. But the power of the low country was still very much in evidence. The governor was permitted to reside where he chose when the legislature was not in session. There were to be two state treasurers, one to reside in Columbia and the other in Charleston; each to collect the revenues from his section to be put into a common treasury. The secretary of state and the surveyor general were required to maintain offices in both cities. The court of appeals was required to sit in Charleston to hear appeals from the three low country districts, while those coming from the four up country districts were to be heard in Columbia.

The governor was left without veto power. The only elective officials were the members of the two houses of the legislature. The right of suffrage was restricted by a property qualification, and the property qualifications for the governorship and for membership in the legislature were high. The membership of the house was fixed at 124, which has not since been changed, but no effort was made to apportion representatives according to population. Each district chose one senator, with the exception of Charleston, which chose two, and a number of others which were combined in twos and threes for the election of one. The people were given the right to elect members of either house from their own district, or outside of it, a feature that might well be embodied in present-day constitutions.

By an amendment passed in 1808 the unjust system of selecting the members of the lower house was modified. Each district was authorized to elect one representative for each sixty-second of the white population of the state it possessed and one for each sixty-second of the taxes of the state it paid. Each district was permitted also to elect one senator, except Charleston, which retained its two until 1895. Under this arrangement the low country kept control of the senate, while the control of the house passed to the up country. In 1810 the state established manhood suffrage.

[1] David D. Wallace, *The South Carolina Constitution of 1895*, Bulletin No. 197 of the University of South Carolina, p. 11.

The people of the up country continued to clamor for the popular election of the governor and the presidential electors, and against the provision for the election of one-half the representatives on the basis of wealth. But with a few more slight amendments the constitution remained unchanged until 1861.

Counties and county courts. In 1785 the state was divided into thirty-four counties largely through the influence of Henry Pendleton of Virginia, and provision was made for a court every three months in each county. These courts were to be presided over by seven justices of the peace of the respective counties. They were never put into operation in the districts of Beaufort, Charleston, and Georgetown. After a trial of fourteen years the system was abolished in 1798.[2]

The justices of the county courts were self-perpetuating bodies, and they held office during good behavior. The districts in which the county courts were not established were those in which the parish system existed.

Districts replace counties. In 1789 the circuit courts which had been established by the act of 1769 were invested with original and final jurisdiction. In 1791 the number of districts was increased from seven to nine. In 1798 these districts were subdivided into twenty-four, and another was created soon afterwards. The new plan contemplated six judges for the twenty-five districts. All the counties were incorporated in these districts.[3] The parish system was rooted so deeply in the low country that the county system could not yet replace it. Since the justices of the peace had jurisdiction over petty cases, since the care of the poor was in the hands of the parish officers, and since the commissioners of the road districts had charge of the roads, there was perhaps no need for more governmental machinery in the low country. The power of the up country was increasing, but the low country was predominant in the affairs of the state.

The constitution of 1790 accorded representation in the General Assembly to forty-five subdivisions called election districts. There were thirty of these election districts in 1776. The election districts comprised nearly all of the old parishes, and many of the counties which had been laid off in 1785 for the establishment of

[2] Thomas, *op. cit.*, pp. 16-17.
[3] Ramsay, *op. cit.*, I, 127 ff.

county courts. The low country in which the county courts had not been established retained for the most part its parish divisions for representative purposes. In the other parts of the state the election districts corresponded in name and territory in most cases with the counties. However, there were exceptions. The county of Lexington was the election district of Saxe Gotha until 1851, when the name of the district was changed to Lexington. Barnwell County was known as the election district of Winton. In 1852 Pendleton was divided into Anderson and Pickens, and Spartan and Kingston became Spartanburg and Horry. In 1861 Claremont and Liberty were changed to Sumter and Marion.[4]

The twenty-five districts which were created in 1798 and 1799 were called judicial districts to distinguish them from the election districts. The number was increased from time to time. Under the provisions of the constitution of 1865 every judicial district became an election district, except Charleston. In 1798 the Charleston judicial district contained ten election districts, while the All Saints election district was partly in the judicial district of Georgetown and partly in that of Horry, after the creation of the latter in 1801. In some instances the judicial and election districts were identical; in others, they were identical except in name. For instance, the Marion judicial district and the Liberty election district were the same. Lexington judicial district, created in 1804, was the same as Saxe Gotha election district.[5] These districts were merely subdivisions of the judicial districts. They bore the same relation to the judicial district, no doubt, as our counties of today bear to their judicial districts. The judicial districts, the subdivisions, and the election districts gradually came to be identical in name and area. Charleston was the last to be changed. However, in the first years of the process it must have been very difficult to keep from losing one's way in trying to distinguish between so many subdivisions, counties, parishes, judicial districts, and election districts.

In that part of the state in which the county courts existed from 1785 until 1798 the justices of the courts exercised some administrative authority in addition to their other duties. However, this authority varied considerably, and towards the close of

[4] Thomas, *op. cit.*, p. 17 ff.
[5] *Ibid.*, pp. 20-21.

the period the justices apparently were relieved of part if not most of it.

Roads and the care of the poor. An act passed in 1786 conferred upon the magistrates of the county courts the powers and authorities of the commissioners of high roads.[6] Where the county courts did not exist, there were the old road districts. The roads in these districts were in charge of commissioners appointed by the legislature.

In 1789 another act was passed conferring upon the justices of the county courts the powers and authorities formerly held by the vestries and churchwardens of the parishes with respect to the care of the poor.[7] Two years later those districts in which there were no county courts were authorized to elect five poor commissioners each, who were to have charge of the poor. In 1793 those districts in which the county courts were established were authorized to elect poor commissioners also.[8] Thus the care of the poor was taken out of the hands of the justices of the county courts after a period of four years.

From 1794 on frequent acts were passed increasing the number of the justices of the peace. The act of 1794 provided that the number of the justices in the counties where county courts were established might be increased from nine to fifteen each. Later acts of such a nature applied as a rule to more restricted areas of the state.

Collection of taxes. In 1797 an act was passed which required that in all counties in which county courts were established the taxes for the support of the poor should be collected by the tax collectors.[9] An act of 1785 specified that the sheriffs should collect the taxes levied by the justices for the purpose of building courthouses and jails. In a part of the state, at least, the sheriffs of the respective counties doubtless became the collectors of the taxes for the support of the poor, but the plan was not uniform.

Popular election of local officials. In 1808 an act was passed authorizing the people of the several districts to elect their sheriffs,[10] and some time later the selection of tax collectors was

[6] *Statutes of South Carolina*, Vol. 4, Act No. 1315.
[7] *Ibid.*, Vol. 5, Act. No. 1459.
[8] *Ibid.*, Vol. 5, Acts Nos. 1500 and 1580.
[9] *Ibid.*, Vol. 5, Act No. 1666.
[10] *Ibid.*, Vol. 5, Act No. 1914.

transferred to the people. This action indicates that at least after the abolition of the county courts in 1798 the tax collectors were separate officials from the sheriffs. The election of other district officials by popular vote may have been provided for during the ante-bellum period.

An amendment to the constitution of 1790, ratified in 1828, provided that all civil officers whose authority was limited to a single election district, to a single judicial district, or to a part of either, should be appointed, hold office, be removed from office, and in addition to liability to impeachment, might be punished for official misconduct in such manner as the legislature might provide previous to their appointment. Since under this amendment the manner of selection of district officials, their tenure, and their powers were placed entirely in the hands of the legislature, it is doubtless safe to say that there was no rigid uniformity to be found in any of these matters. The constitution of 1790 with its amendments left the problems of local government wholly with the legislature. Towns and cities were incorporated under it, but no county or district was given corporate powers.

Schools. In 1811 through the influence of Hon. Stephen Elliott of Charleston, who is known as the father of the public school system of the state, an act was passed providing state support for public schools. The act provided that the number of schools in each election district should equal the number of members to which the district was entitled in the lower house of the General Assembly. An appropriation of $300 per annum was made for each school. Elementary education was to be imparted to all pupils free of charge, though preference was to be given to poor orphans and children of indigent parents. At first these schools were patronized mainly by the children of the indigent whites. Some progress began to be made, however, after 1830. By 1860 the attendance had reached 20,000, and support amounted to $200,000.[11]

The schools in each election district were under the control of three commissioners appointed by the General Assembly. They were charged with the duties of establishing schools in each district, of examining, appointing, with the aid of local trustees, and

[11] Thompson, *op. cit.*, p. 6 ff.

removing teachers, and of the general supervision of all free school interests in the districts.[12]

The patrol system. The patrol system as developed during the colonial period remained largely unchanged up to the War Between the States.

The close of the ante-bellum period. When the War Between the States came on, county or district government had made little advance over that of the colonial period. There were, however, election and judicial districts throughout the state. The electors of the judicial districts chose their sheriffs, tax collectors, and commissioners of the poor. In some cases other district officials may have been chosen by popular vote. There were school commissioners in each election district; there were road districts with their road commissioners; there were numerous other officials. These officials were as a rule appointed by the legislature. All district officials, whether appointed or elected, were required to report to the legislature, and their instructions came from it. All local affairs, except those of towns and cities, were in the hands of the legislature.

New Constitutions

Within a period of fourteen years from 1776 the state of South Carolina adopted three constitutions successively. Within a period of seven years, beginning with 1861, the state adopted successively three other constitutions.

The Confederate constitution adopted in 1861 differed in no material way from that of 1790 for the purposes of this study. In 1865, after the close of the war, a second constitution was adopted, which was in operation about one and a half years. This constitution was to a large extent merely the constitution of 1790 amended. Traces of the dual location of government were abolished. The judicial districts became election districts, and thus the parishes lost the political distinction they had held since colonial days. The property qualification for office holding was abolished. The people were required to elect their representatives from their own districts. The governor was to be elected by the people for a term of four years, and he was given the veto again, though it might be overridden by a majority vote of the members of each house. Special county courts were set up for the trial of cases involving

[12] Edgar W. Knight, *Reconstruction and Education in South Carolina*, p. 3.

Negroes, and the establishment of these courts along with the rejection of the fourteenth amendment by the legislature helped to prepare the way for Reconstruction and the constitution of 1868, which provided county government.

Under the constitution of 1868. The constitution of 1868 marks the most violent change in the constitutional history of the state. Even leaving aside the cataclysmic results of the enfranchisement of the Negro, the new instrument merely as a system of constitutional law marks the assimilation of South Carolina to the modern American style. This is natural enough. Her former constitutions had been the work of her own leaders, evolved from her own experience, and expressive of her own ideals of law and of civilization so far as enshrined in constitutional forms. They were of course marked by the brevity and flexibility of the early state constitutions; but as others changed, South Carolina had become more distinctly South Carolina. The constitution of 1868 was merely a well-balanced copy of the ordinary American state constitution of the period.[13]

The constitution of 1868 did not increase the membership of the lower house of the General Assembly, but it did provide that the representatives should be apportioned among the counties according to the number of inhabitants in each. The senate was to contain one member from each county.

The name county restored. The subdivisions of the state had been called districts since 1800. The constitution of 1868 restored the name county. The change marked by the adoption of the new constitution was perhaps not so violent in its provisions relating to county government, though it did provide that

. . . the qualified electors of each county shall elect three persons for the term of two years, who shall constitute a board of county commissioners, which shall have jurisdiction over roads, highways, ferries, bridges, and in all matters relating to taxes, disbursements of money for county purposes, and in every other case that may be necessary to the internal improvement and local concerns of the respective counties; provided, that in all cases there shall be the right of appeal to the state courts.[14]

Other sections of the same article provided for a court of probate with an elective judge, a competent number of justices of the peace and constables, to be chosen by the qualified electors in the manner provided by the General Assembly. The qualified

---

[13] Wallace, *op. cit.*, p. 21.
[14] *South Carolina Constitution of 1868*, Art. IV, sec. 19.

electors of each county were to choose a clerk of the court of common pleas, a sheriff, and a coroner. The jurisdiction of the courts of probate and of the justices of the peace was prescribed. The duties of the former district ordinaries devolved upon the judges of probate. The clerk of the court of common pleas, by virtue of his office, was to be the clerk of all other courts of record in his county, unless the General Assembly provided for the election of a clerk for each of the other courts, or unless it authorized the judge of probate to perform the duties of clerk of his own court. Under the new constitution there was a considerable degree of uniformity in the organization of county government; much more in fact than there was in the machinery for handling district affairs under the constitution of 1790, or, for that matter, than there is in county government machinery under the constitution of 1895.

No county taxes were levied before 1868. The new constitution provided that the corporate authorities of counties, townships, school districts, cities, towns, and villages might be vested with power to assess and collect taxes for corporate purposes.[15]

Following the adoption of the constitution, the legislature of 1868 passed an act setting up an elaborate scheme of township government, modeled on that of the New England town. Since it was not adapted to South Carolina conditions and was contrary altogether to South Carolina traditions, the plan would not work and the law was repealed in 1870.[16] The legislature authorized the county commissioners to appoint a treasurer, who should keep and disburse all county funds. His compensation was to be two per cent for receiving and the same for disbursing the funds.[17]

Education. The constitution of 1868 was the first constitution of the state to make mention of a state system of public schools. It provided for one school commissioner to be elected biennially in each county.[18] It also provided that there should be assessed an annual poll tax of one dollar to be applied solely to educational purposes, and it directed the General Assembly to levy at each regular session an annual tax on all taxable property throughout the state for the support of public schools. This tax was to be

[15] *Ibid.,* Art. IX, sec. 8.
[16] John S. Reynolds, *Reconstruction in South Carolina,* p. 116.
[17] *Ibid.,* p. 97.
[18] South Carolina Constitution of 1868, Art. X, sec. 2.

collected at the same time and by the same agents as the general state levy and paid into the treasury of the state.

The constitution directed the General Assembly to provide for a liberal and uniform system of free public schools throughout the state, as soon as practicable after the adoption of the constitution, and also for the division of the state into suitable school districts. One or more schools in each district were to be kept open for at least six months in each year; and all schools supported in whole or in part by public funds were to be open to children of both races.[19] Local districts were authorized to levy taxes for school purposes.

But owing to the prostrate condition of the state, to the provision in the constitution requiring that the schools be open to both races, and to the ignorance and extravagance of most of the state and county officials, the system of education set up accomplished little else for the first ten years of its existence than the saddling of debt on the counties. In 1877 the law authorizing districts to levy taxes for school purposes was repealed. The same year a constitutional amendment was passed which provided for a state levy of not less than two mills for the support of the schools. This levy was to be made by the boards of county commissioners, and the tax was to be collected at the same time and by the same officers as the other taxes for the same year. The proceeds were to be held in the county treasury and distributed to the several school districts in proportion to the number of pupils attending the public schools.

The legislature of 1878 created the state board of examiners, which in turn appointed the county board of examiners. These county boards were required to examine all teachers, to divide the counties into school districts, and to appoint three trustees for each district to serve for terms of two years each. The trustees were to have control of all educational interests in their respective districts under the supervision of the county board.[20] This action was made necessary because of the proved incompetence of the county school commissioners provided for in the constitution. The legislature repealed a former law which required the state to provide textbooks to those children whose parents refused or neglected to provide them, and another which required a census of

[19] *Ibid.*, sections 3, 4, 5, and 10.
[20] Thompson, *op. cit.*, p. 24.

school children to be made by local authorities. From that date up until 1930 no census by local authorities was required.

While the two-mill levy for schools was to be distributed to the districts in proportion to the pupils attending the public schools, the poll tax was to be distributed in the district in which it was collected.

Though the law authorizing school districts to levy taxes for school purposes had been repealed in 1878, a special act was passed authorizing Winnsboro to levy a special tax for schools. Charleston had already adopted the plan of local taxation for school purposes. After 1883 this method of school support spread rapidly.

The constitution of 1868 lasted twenty-seven years, and might have served the people of the state acceptably much longer but for the democratic movement of 1890 and the fear which the white masses entertained of the potential Negro vote in the state. The white masses feared competition with the Negro. When Colonel A. C. Haskell, with the support of a large part of the old aristocracy, made a direct appeal to the Negro vote, the leaders of the Tillman movement determined upon the constitutional elimination of the Negro from politics.[21]   The result was the constitution of 1895, though the popular referendum on calling the constitutional convention showed the voters almost evenly divided.

Under the constitution of 1895. The constitution of 1868 marked a change from an aristocratic commonwealth to a democratic one with no restrictions upon the right of suffrage or of office holding. The movement coming in the 1890's, which produced the present constitution, is referred to also as a democratic movement. But in fact it was a reaction against an excess of democracy. However, it proposed to guarantee white supremacy and in that respect it represented the views of the white masses. The aristocratic element was determined upon white supremacy also, but it had no fear of Negro competition. It proposed to be supreme through political manipulation rather than through constitutional guarantee.

The constitution of 1895 limits suffrage with an alternative educational or property qualification. It set up, according to Dr. Wallace, a paralyzed state executive department, and substituted for the "old time state sovereignty, not county sovereignty, but a

21 Wallace, *op. cit.*, p. 27.

kind of county officer sovereignty."[22]   It overburdened the legislature by heaping on it a vast mass of local laws, and at the same time showed its distrust of the legislature by numerous limitations placed upon it.   By reducing the term of office of the judges, it denied them proper power and independence.   The county was made the territorial basis in state administration for practically all purposes.   But the whole system presents two improprieties:

The executive authorities of the state have no adequate means of administering state law, as that is committed to county officers over whom they have no means of making good the control that the law directs the former to exercise and the latter to obey.   On the other hand, the county is not guaranteed any freedom in managing its own local affairs, but is subject completely to the authority of the state legislature.   The county is allowed power to cripple the state's administration, and the state is given complete power to meddle in the affairs of the county, but neither is afforded proper means for managing its own affairs.   The whole system is an inconsistency.[23]

The measure of truth in this succinct statement, it is hoped, will be revealed in the course of the present study.

The county and township.   The provisions in the constitution of 1895 concerning county government are not numerous.   Each county was constituted one election district, and a body politic and corporate.[24]   Each township, as established at the time, was constituted a body politic and corporate also, though the right of the General Assembly to organize other townships and to change boundaries of those already existing was reserved.

Provision was made also for the creation of new counties.   A new county could be created on petition of one-third of the electors within the area of the proposed new county, provided that upon submission of the matter to the qualified voters two-thirds of them cast their ballots in favor of its establishment.   Certain limitations were placed upon this provision.   No new county might contain less than one one-hundred-and-twenty-fourth part of the whole number of inhabitants of the state; neither might it have less taxable property than $1,500,000, nor an area of less than 400 square miles.   Old counties might not be reduced to less than 500 square miles in area; their assessed taxable property might not be

[22] *Ibid.,* p. 43.
[23] *Ibid.,* p. 91.
[24] South Carolina Constitution of 1895, Art. VII, sec. 9.

reduced to less than $2,000,000, nor their population to less than 15,000. No old county might be cut within eight miles of its courthouse building.[25]

Consolidation of counties. A wise provision of the constitution in the light of present conditions is that which authorizes the General Assembly to provide for the consolidation of two or more existing counties. The action of the General Assembly, however, is contingent upon the action of the majority of the qualified electors in each county concerned.[26]

Taxation and bonded debt limits. The corporate authorities of counties, townships, school districts, cities, towns, and villages may be vested with power to assess and collect taxes for corporate purposes. The bonded debt of any one of these subdivisions shall not exceed eight per cent of the assessed value of the taxable property within it. But whenever several subdivisions cover the same territory the debt may be increased to not more than fifteen per cent upon any area.[27]

The General Assembly was authorized to provide for the assessment of all property for taxation. Taxes for the subdivisions were required to be levied on the same assessment, but they were to be levied and collected by the respective fiscal authorities of the subdivisions. The constitution did not establish the fiscal authorities of the subdivisions. It left that matter to the General Assembly.

County courts. The constitution provided for a sufficient number of magistrates to be appointed by the governor with the advice and consent of the senate. These magistrates were to take the place of the trial justices already existing and each was to be paid a salary in lieu of all fees in criminal cases. Each was given authority to appoint one or more constables under such regulations as may be provided now or hereafter by law. The civil jurisdiction of the magistrates was limited to cases in which the value of the property in controversy or the amount claimed did not exceed $100. Their jurisdiction does not extend to cases in which the title to real estate is in question, nor over cases in chancery. The General Assembly may prescribe their criminal jurisdiction, except that it may not extend to cases in which the punishment exceeds a fine of $100 or imprisonment for 30 days.[28]

[25] *Ibid.*, Art. VII, secs. 1-5.
[26] *Ibid.*, sec. 10.
[27] *Ibid.*, Art. X, sec. 5.
[28] *Ibid.*, Art. V, secs. 20 and 21.

No change was made in the court of probate as it existed in the county of Charleston. Neither was an immediate change made in that of the other counties of the state, but the General Assembly was given authority to vest jurisdiction in all matters testamentary and of administration, in business appertaining to minors and the allotment of dower, in cases of idiocy and lunacy, and persons *non compos mentis* in other courts.[29]

The General Assembly was also authorized to establish county courts, municipal courts, and such courts, inferior to the circuit courts, in any and all of the counties as may be deemed necessary. But a county court may not be established in any county until it is submitted to the qualified electors of the county and voted upon favorably by a majority of them.[30]

Juries are provided by the constitution. The jury in cases in all courts inferior to the circuit courts consists of six men. The grand jury of each county must consist of eighteen men, twelve of whom must agree on a matter before it can be submitted to the court. The petit jury must consist of twelve men, all of whom must agree to a verdict in order to render it. No qualification for jurors is set up other than that they must be qualified electors between the ages of twenty-one and sixty-five and of good moral character.[31]

The provision concerning the clerk of the court of common pleas is the same as that contained in the constitution of 1868; that is, one is to be elected in each county every four years. By virtue of his office he is to be clerk of every court of record in his county, though the General Assembly may provide for the election of a clerk with the same term of office for each or any of the courts of record, and may authorize the judge of probate to perform the duties of clerk of his own court.

Other elective county officials. The qualified electors of each county are required to elect a sheriff and a coroner for a term of four years each. These officials are disqualified for office a second time if it appears that they are in default of moneys collected by virtue of their respective offices.

Election officials are to be provided by the General Assembly, though the first county boards of registration were to consist of

[29] *Ibid.*, sec. 19.
[30] *Ibid.*, Art. V, sec. 1.
[31] *Ibid.*, Art. V, sec. 22.

three "discreet persons" each, to be appointed by the governor with the advice and consent of the senate.

Education. For some undiscoverable reason the constitution provides that the salaries of state and county school officials for collecting and disbursing school funds shall not be paid out of school funds.[32] In providing for a liberal system of free public schools for all children between the ages of six and twenty-one years, and in dividing the counties into suitable school districts, the constitution unfortunately limited the area of the district instead of leaving it to the discretion of the state department of education, or to the county school authorities. No district may be less than nine square miles nor greater than forty-nine square miles in area, except in the case of all cities of 10,000 or more inhabitants.[33]

By an amendment to the constitution ratified in 1929 the constitutional limitation on the size of school districts in Fairfield and Union counties was removed. In the future the size of the districts in these counties will be prescribed by the General Assembly or the county board of education. It seems safe to say that it will be done by the former.

The county officers vested with the powers and duties of the county boards of commissioners are required to levy an annual tax of three mills for schools. This tax is to be collected and put into the county treasury of the respective counties and distributed among the districts in the county in proportion to the number of pupils enrolled in the public schools. The trustees for each district are required to be selected as the General Assembly may determine, except in the case of special districts. The manner of selection need not be uniform throughout the state, according to the constitution, and it is not. These trustees shall disburse the school funds of their respective districts.[34]

The constitution names no county school officials. It specifies three district trustees, except in special districts already existing. These are under the provisions of special acts of the General Assembly. The number, method of appointment, qualifications, powers, duties, compensation, and terms of office of all other necessary county school officials are left in the hands of the General Assem-

[32] *Ibid.*, Art. XI, sec. 4.
[33] *Ibid.*, sec. 5.
[34] *Ibid.*, Art. XI, secs. 4-6.

bly.[35] But for the constitutional limitations upon the size of the districts, the provisions concerning county educational affairs are such that the reorganization of the county school system might be readily accomplished on popular demand.

The care of the poor. No provision concerning the poor is made other than that the counties are authorized to make such provisions for their poor as may be determined by law.[36]

The present constitution of the state deals rather briefly with the subject of counties and county government. It provides no county boards for general purposes, for roads, for schools, for health, for public welfare, or other things. There are four constitutional officers to be elected by popular vote: the clerk of the court of common pleas and general sessions, the judge of probate, the sheriff, and the coroner. There must be also a sufficient number of magistrates to be appointed by the governor with the advice and consent of the senate, and three trustees for each school district in the state, other than special districts, to be appointed as the General Assembly may direct. The jurisdiction of the magistrates, and the duties of the judge of probate in the single county of Charleston are fixed. All else pertaining to county government and county affairs is left in the hands of the legislature. It is in fact a system of county government by the state legislature. The further course of the study should indicate the virtues and defects which are inherent in the system, as well as show to what extent it is handicapped by "county officer sovereignty."

[35] *Ibid.,* Art. XI, sec. 3.
[36] *Ibid.,* Art. XII, sec. 3.

PART II

THE COUNTY GOVERNMENT AND ADMINISTRATION

CHAPTER III

THE COUNTY GOVERNMENT ORGANIZATION

The adoption of the constitution of 1895 in so far as it concerned the county government organization was a step backward. The constitution of 1868 provided for a county board of commissioners, composed of three members, to be chosen by the qualified voters of each county. This board was an imported political device and had associations which were doubtless very distasteful. The new constitution did not provide for the board. Established custom was responsible for the provision in the constitution calling for the election by the qualified electors of the respective counties of a judge of probate, a sheriff, a clerk of the court of general sessions and common pleas, and a coroner. The more important county officials and the duties of practically all of them were left to the mercy of the state legislature. This was in keeping with ante-bellum practices in the state.

It is easily understood why the question of unity and uniformity in and simplification of county government machinery did not present itself to the framers of the new constitution. There were perhaps just three major reasons. Long established custom was one; then, at that time county government was a relatively simple matter, and no one was giving much thought to it. In the last place, there was the race problem, which cast all else into deep shadow. The county board as it existed under the constitution of 1868 was a step in the right direction, but it was omitted from the new constitution. As a result, the state legislature has spent innumerable hours since on county boards, in establishing and abolishing, in appointing and authorizing election by popular vote, in changing the number of members and the length of their terms, in requiring the selection to be made by district or from the county at large, in creating the office of supervisor here, in abolishing it or leaving it out there, and so on. The expenditure of all this time and energy has been productive of no good results so far as one can tell. But legislation dealing with county boards makes only a minor part of that vast mass of local matters to which the General Assembly must give time under the present system.

Before taking up the county government organization more in detail, it is necessary to point out a peculiarity of the system which is perhaps unique among American states. The powers and jurisdiction of local governments are delegated by the states. They may be provided for in the fundamental law or by legislative act. In any and every case the state is supreme. But here the similarity ends. Numerous local officials are state officials also. There is scarcely to be discerned any line of demarcation between state and county affairs, and the county legislative delegations, by virtue of the fact that they make up the dominant body in the government of the state, work their wills virtually unhindered over the whole wide field. The members of the state legislature are state officials. In practice they are no less county officials. Their field of operations, because of their peculiar relations to it, is one that adapts itself especially to innumerable petty and often obscure performances and consequently to much evasion of responsibility on the part of these officials. Because of the peculiarity of the system, it is necessary to begin an examination of the county government machinery with an examination of the supreme power in it.

THE COUNTY LEGISLATIVE DELEGATION

In common with three other states South Carolina assigns one senator to each county. This equality of counties in the senate originated in 1808, though Charleston was permitted at that time to have two. Dr. Wallace remarks that this arrangement is one of the most flagrant violations both of democratic principles and ordinary common sense that the constitution contains.[1] The senators are chosen by popular vote for terms of four years each. Each county is given in addition to its senator one representative for each one-hundred-and-twenty-fourth part of the population of the state it contains; that is, one representative for about 15,000 inhabitants, though every county shall have at least one representative. Representation in the lower house ranges from one member each for the less populous counties such as Jasper and McCormick to seven each for the counties of Greenville and Spartanburg. Consequently, the county legislative delegations range in size from

[1] Wallace, op. cit., p. 59.

two to eight members each. The senator's position among the
members of the delegation is the most powerful, politically speaking, by virtue of his membership in the upper house.

The legislative delegation itself can not enact laws, but it has
by long established custom largely assumed the direction of county
affairs. It helps to prepare the county supply bill, which purports
to be a kind of operating budget for ordinary county affairs for the
year. Thus the delegation hears all requests for appropriations

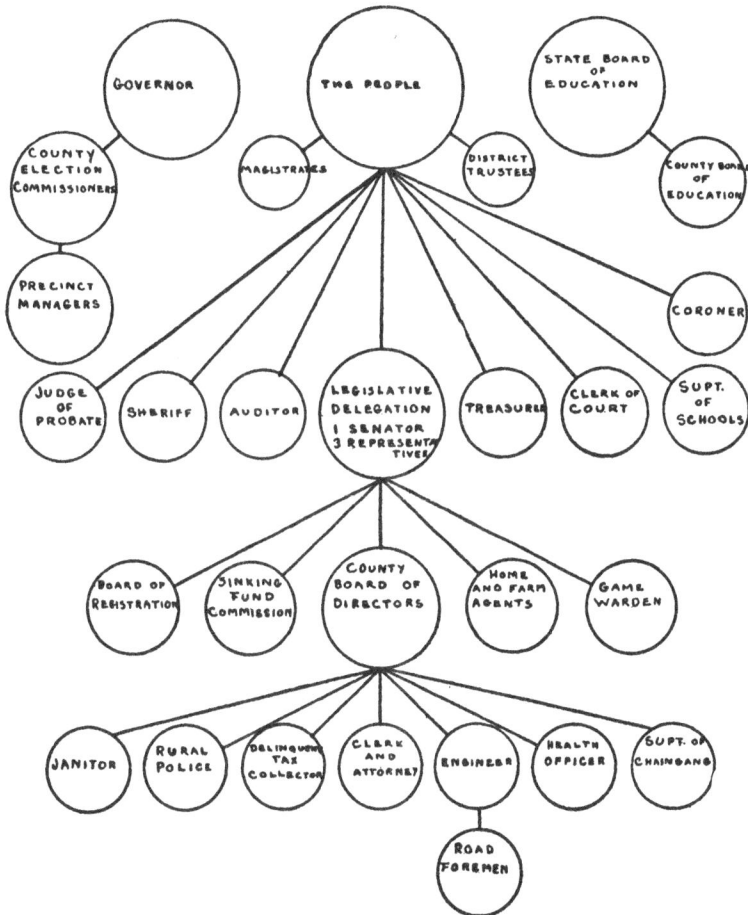

DIAGRAM I

THE COUNTY GOVERNMENT ORGANIZATION
Darlington County, South Carolina

whether for roads, bridges, for increase in salary, for clerical help, for some new activity, or what not. Such items and measures as the delegation, or the senator and a majority of the representatives, agrees upon the legislature passes as a matter of course, provided they are of a local nature. Whoever wants something goes to the delegation. Consequently, much of its time must be given to conferences with individuals and groups about matters of local interest. The members of the delegation are besieged both at Columbia and when at home by persons who may have some selfish interest in local affairs. Frequently important local matters may be settled in secret conferences in the capital city or elsewhere. The legislature passes the measures, if no opposition arises in the delegation. Local public opinion frequently has no chance to be heard. The legislature and the governor can hardly do otherwise than follow the advice of the delegation in matters of local legislation.

Because of these facts much time of the legislature that should be given to matters of statewide importance is given to petty local affairs, and many measures are made into laws which would not have been considered seriously if the delegation could be held directly responsible for them. Dr. Wallace suggests that it would be much better from every standpoint to have local legislation enacted by the county delegation of its own authority openly in the county court room.[2] Probably no such county legislature is anywhere in existence, though it would be a modification of the New England town meeting applied to the county. Doubtless such a plan would work with the county manager, and thus effect a saving in the number of officials to the extent of those making up the county board. The genius of South Carolina is peculiar among the American states. The state might well be able to develop a democratic and at the same time responsible and more or less efficient system of county government by taking this extraordinary course. It seems clear, however, that it would be necessary for numerous constitutional restrictions to be placed upon the law-making power of the delegations, and that a uniform frame-work of county government be provided for all rural counties.

The legislature has in the main handled local affairs since the first settlement in the colony. The more recent constitutions and statutes, however, have definitely conferred certain powers on it

<hr />

[2] *Ibid.*, p. 93.

with reference to local affairs. Some of these powers are conferred upon the senate and some upon the General Assembly as a
whole. Most of them have to do with the appointment of local
officials. If the power is conferred upon the senate, it is the individual senator who really exercises it; if upon the General Assembly, the county delegation exercises it.

The general law of the state provides that the governor shall
appoint the board of registration, the county auditor, the county
treasurer, the magistrates, and the master in equity with the advice
and consent of the senate.[3] In every case there were some exceptions. And popular demand has caused changes in practice, if not
in the law. The treasurer, the auditor, and the magistrates in
nearly all the counties are now nominated in the primary. Those
receiving a majority vote are recommended to and appointed by
the governor. Thus the senators have yielded some of their power
to the people. Township, district, and special boards of tax assessors are appointed by the governor on the recommendation of
a majority of the legislative delegation.[4] There are numerous exceptions to this provision. In a few counties there are district
boards of assessors rather than township boards. These district
boards may be the school district trustees, who are in numerous
cases elected by popular vote. In some towns and villages there
are special boards of assessors, and these are frequently appointed
by the board of aldermen. Exceptions to the general law tend to
increase.

The general law concerning county boards of commissioners
provides for a supervisor for each county, to be elected by popular
vote, and two commissioners to be appointed on the recommendation of the majority of the county legislative delegation.[5] Several
counties were excepted from the provisions of the law to begin
with, and now there are only fifteen counties out of the forty-six
with a supervisor and two commissioners each. And the manner
of selecting the commissioners may not be uniform in these
counties.

The county board of education is composed of the county
superintendent of schools, chosen by popular vote, and usually
two other members appointed by the state board of education. The

[3] Code, 1922, Vol. 3, secs. 204, 433, 491, 2241, and 2219.
[4] *Ibid.*, sec. 469.
[5] *Ibid.*, sec. 1061.

law does not specify upon whose recommendations these appointments shall be made. Frequently the senator or the delegation is consulted in the matter. Health officers in certain counties are appointed on the recommendation of the delegation.

The law provides that the governor shall appoint three county election commissioners for state and county offices and three for federal offices.[6] He necessarily turns in most cases to the county senator or the delegation for advice in making these appointments, though the law does not anywhere provide that he shall do so.

The constitution specifies four county officials who shall be elected by popular vote. In addition, through statute and custom four others are virtually chosen in the same manner. The county supervisor, the county superintendent of schools, the auditor, and the treasurer make up the latter group. The treasurer and auditor are nominated in the primary only. Practically all other county officials are directly at the mercy of the legislative delegation. As a matter of fact the county supervisor has been the subject of a great deal of local legislation. Up to the present the auditor, the treasurer, and the superintendent of schools have been relatively free from legislative attention. The two former are as a rule the best paid officials in the county. Each draws two-thirds of his salary from the state.

The extent to which the legislative delegations go in legislating about county officials may be readily illustrated. Twenty-nine of the forty-six counties have supervisors, though the title is not always the same. In these counties the number of commissioners ranges from two to eight each. In some cases they are elected; in others, appointed. In some cases they are chosen by district; in others, from the county at large. In the remaining seventeen counties the boards range in size from three to seven members each, though two-thirds of them have either three or five members. Some of these boards are elected, and some appointed; some are chosen by district, and some from the county at large. When we come to minor county officials, there is even more variety.

Despite numerous establishings and abolishings, twenty-two counties now have rural police. The number per county ranges from one policeman each in Marion and Dillon counties to fourteen in Charleston County. In five of the twenty-two counties police

6 *Ibid.*, sec. 234.

commissions have been set up. The act for Fairfield County provides for a commission composed of the sheriff ex-officio, who is the chairman, and five other members selected from different sections of the county. These five are appointed by the governor on recommendation of the county legislative delegation or a majority of it. It is the duty then of the commissioners to recommend two men from different sections of the county to the governor to serve as rural policemen. The governor appoints them, they serve under the direction of the commission, and report each Monday to the sheriff.[7]

Cherokee County has two officers called rural policemen and a third who is called a motorcycle policeman. Their salaries are specified in the county supply bill. The rural police receive $160 more each per year than the motorcycle policeman. One of them must reside in Cherokee Township and the other two in Limestone Township. There is no separate body of police commissioners. The sheriff is authorized to appoint and remove them for cause; he makes all rules and regulations for them not inconsistent with the provisions of the act.[8] In Oconee County the governor appoints three or more men of good habits as rural policemen upon the recommendation of a majority of the county legislative delegation. They work under the direction of the sheriff, who must report any misconduct on their part to the legislative delegation.[9] In Marlboro County "on some convenient date" between the first day of January and the first day of April of each year, to be fixed by the supervisor of the county, the county legislative delegation, and the sheriff shall meet "at some convenient place" and elect four rural policemen. The policemen operate under the general direction of the sheriff.[10] In Darlington County the county board of directors appoints the rural police and receives regular reports from them. In Orangeburg County the rural police report to the clerk of the court the first of each month.

Here are five more or less distinct plans for the appointment and regulation of the rural police. There are other variations, but these are sufficient to show the lack of uniformity in a matter in which there can be no necessity for such a condition.

[7] Acts and Joint Resolutions, 1930, Act No. 969.
[8] Ibid., Act No. 369.
[9] Acts and Joint Resolutions, 1928, Act No. 974.
[10] Acts and Joint Resolutions, 1927, Act No. 476.

Magistrates and constables, deputy sheriffs, superintendents of poor farms and homes and of chaingangs, delinquent tax collectors other than sheriffs, county health departments, county physicians, and even courthouse janitors frequently receive the attention of the legislative delegations.

In local matters other than the appointment of county or district officials the delegations take a large part. The following illustrations will show to what extent they deal even in the most trifling details of county affairs.

Each year the legislature passes forty-six county supply bills, one for each county in the state. The respective delegations assist in the preparation of these bills. Some of them specify the objects for which appropriations are made much more in detail than others do. Frequently many other unrelated matters are included in the act by which the bill is passed.

The 1930 supply bill for Fairfield County sets up one miscellaneous contingent fund to the amount of $4,000. This fund is to be expended with the consent of a majority of the delegation. The Aiken County bill for the same year contains four contingent funds. In addition, it has appropriations for office supplies for each of two county offices, and an additional appropriation of $600 for miscellaneous office supplies. The Anderson County bill provides a miscellaneous contingent fund and authorizes the county board of commissioners to pay out of it such expenditures as it sees fit. The Barnwell County bill provides that the ladies' rest room in the courthouse at Barnwell be placed in the custody of a particular lady, who shall receive a salary of $100 for maintaining the same. This bill also provides that the chairman of the board of regents of the county poor home shall receive an annual salary of $200, that the said board is authorized and directed to purchase all groceries and supplies for the county poor home and to have absolute supervision of it. The board may employ a physician for the poor home at a salary not to exceed $200 per annum. The Beaufort County bill makes an appropriation for a mimeograph machine and provides that it shall be available for the use of other officials of the county, but shall remain in the office of the farm and home demonstration agents. It contains also an appropriation of $300 for three bullet-proof vests at not more than $100 each for the sheriff and his deputies.

The Berkeley County bill appropriates $300 for the clerk to the board of county commissioners, to be paid to a woman, whose name is given in the bill, and to no other. The same bill provides that the commutation road tax and all fines collected by the magistrates and the clerk of the court shall be placed in the Peoples Bank of Monck's Corner, South Carolina, together with the convict hire funds, to be disposed of at the direction of the county legislative delegation, and also that all funds now on hand as a sinking fund shall immediately upon the passage of this act be turned over to the treasurer of the county to the account of the general county fund and expended in due course at the direction of the county legislative delegation. The treasurer is also authorized to use all funds now in his hands and not specifically appropriated for some other purpose, including reimbursement funds of the county, in the settlement of all claims against the county, at the direction of the county legislative delegation.

The Calhoun County bill appropriates $200 for painting the exterior of the courthouse in lieu of beautifying the grounds. The Cherokee County bill provides that the sheriff of the county shall be paid 75 cents per day for dieting each prisoner in the county jail and that he shall receive the fees provided by law for doing the constable's work for each of the two magistrates in the city of Gaffney; that the court crier, jury boy, and bailiffs shall be paid a per diem of $3.00 for the actual number of days served; that the fee for holding post mortem examinations shall be $5.00 for each examination, and that the county board shall employ a county physician or physicians whose duties shall be prescribed by the said board and whose compensation shall be fixed by the said board, not exceeding the amount herein appropriated. Another provision in the same act has to do with the management of the county chaingang. The chaingang is to be under the direct supervision and management of the county supervisor. It is his duty to employ and discharge the superintendent of the chaingang and the other employees, but before he may do either his action must meet with the approval and sanction of the county board of township commissioners. When differences arise between the supervisor and the commissioners, a majority vote of the commissioners shall control. Still another provision is added just at this point. It is to the effect that the rural mail carriers shall notify the supervisor or a township commissioner when a bad place occurs in any mail road, and the said supervisor or commissioner shall send some one to fix same. No differences may arise between the supervisor and the commissioners as to repairing bad places in the mail roads. The bill contains an appropriation of $2,500 to be paid over to the judge of probate to be expended on the order of the county physician for hospitalization of the indigent sick.

The Chesterfield County supply bill provides that the cotton weighers of the county shall receive twelve cents per bale for each bale weighed by them, one-half to be paid by the seller and the other half by the buyer. It also provides that no county warrant shall be issued by the board of commissioners until the claim which is the basis of said warrant shall have been endorsed in writing by the county attorney as a valid and legal obligation of the county, provided the majority of the legislative delegation or the clerk of the county board of commissioners shall have first made a written request to the county attorney asking that all claims filed against the county be approved by him as to their legality. The county board is required also to make a contract with some practicing physician to furnish medicine and professional services to the inmates of the county home for the fiscal year 1930. The Colleton County bill contains an appropriation of $50 for the county expert. It is his duty to advise the grand jury. The bill also specifies twenty-seven highways and directs the supervisor to proceed at once with the chaingang to construct them in the order named.

The bill for Edgefield County empowers the board of county commissioners to elect a county dentist. It also appropriates the sum of $100, if so much be necessary, to pay him to do all dental work for the inmates of the county home and county jail and for the convicts on the county chaingang for the year 1930. Another provision of the bill is that all persons and officers of the county are hereby prohibited from using any automobile or other equipment and from buying gasoline for any purpose, except on official duty. No local insurrection followed the enactment of this section of the bill.

The Jasper County bill authorizes the county supervisor to select not more than one county convict, who can be trusted, to remain in the county under the supervision of the county supervisor. It also validates the action of the county supervisor and the county board in keeping a convict in the county a part of the previous year. The Laurens County bill names the county physician, authorizes the delegation to name the courthouse janitor and to fix his duties and salary. It also contains an appropriation of $900 for constructing a suitable front porch to the county jail, to be built by contract approved by the sheriff and the foreman of the grand jury. The Lexington County bill contains an appropriation of $2,400 for salary of a registered nurse, payable on written approval of the county senator. The McCormick County bill authorizes the auditor to levy a tax sufficient to raise the money to meet the appropriations made by law, and then adds that any change he may make in the amount of the levy shall be made only on the written approval of a majority of the county legislative delegation. This written approval must be filed in the office of the clerk of the court. The Marion County bill requires all county officers to open their offices at nine o'clock, A. M., and to keep them open until 5:30 P. M., except on Sundays and legal holidays. On Saturdays the offices may be closed at 3 o'clock P. M. The Newberry County bill provides that the sheriff shall receive ten cents for entering each tax execution returned nulla bona, and ten cents for each nulla bona return on tax executions. The Pickens County bill authorizes the county auditor to appoint the trustees of the several school districts in the county as equalization boards for such districts for the year 1930. It shall be their duty to equalize all property returned in said districts and to return any property or persons not returned. These boards are required to report to the county auditor. The Richland County bill makes appropriations for a health unit with a staff of four persons, and in addition provides for two county physicians at $900 per year each. The Saluda County bill provides for various improvements to the county courthouse and grounds, and authorizes the foreman of the grand jury and the clerk of the court to contract for and supervise the work.

These petty details are taken at random from the county supply bills, or appropriation bills, as found in the Acts and Joint Resolutions of the General Assembly for the year 1930. These bills set up the appropriations for the various purposes under the head of ordinary county affairs. They may be expected to contain many details, the number depending, in part at least on how minutely the appropriations are definitely fixed in the bill. Some of the bills specify just what the salary of each magistrate and constable in the county shall be. Some of the constables receive $12.50 per quarter. In other bills the pay of these officials is set up in one lump sum, leaving the details to be settled by some one else, or at least in some other manner. These bills have nothing to do with school affairs, except that generally they make an appropriation for the salary of the county superintendent of schools.

The details already given are to be found in one class of local bills only. In 1930 the General Assembly passed 566 bills in addition to the 46 county supply bills. From 300 to 400 of these were also of a local nature. A few illustrations will show the range and importance of these acts.

Act No. 1067 requires the maintenance officer chosen by the Newberry County Highway Commission and the chief mechanic in charge of the Newberry Highway Garage to give bond in a surety company, to be approved by the county attorney, in the sum of $1,000 each. The premiums on the bonds are to be paid out of the county treasury. No. 1081 authorizes the County Highway Commission of Orangeburg County to use the county chaingang for certain work on the grounds of the Orangeburg County Fair Association. No. 1089 is an act to fix the compensation of the clerk of the sheriff of Pickens County. No. 1127 is an act to authorize and direct the county board of Spartanburg County to borrow $400,000 to pay current county expense. No. 1136 is an act to create a delinquent tax commission for Sumter County and to define its powers and duties. No. 1160 authorizes the board of trustees of the Wee Nee school district in Williamsburg County to borrow a sum not exceeding $200, to issue its note for the payment thereof, and to provide a tax levy out of the proceeds of which to pay the same. No. 1180 authorizes the treasurer of Union County to transfer any credit balance of any county account for any fiscal year to such other accounts as may have deficits. No. 886 authorizes and directs the Beaufort County board of directors to maintain a certain road in the county. No. 675 provides for the nomination and appointment of trustees for Luray school district No. 10 in Hampton County. No. 666 is an act to fix the salaries of the magistrate and constable at Langley in Aiken County.

These are only a few acts picked at random, but taken with the details given from the county supply bills they give ample evidence that no matter pertaining to county affairs is too minute to demand the attention of the county legislative delegations. With such a condition existing in the state one might be led to expect a large measure of uniformity in county government affairs. But there is very little; in fact, there is probably no more than there would be with 46 separate and distinct county legislatures in the state. The county delegation, not the legislature, is in fact the head of county affairs. Yet, by virtue of the preëminence of the legislature in state affairs and of the courtesies the members of the county delegations enjoy as members of the legislature, the delegations can

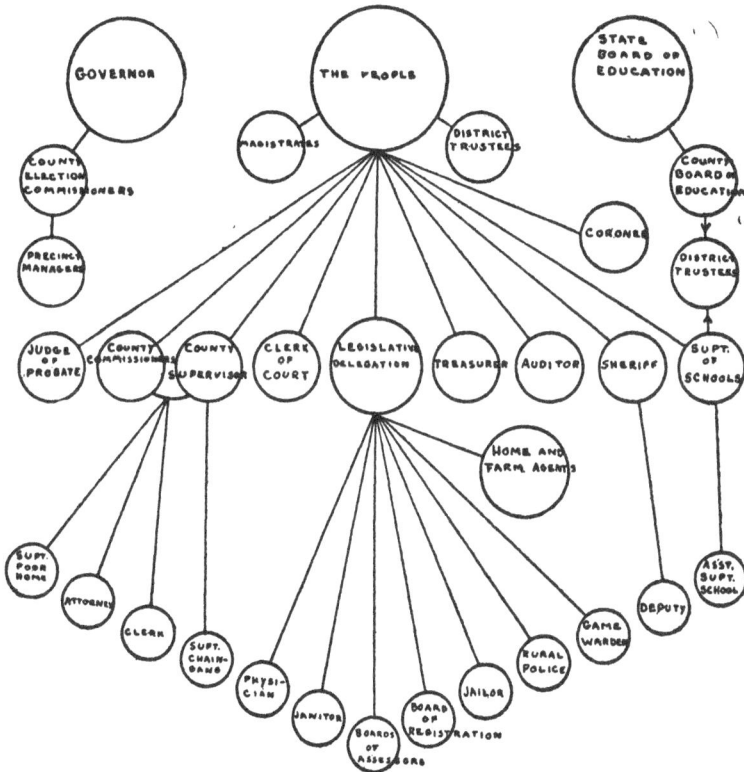

DIAGRAM II
THE COUNTY GOVERNMENT ORGANIZATION
Laurens County, South Carolina

not readily be called to account. They delegate such powers and
duties in local affairs as they do not wish to assume to numerous
commissions and individuals through various and complex methods
of appointment with the result that powers and duties are widely
scattered, responsibility nowhere definitely fixed, and the growth
of local political organizations inimical to the delegation prevented
or easily checkmated. Of course, the purposes of most of the
members of these delegations are not sinister. But they have
power and will retain it at the price of confusion and waste in
county government affairs.

THE COUNTY BOARD OF COMMISSIONERS AND SUBORDINATE OFFICIALS

The general law of the state provides that there shall be in
each county a county board of commissioners composed of the
county supervisor, who is elected by the people, and two commissioners appointed by the governor upon the recommendation of
the General Assembly. The supervisor was to be elected in every
case. With respect to the two commissioners and their mode of
selection there were numerous exceptions in the original law.
They were to be elected by popular vote in Bamberg, Laurens,
Oconee, and McCormick counties. In Richland County one was
to be elected from each township. In Florence County there were
to be three, in Lee five, and in Jasper four commissioners.[11]

According to the law the general jurisdiction of the supervisor
extended over all public highways, roads, bridges, ferries, over
paupers, and in all matters relating to taxes and disbursements of
public funds for county purposes, in his county, and in any other
case that might be necessary for the internal improvement and
local concern of the county. He was given the power to administer oaths also.[12] The law also provided that the board should
submit an annual report on the first day of the first term of the
court of general sessions to the presiding judge. The report was
to cover all expenditures ordered to be paid for the preceding year,
and also the condition of the highways, bridges, the poor farm, and
any other matter concerning the welfare of the county. The judge
then submitted the report to the grand jury. In a few counties
quarterly statements of receipts, disbursements, balances, and debts

[11] Code, 1922, Vol. 3, sec. 1061.   [12] *Ibid.*, sec. 1059.

were required. All claims against the county were required to be presented to the board. When they were approved, the supervisor was authorized to draw his warrant upon the county treasurer in payment of them.

The powers of the board were lodged mainly in the hands of the supervisor. The two commissioners were principally advisory in capacity. Their approval of claims and other matters was little more than a formality.

Reference to Table I will show the present composition of the county boards. There are only sixteen counties with boards as provided for under the general law, and the commissioners in six of these are now elected by popular vote. The county boards may be divided roughly into two classes. Twenty-nine of the forty-six counties have boards consisting of a supervisor and from two to eight commissioners each. The power of the commissioners varies somewhat. In Colleton, Laurens, and Williamsburg counties it is purely advisory. In Fairfield County a board of four members has been recently re-established, and it exercises some restrictions over the supervisor. The supervisor and at least two members must approve all claims, and the whole board is required to make all purchases of supplies from the lowest competent bidder.

The second class is made up of the remaining seventeen counties of the state. These counties have no supervisor. Their boards consist of from three to seven members each. In some instances they are appointed at large from the county, as in the cases of Allendale, Lexington, and Sumter. In Dorchester four members of the board are appointed by district, while the fifth is elected at large from the county. This is a slight modification of the supervisor plan. In Darlington and Georgetown counties the members of the boards are appointed by district. In Orangeburg the board is elected at large from the county, while in Aiken, Dillon, Richland, and one or two others the board members are elected by district.

In neither class is there much uniformity in the number of members comprising the boards, in the manner of selection, or in the length of term. However, the term of office in every case is either two or four years. The counties with the larger boards in nearly every case will be found to be those in which the members are chosen by township. Among these are Charleston, Dillon,

48   County Government in South Carolina

TABLE I
COUNTIES AND COUNTY OFFICIALS

A = appointed.   L = at large.
E = elected.   D = by district.

COUNTIES	No. of County Commissioners	County Supervisor E		Auditor Nominated in Primary	Treasurer Nominated in Primary	Clerk of Court E	Judge of Probate E	Sheriff E	Superintendent of Schools E
1. Abbeville	2	A	L	1	1	1	1	1	1	1
2. Aiken	3	E	D		1	1	1	1	1	1
3. Allendale	3	A	L	..	1	1	1	1	1	1
4. Anderson	4	A	D	1	1	1	1	1	1	1
5. Bamberg	2	E	L	1	1	1	1	1	1	1
6. Barnwell	5	A	D	1	1	1	1	1	1	1
7. Beaufort	5	A	D	1	1	1	1	1	1	1
8. Berkeley	3	A	L	..	1	1	1	1	1	1
9. Calhoun	2	A	L	1	1	1	1	1	1	1
10. Charleston	8	A	D	1	1	1	1	1	1	1
11. Cherokee	6	E	D	1	1	1	1	1	1	1
12. Chester	3	A	L	1	1	1	1	1	1	1
13. Chesterfield	3	E	D	1	1	1	1	1	1	1
14. Clarendon	2	A	L	1	1	1	1	1	1	1
15. Colleton	2	E	D	1	1	1	1	1	1	1
16. Darlington	5	A	D	..	1	1	1	1	1	1
17. Dillon	6	E	D	1	1	1	1	1	1	1A
18. Dorchester	5	1E / 4A	L / D	..	1	1	1	1	1	1
19. Edgefield	2	A	L	1	1	1	1	1	1	1
20. Fairfield	4	A	D	1	1	1	1	1	1	1
21. Florence	6	E	D	..	1	1	1	1	1	1
22. Georgetown	7	A	D	..	1	1	1	..	1	1
23. Greenville	2	A	L	1	1	1	1	1	1	1
24. Greenwood	2	A	L	1	1	1	1	1	1	1
25. Hampton	2	A	L	1	1	1	1	1	1	1
26. Horry	3	A	L		1	1	1	1	1	1
27. Jasper	4	E	D	1	1	1	1	1	1	1
28. Kershaw	4	E	D	..	1	1	1	1	1	1
29. Lancaster	5	A	L	..	1	1	1	1	1	1
30. Laurens	2	E	L	1	1	1	1	1	1	1
31. Lee	3	A	L	..	1	1	1	1	1	1
32. Lexington	5	A	L	..	1	1	1	1	1	1
33. McCormick	2	E	L	1	1	1	1	1	1	1
34. Marion	4	A	L	..	1	1	1	1	1	1
35. Marlboro	2	A	L	1	1	1	1	1	1	1
36. Newberry	2	E	D	1	1	1	1	1	1	1
37. Oconee	2	E	L	1	1	1	1	1	1	1
38. Orangeburg	5	E	L	..	1	1	1	1	1	1
39. Pickens	2	A	L	1	1	1	1	1	1	1
40. Richland	7	E	D	1	1	1	1	1	1	1
41. Saluda	3	E	L	..	1	1	1	1	1	1
42. Spartanburg	3	A	L	..	1	1	1	1	1	1
43. Sumter	7	A	L	..	1	1	1	1	1	1
44. Union	4	A	L	1	1	1	1	1	1	1
45. Williamsburg	5	E	D	1	1	1	1	1	1	1
46. York	2	A	L	1	1	1	1	1	1	1

Note: Certain officials, institutions, and agencies are found in a few counties. See list below:
Sanitary and Drainage Commission: Has charge of county Highways—Charleston County.
Charities and Corrections Commission: Greenville County.
Supervising Auditor: Spartanburg County.
County College: Charleston County.
Register Mesne Conveyance: Charleston, Greenville, Spartanburg counties.
County Library: Allendale, Dillon, Laurens, Newberry counties.
County Court: Florence, Greenville, Orangeburg, Richland.
Master in Equity (A): Aiken (E). Charleston (2), Dorchester, Greenville, Horry, Spartanburg, Sumter counties.
Police Commission (Rural) A: Charleston, Chester, Fairfield, Orangeburg, Spartanburg counties.
County or District Hospital: Aiken, Anderson, Greenville, Marlboro, Newberry, Spartanburg.

TABLE I
COUNTIES AND COUNTY OFFICIALS (Continued)

Counties	Board of Education (Members) A	Boards of Assessors A and E	Health Departments A	Rural Police A	Highway Engineer A	Sinking Fund Commission (Not ex-officio) A	Delinquent Tax Collector (Not Sheriff)	Poor Home and Farm	County Chaingang
1	3	District	....					1	
2	3	Township	1	2				1	1
3	3	Township	....					1	1
4	3	Township	1				1	1	1
5	3	Township	....						1
6	3	Township	Nurse only					1	1
7	3	Township	1					1	
8	3	Township	Nurse only					1	
9	3	Township	....					1	1
10	3	County E	1	14	1				1
11	3	Township	1	3		1	1	1	1
12	3	Township	Nurse only	2	1		1	1	1
13	3	Township	....			1	1	1	1
14	3	District	....	2					1
15	3	Township	....					1	1
16	3	District	1	3	1	1	1		1
17	4	Township	1	1			1		
18	3	Township	Nurse only	3					1
19	3	Township	....				1	1	1
20	3	Township	1		1		1	1	1
21	3	District	Nurse				1	1	1
22	3	Township	....	2					
23	5	Township	1		1	1	1	1	1
24	3	Township	1	2				1	1
25	3	Township	....					1	1
26	3	Township	1	3	1E				1
27	3	Township	....					1	
28	3	Township	Nurse	4				1	1
29	3	Township	Nurse only						
30	3	Township	....	6				1	1
31	3	Township	....	4				1	1
32	3	Township	Nurse only					1	1
33	3	Township	....						
34	3	Township	Nurse only	1			1	1	
35	3	Township	Nurse only	4			1	1	1
36	3	Township	1					1	1
37	3	Township	....	4		1		1	1
38	3	Township	1	6	1			1	1
39	3	Township	....					1	1
40	3	Township	1	8					1
41	3	Township	Nurse only				1	1	1
42	5	Township	1	11			1	1	1
43	3	Township	....	3	1			1	
44	3	Township	....	3				1	1
45	3	Township	....						1
46	3	Township	....	4				1	1

Georgetown, Richland, Cherokee, and a few others. The Charleston board consists of the supervisor and eight commissioners. The eight commissioners are the chairmen of their respective township boards of assessors. The county highways are under the jurisdiction of the Charleston Sanitary and Drainage Commission. Thus the supervisor has been stripped of his most important duties, and now he is concerned with care of the public buildings of the county and some other minor county matters.

A few of the counties have township road commissioners or supervisors. These officials are given jurisdiction over certain roads and over the expenditure of certain road funds. In Spartanburg County the township road supervisors are nominated in the primary and then appointed by the governor. In York they are appointed on the recommendation of the county legislative delegation, while in Hampton they are appointed by special act.

The legislature of the state has had and yet has plenty of freedom in which to experiment with the county board, and it has done no little experimenting, if shifting the number of members, the manner of selection, the name of the board, and such insignificant matters can be called experimentation. With so much freedom to experiment it would seem that in a period of thirty-five years a definite and uniform type of county board suitable to rural counties might now be emerging, but if so one fails to discover it. The development of such a board has apparently not been the motive responsible for the numerous changes that have been made. The confusion that exists in the matter is the direct result of county government by county legislative delegations, and a vast majority of the changes that have been made were made for political purposes. There can be little doubt but that, with the possible exceptions of Charleston, Richland, Greenville, and Spartanburg counties, the board as constituted in the general law would have served the counties just as well as they have been served by boards undergoing constant change. But even at that the board as constituted under the general law was not adapted to a centralized county government with responsible headship.

OFFICIALS SUBORDINATE TO THE COUNTY BOARD

There are numerous employees subordinate to the county board of commissioners, but they are not always chosen by the board. Only the more important ones will be given here.

The clerk to the county board. A very important county official is the clerk to the county board or to the supervisor. He is usually employed by the board. He keeps the minutes of the board meetings and such other records as the board may require. Usually he keeps a record of county bonds and notes. He keeps a record of all claims against the county and of warrants issued to the treasurer in payment of them. He may be also clerk to the county warehouse and purchasing agent to the board, as in Aiken County.

He may be clerk to the county board and county attorney, as in Darlington County. In the latter instance he hires an assistant to keep the books for the board. In some instances he assembles and audits the claims against the county for the attention of the board at its monthly or bi-monthly meeting.

The county highway engineer. The county highway engineer is found in about one-fourth of the counties. As a rule he is a trained engineer. In many of the counties having a supervisor the supervisor is essentially the highway engineer. This is the case in Colleton and Williamsburg counties, where the supervisors are practical road builders and have charge of all road work in their respective counties. Fairfield County has both the supervisor and the engineer, and responsibility for road work is divided. Laurens County has the supervisor also, but the law requires that part of the road work in that county shall be done by contract. The two county commissioners are paid a small sum for inspecting this work. In Darlington County the engineer is hired by the county board of directors and has charge of the county chaingang and all road work in the county. Horry County has a road commissioner, who is nominated in the primary and then recommended and appointed. As in other matters, there is little uniformity in the manner and methods of handling road work, and it is well to keep in mind that what is found in any county at one time may be changed at the next meeting of the General Assembly.

The superintendent of the county chaingang. Thirty-four counties have chaingangs. In some cases the chaingang is divided. In Aiken County it is divided into three approximately equal sections with a superintendent over each. As a rule, the superintendent is chosen by the county board, though he may be chosen by the county supervisor or the engineer. He may be authorized to purchase supplies for the chaingang, as in Fairfield County.

The superintendent of the county poor home and farm. Thirty-four counties still maintain poor homes and farms. In some counties the home and farm are under the general direction of a board. In Barnwell County the board is known as a board of regents, and it does all purchasing for the home. The Greenville County home is in care of the county Charities and Corrections Commission. This commission has charge also of the county jail and the hospitalization of charity patients. In Laurens County there is a superintendent for the home chosen by the county board, who does all the purchasing for the home in any manner he sees fit. In Colleton County the home and farm are under the general care of the county supervisor. He purchases all supplies for the home.

The county attorney. Every county has its attorney or legal advisor. He is chosen by the county board as a rule. Frequently the attorney is influential in his profession and in county affairs generally. He is in position to render valuable service to his county. The salary paid is small, but nevertheless the place is sought for.

The county physician. The county physician is to be found in practically every county, even in those with health units. He is usually hired by the county board, though he may be appointed by the legislative delegation as in Laurens County. In at least one instance he is hired on bid. His duties are confined to giving medical attention to inmates of the county jail, poor home, and the chaingang. This is a county official that probably should go into the discard along with the coroner.

COUNTY FINANCE OFFICIALS

Perhaps the most important single group of county officials is that made up of the county finance officials. They consist of the county auditor, the county treasurer, the township or district boards of assessors, the county board of equalization, the delinquent tax collector, and the sinking fund commission.

The county auditor. The general law provides that the county auditor shall be appointed by the governor with the advice and consent of the senate for a term of four years. But a few exceptions were made to begin with. The term was limited to two years in Bamberg, Berkeley, Horry, Lexington, and Williamsburg counties. In Beaufort County he was to be elected by popular vote for a four-year term.[13] Probably a few other changes have been made since the enactment of the general law. However, as a rule now the auditor is nominated in the primary, recommended by the senator, and appointed by the governor. He is both a state and county official, and receives two-thirds of his salary from the state treasury.

His duties are confined in the main to the assessment of prop-

[13] *Ibid.,* sec. 433.

erty for taxation. His position among the county officials is one of major importance. How great the county's local revenue may be and how equitably local tax burdens are distributed in the first place depends in a large measure upon his initiative, his knowledge, his industry, his efficiency, and his incorruptibility. Though he is only one of numerous officers concerned with the assessment and collection of taxes, he is first in rank and importance. The law appears to give him wide powers in the assessment of property, though they are in part balanced by those given to the county board of equalization.

The assessment of property is deemed a step in the collection of taxes, and the county auditor is given full and complete power, independent of any right conferred upon any county boards of assessors or other officers, to secure full and complete returns of property taxation. The auditor has a right to examine a party in case of evasion of tax return or false return. He may add a penalty of 50 per cent for false return or refusal to return, and the cost of examination of the party making the false return, including expenses of witness and sheriff, must be borne by the party. The auditor's action in such matters shall not be interfered with by any court in the state by mandamus, summary process, or any other proceeding. The only right possessed in such matters by the taxpayer is to pay under protest.[14]

Briefly stated, the auditor's duties are as follows: He receives tax returns from taxpayers from January 1 to February 20. In some counties he is required to attend convenient places in each township or district, after giving thirty days' notice, for receiving tax returns. In other counties he receives returns only in his office. When the returns are in, he hands them over to the township or district boards of assessors. From these boards the returns come back to the auditor, then pass to the county board of equalization, of which the auditor is secretary. When the county board of equalization has completed its work, the auditor proceeds to complete his tax duplicates and abstracts. These records must sometimes wait on the valuations of corporation property, which must come to the auditor from the State Tax Commission by way of the comptroller general of the state. When the auditor has completed his tax duplicates, the law requires that he report to the

[14] *Ibid.*, secs. 451-456.

county superintendent of schools, by school district, the names listed for poll tax, and the amount of taxable property when there is a special levy.

The tax books of the county are required to be completed on or before the 30th day of June, and on the same day the auditor is required to transmit to the comptroller general of the state and to the county commissioners an abstract showing the real property in both town and country and the various kinds of personal property in each district. The auditor is required to enter omitted property on the tax duplicates. He is required also to keep a record of sales and conveyances of real estate in his county. The register of mesne conveyances, who is usually the clerk of court, must have the auditor's endorsement on every deed of conveyance for real property before it can be placed on record. When the state, county, and district levies for the year have been made, the auditor completes his tax records. On or before September 30 he forwards to the comptroller general a complete abstract of the duplicate of his county and an abstract of personalty as well. He prepares also the treasurer's duplicate, which is an abridged form of his own. When he turns the duplicate over to the treasurer, he charges him with the total assessment for the year. On the settlement sheets, as prepared at the end of each fiscal year, the charges appear under the three heads of state, county, and school assessments.

Usually the last act of the auditor for any fiscal year is his settlement with the county treasurer. These settlements show the assessments and penalties charged against the treasurer and all receipts from whatever source, and the items for which he is given credit. These are taxes collected and expended or held in banks to the credit of the county, adjustments and abatements of taxes made by the county auditor and the comptroller general, and the tax executions turned over to the sheriff or to the delinquent tax collector, if other than the sheriff. The law requires that the settlement sheets be signed by the county commissioners or supervisor, the county treasurer, and the county superintendent of schools, and certified by the county auditor. The comptroller general or his representative and the foreman of the grand jury are also required to be present to witness the settlement.

The original method of appointing the auditor was perhaps

the better one. But popular pressure has led to a modification of the method to what virtually amounts to election by popular vote. At best, the most difficult problem facing local government is the assessment of property for taxation. It can scarcely be doubted that as a general rule the direct responsibility of the tax assessors to the local electorate makes the problem still more difficult.

Township and district boards of assessors. According to the law property must be assessed for taxation in all counties by township boards of assessors, special boards of assessors for cities and towns, and county boards of equalization. Generally, these boards are appointed by the governor every two years upon the recommendation of the respective county legislative delegations. The principal exceptions to the general law are as follows: In Horry, Newberry, and Pickens counties the township boards are appointed on the recommendation of the county auditor. In Berkeley County the board consists of one person from each parish appointed by the governor. In Darlington and Abbeville counties the trustees of the respective school districts are the boards of assessors. The same is true of Richland County outside of the city of Columbia. The trustees of many of the districts in these counties are elected by popular vote. In Saluda County the chairmen of the district trustees are the assessors. In Hampton County one person in each school district, appointed by the governor, is the assessor. In Marlboro County the governor may appoint three men in each school district who shall constitute a board of assessors. In Cherokee County the township boards of assessors consist of the township commissioner and two competent persons appointed by the governor. In Barnwell and Chester counties the duties of township boards of assessors are devolved upon the township boards of commissioners.[15]

In Charleston County the board of assessment consists of eight members, five of whom must be citizens of the city of Charleston. This board is elected by popular vote. It constitutes three bodies in one: the county board of assessment, the county board of equalization, and with the supervisor, the county board of commissioners.

The boards most frequently found are the township boards. With few exceptions these boards consist of three members each,

[15] *Ibid.*, secs. 469-471.

appointed by the governor on the recommendation of the legislative delegation. Three townships in Newberry County have boards of five members each, and there may be other exceptions. In at least four counties the school district trustees are the boards of assessors. Many of these are elected by popular vote. Some city school districts have boards appointed in very complicated ways. For instance, the district for the city of Chester has a board of three members, one appointed by the city council, one by the trustees of the school district, and one by the county board of directors. The district for the city of Florence has two boards. The board for the part of the district within the city is appointed by the city council. That for the part of the district without the city is appointed by special act. Several towns have special boards of assessors. As a rule, these boards are appointed by the town councils, though not always. Certain counties, as has already been pointed out, have special plans at variance with the two most commonly found. The legislative delegations are instrumental in the appointment of all boards, except in those cases where they are elected by popular vote or are chosen by town or city councils. Frequently the delegation consults the county auditor before making recommendations.

These township or district and special boards, together with the county auditor, are required by law to seek and discover, on or before the first Tuesday in March of each year, all property subject to taxation and not previously returned. The boards themselves have the right to increase or lower the valuation of any property as fixed by the county auditor or as returned by any person. But they may not reduce the aggregate below the aggregate as returned by the county auditor. The board may assess real estate and improvements which have not been returned or assessed previously.[16] The county auditor is required to prepare an alphabetical list of the property holders of each township or district for the use of the chairmen of the boards. With the assistance of the list each township or district chairman is required to canvass his territory immediately after February 20 of each year in order to discover property or polls not returned to the auditor.

The township or district boards of assessors stand next to the county auditor in importance as cogs in the tax assessing machin-

[16] *Ibid.*, sec. 475.

ery. These boards work in rather restricted areas. The school districts as a rule are smaller than the townships, but in either case the area is not very large. Since the boards are made up as a rule of three men, who are residents of their respective districts, there seems to be no sound reason why any tangible property should escape. If such boards have anything in their favor, it lies in the fact that they are sufficiently familiar with their districts to know the persons and property to be found in them. They are weak in that they are not familiar with expert methods in assessing property and especially in the fact that they are too close to the people whose property they must assess. Add to that the fact that in some districts the boards are chosen by popular vote, and one could scarcely imagine a more undesirable method of assessing property for taxation. However, what is accomplished depends to a great extent upon the county auditor.

The county board of equalization. The county board of equalization is made up of the chairmen of the township or district and special boards, except in the counties of Charleston, Berkeley, Saluda, and Hampton. However, in every case the board is either a part of the assessing machinery or all of it, so that in fact we are dealing with boards which are the same except for certain purposes only. The law requires that the auditor shall add to or deduct from the value of real estate or personal property as directed by the board of equalization.[17] The work of the county board of equalization is less important than that of the boards of assessors. Its principal duty is to hear protests against increases in valuation of $100 or more made by the boards of assessors or the assessor, as the case may be. However, it does make changes in individual returns and it may equalize as between townships or districts.

The county treasurer. From the officials concerned with the assessment of property for taxation we turn next to those concerned with the collection of taxes. The county treasurer is the tax collector for the county. When he receives his tax duplicate from the auditor, he begins to prepare his tax receipts; or he may, as in Darlington County, where a special form of tax receipt is used, prepare his receipts in quadruplicate from the auditor's duplicate. When the tax receipts have been prepared, the tax books are open and the treasurer is ready to receive taxes. The usual date for opening the books is October 15.

[17] *Ibid.*, sec. 489.

The treasurer is both a state and county official. Two-thirds of his annual salary come from the state treasury. Under the general law he too was to be appointed by the governor with the advice and consent of the senate, except in Beaufort County, where he was to be elected by popular vote. But as a result of popular demand he is now nominated in the primary, recommended by the senator, and appointed by the governor in most cases.

There are many provisions in the law concerning the duties of the treasurer. In some counties he may attend certain convenient places, after giving twenty days' notice, in order to collect taxes. As a rule, this provision is ignored. The law requires that he forward state taxes collected to the state treasurer on the first and fifteenth of each month; that he report on collections to both the county commissioners and the county superintendent of schools on the first and fifteenth of each month; that he make a report of collections, disbursements, and cash balances to the comptroller general on the first of each month. He is required to deposit any sums not to be demanded for six months or more in some chartered bank at interest, and he may require a depositor's guaranty bond for the same. He is also required to make an annual report to the county superintendent of schools on the first of November, showing the taxes collected by district. Still another report required by the law is one to the judge of the court of general sessions. This must be made at the second term after January first, and must cover all county and school claims paid for the previous fiscal year. The judge then submits the report to the grand jury.[18] For the most part these requirements are ignored. If not, they are observed in a perfunctory manner only.

The treasurer receives taxes from October 15 to March 15. When the latter date arrives, if the time for the payment of taxes has not been extended, he issues executions against the unpaid taxes and turns them over to the delinquent tax collector.

The delinquent tax collector. Originally the sheriff was the delinquent tax collector. But the collection of delinquent taxes has been the subject of legislative changes. Table I shows thirteen counties in which the collection of delinquent taxes has been taken out of the hands of the sheriff and lodged in a special de-

[18] *Ibid.,* secs. 499-504.

linquent tax collector appointed by the county board of commissioners, or on the recommendations of the county legislative delegation.

There are many provisions of the law concerning the duties of the delinquent tax collector. One is that the sheriff must make return of all tax executions to the treasurer within ninety days after they have been issued to him, designating such as may be nulla bona and such as may have been collected by distress or sale. Within the same time he must pay over to the treasurer all taxes and penalties collected. The treasurer is then directed at the last term of the circuit court of each year to deliver to the foreman of the grand jury a complete list of all tax executions not collected. The grand jury is required to examine the list and to present the sheriff for any default or neglect of duty in the enforcement of such executions.

If the sheriff makes default in paying over in the required time any moneys collected on the executions, the treasurer is directed to bring suit against him in any court of competent jurisdiction. The sheriff is liable for treble the amount for which he has defaulted. In case the county suffers loss because of the failure of the treasurer to perform his duty in the matter he becomes liable therefor.[19]

These provisions of the law apply to special delinquent tax collectors as well as to the sheriffs. As is the case with so many laws concerning county affairs, these are little more than dead letters.

The plan of taking the collection of delinquent taxes out of the hands of the sheriff, who is an elective officer, and placing it in the hands of an appointive official is undoubtedly sound in theory. Unfortunately, in actual practice it shows no better results than the old plan in those cases studied. Aside from the force of custom and whatever virtue there may be in the multiplication of county officials and the sharing of their duties, there seems to be no sound reason why the collection of all taxes, whether delinquent or not, should not be made by the same official.

The sinking fund commission. Every county has its sinking fund commission. Some of them have many. For instance, the school district trustees in Laurens County are also sinking fund

19 *Ibid.*, sec. 527.

commissions for their respective districts. The sinking fund commission is an important body in those counties which have issued term bonds in large sums. In the majority of counties the sinking fund commission is an ex-officio commission composed of the county treasurer, the county auditor, and the clerk of the court. In five counties the ex-officio commissions have been replaced by commissions appointed on the recommendation of the respective legislative delegations. This plan is an improvement over the original one in certain respects, but it is objectionable in that it serves to increase the number of county officials, a number already too large.

The county sinking fund commission is the forfeited land commission also in those counties having an ex-officio commission. In the other counties the latter is composed of the auditor, the treasurer, and the clerk of the court. The duties of the land commission are not onerous. It bids off for the state sinking fund commission land sold for taxes, when there are no other bids or when the bids do not cover the tax charge. It also disposes of such lands for the state sinking fund commission. The actual bidding off of the land sold for taxes usually falls to the county auditor. After the expiration of a certain period the commission is supposed to take title to the land which has been bid off and which has not been redeemed. Such action, however, is rarely taken.

COUNTY SCHOOL OFFICIALS

The so-called weak county unit school system is found in the state. In general the machinery of the system is made up of the following: an elective county superintendent of schools, a board of education composed of the superintendent and two other members appointed by the state board of education, and boards of district trustees elected by popular vote or appointed by the county board. The system is weak however in that the powers and duties of the school officials are so divided between the county superintendent and the county board, on the one hand, and the district trustees, on the other, that there is no single school authority who may direct school affairs and who may be held responsible for them. The system is weak also in that the county superintendent must be elected by popular vote.

The machinery of the county school system is subject to frequent change by the legislature. The manner of selecting the district trustees is subject to most frequent change. In 1930 the legislature passed 108 local laws relating in the main to local districts and district trustees. The tendency to select district trustees by popular vote seems to be growing. The constitution of 1895 provided that the manner of selecting trustees in special districts already established was not subject to change by legislative enactment. Not satisfied with this limitation on its power, in 1930 the General Assembly proposed a constitutional amendment to remove it. If the proposed amendment is finally ratified, the trustees of all school districts in the state will join the county boards of commissioners, the rural police, and other county and district officials as objects upon which the legislature may spend many additional hours.

The county superintendent of schools. The law requires the election of a county superintendent of education in each county, whose term of office is four years. As is to be expected, there are some exceptions. Most of these have to do with the term of office. In Bamberg, Berkeley, and perhaps other counties the term is two years rather than four.[20] In Dillon County the superintendent of schools is appointed by the governor upon the recommendation of the county board of education.

The law sets up no qualifications for the office of county superintendent. Numerous duties are required of him by the law. He must visit the schools of his county at least once each year and more often, if practicable, and he should make suggestions to the teachers concerning discipline, methods of instruction, courses of instruction, classification of pupils, and any other matter which he thinks may be improved. He is required to attend the annual settlement of the county treasurer with the auditor and comptroller general. He is required also to file an annual report of claims filed, audited, allowed, and ordered to be paid during the fiscal year, to the presiding judge at the third term of the court of general sessions held after the first day of January in each year. The judge submits the report to the grand jury, and the grand jury may report back to the judge on any matter in the report which seems worthy of the attention of the court. The report must then be filed in the office of the clerk of the court. It is

[20] *Ibid.,* sec. 2566.

needless to say that this report is not made. It is the duty of the superintendent to report to the county treasurer on or before the 15th of July in each year all school claims approved during the preceding fiscal year. These claims must be reported by school district.[21]

Perhaps the most important single duty of the superintendent according to the law is that of approving school warrants. No warrant against any public school fund may be paid by the county treasurer until it has been approved by the county superintendent.[22] This provision of the law does not apply however to funds of districts created by special acts. Through this provision of the law the superintendent may exercise some control over the expenditure of district funds. But the good results that might accrue from this provision of the law are largely nullified by that which requires that the superintendent be elected by popular vote. If he refuses to approve warrants drawn by the district trustees, he makes political enemies. Therefore, if he wishes to retain his office, he is likely to approve the warrants presented to him. Sometimes he approves them when the funds are exhausted. The problem is then shifted to the shoulders of the treasurer. The superintendent apportions the proceeds of the three and four mill taxes and the state aid received to the various districts in his county.

The county board of education. The county board of education is composed of three members, one of whom is the county superintendent of schools. The members of the board hold office for terms of four years usually. They are appointed by the state board of education at its meeting in June every fourth year.[23] The most striking exception to the general law is to be found in the case of Dillon County. The board in Dillon is composed of three members appointed by the state board of education upon the recommendation of the county legislative delegation. One member is chosen chairman at a salary of $150 per year. He serves for three years, while the other two serve for terms of one and two years respectively. The county superintendent is an ex-officio member of the board. He has an equal vote with the other members, according to the law, but in case of a tie the recommendation of the appointed members prevails. This is an unusual arrange-

[21] *Ibid.*, secs. 2568, 2569, 2570, 2571, 2573.
[22] *Ibid.*, sec. 2628.
[23] *Ibid.*, sec. 2588.

ment, which seems to guarantee the control of county school affairs by the board, if they can agree. In this case the board recommends the county superintendent and the governor appoints him.

In Marion and Greenville counties the boards consist of five members each, one of which is the county superintendent. The other four members in each case are chosen on the recommendation of the county legislative delegations.

The law states that the county board of education constitutes an advisory body with whom the county superintendent shall have the right to consult when he is in doubt as to his official duty, and also a tribunal for determining any matter of local controversy in reference to the construction or administration of school laws, with the power to summon witnesses and take testimony, if necessary. When the board makes a decision, it is binding on the parties to the controversy, though either party may appeal to the state board through the county board.[24]

The board is required to meet at least twice each year for the purpose of examining applicants for teachers' certificates and the transaction of other business. The board together with the district trustees is required to see that the subjects prescribed by law are taught in the public schools. The county boards divide their counties into convenient districts within the limitations as to size prescribed by the constitution. But new districts may be created only on petition of at least one-third of the qualified voters in the proposed district. Consolidation of existing districts may be made in the same manner, though the size of them may not be greater than that specified in the constitution. The sale of school property in any district can be made by the district trustees only on consent of the county board. The board may transfer pupils from one district to another, even if the trustees of the latter do not consent. But such pupils must pay, if financially able, tuition equal in amount to the per capita expenditure from the special tax for operating the school to which the pupils are transferred.

The county boards are authorized to set aside annually a sum equal to five per cent of the entire public school funds of their respective counties for the purpose of encouraging and aiding in the construction of adequate school buildings.[25]

24 *Ibid.*, sec. 2597.
25 *Ibid.*, secs. 2598, 2599, 2618, 2619, 2620, 2631.

The general law authorizes the county boards of education to appoint three trustees for each school district in their respective counties for overlapping terms.[26] This provision does not apply to many districts in the state. Numerous districts have been authorized by special act to elect their trustees, while certain county boards of education have been directed to order special elections for trustees on petition of a majority of the qualified electors in any school district. School districts created by special act may elect their trustees, or may have them appointed, or some may be elected and some appointed, as is the case in at least one instance.

District trustees. The district trustees must be chosen from the qualified electors and taxpayers of their respective districts. The law declares that they shall take the management and control of local educational interests, shall visit each school at least once in every school term, and shall be subject to the supervision and orders of the county board of education.[27] Despite the provision that the trustees shall be subject to the supervision and orders of the county board of education, they are in position without doubt to determine very largely the educational policies of their respective counties by virtue of the powers conferred on them and the political pressure they can bring to bear on the system. They are authorized to provide schoolhouses, to employ and discharge teachers, to suspend or dismiss pupils, to call meetings of the qualified electors of their respective districts, to control school property, to visit the schools from time to time, to charge and collect matriculation and incidental fees from pupils, when such are allowed by the General Assembly, and to arrange for medical and dental inspection of pupils.[28]

Their power to employ and discharge teachers, however, has been held by the courts to be subject to the supervision and orders of the county board of education. The attorney general of the state has given it as his opinion that the discipline necessary to get a pupil to obey the rules of the school is left to the wise discretion of the teacher. On the other hand, he has given it as his opinion also that the trustees should determine the length of the school

---

[26] Acts and Joint Resolutions, 1922, Act No. 459.
[27] Code, 1922, Vol. 3, sec. 2616.
[28] *Ibid.*, sec. 2630.

day.[29]   The county board of education is empowered to regulate the opening and closing of the school terms.   The district trustees may not make contracts in excess of the funds apportioned to their districts, nor shall they employ persons related to themselves within the second degree as teachers without the written approval of the county board of education or the written request of a majority of the parents or guardians of the children attending the school.   They may transfer pupils from one district to another under certain conditions, and they may condemn property for school purposes.   They may purchase textbooks for the children of indigent parents, but the sum so expended may not exceed five per cent of the total school funds for any one year.[30]

Other school officials.   Other school officials are found in nearly every county.   With very few exceptions the county superintendent has a full-time or part-time clerk who keeps the statistical and financial records for the superintendent's office.   Assistant superintendents are found in only three counties, and in one of these the official so designated is merely a clerk.   Attendance officers are found in two counties only.   A rural and mill school supervisor is found in Spartanburg County.

COURT AND LAW ENFORCEMENT OFFICIALS

The clerk of the court of common pleas and general sessions. The clerk of the court is one of the four constitutional county officials.   The state is divided into fourteen judicial circuits.   Each circuit is composed of a number of counties.   Circuit court is held in each county usually five times each year.   There are, as a rule, three terms of the court of general sessions, the criminal court, and two terms of the court of common pleas or civil court.   The judges who preside over these courts are chosen by the state legislature, but each county elects its own clerk by popular vote for a term of four years.   Unless there is a special act making other provisions, the clerk has charge of the county courthouse and hires the janitor.

He keeps the criminal and civil dockets and other records of the circuit courts.   In some counties he issues marriage licenses, while in others this duty is performed by the judge of probate. The law requires him to report once each month to the auditor and

[29] *General School Law of South Carolina,* pp. 48-49.
[30] Code 1922, Vol. 3, sec. 2684.

treasurer the amount of money collected on account of licenses, fines, penalties, and forfeitures for the preceding month.[31]

His compensation is largely in fees, though the county supply bill may contain an appropriation for salary or for clerical help for his office. Except where special sinking fund commissions have been set up, he is an ex-officio member of the county sinking fund commission. He is also a member of the forfeited land commission of his county.

The clerk of the court is register of mesne conveyances for his county, except in the counties of Charleston, Greenville, and Spartanburg. In those counties the register of mesne conveyances is a separate official elected by popular vote. The clerk's duties as register of mesne conveyances consist in recording deeds, marriage settlements, conveyances, mortgages, renunciations of dower, crop liens and the like.

The clerk of court may be master in equity also, though that is a separate appointive office in six counties and an elective one in one county. Charleston County has two masters. In Darlington, Colleton, and certain other counties the judge of probate is master in equity. As master in equity the clerk may hear motions and make orders in causes praying equitable relief, may extend the time to answer or demur, may grant leave to amend pleadings and to make new parties, may appoint guardians *ad litem* for infants, and make all orders necessary for the service publications of absent defendants. He has power also to make orders of reference in matters of account, reserving all the equities of the parties, and may grant all such orders of an interlocutory character as may be necessary to prepare such causes for a hearing on merit. All his orders are subject to revision by the circuit judge. He must execute and perform all orders of the court upon reference to him in conformity to the practice of the court. He may administer oaths, take depositions, affidavits, renunciation of dower, probate deeds and other instruments, and take testimony by commission. He may also grant orders in partition and dower.[32]

The judge of probate. A second constitutional officer is the judge of probate, who is chosen by popular vote for a term of four years. In several counties he is also master in equity. He pro-

---

[31] *Ibid.*, sec. 2156.
[32] *Ibid.*, secs. 2233-2235.

bates wills, and has jurisdiction in all matters testamentary and of administration, in business pertaining to minors and allotment of dower, in cases of idiocy and lunacy and persons *non compos mentis.* He has jurisdiction in relation to the appointment and removal of guardians and the management and disposition of the estates of their wards. He exercises original jurisdiction in relation to trustees appointed by will.[33]

He is required by law to hold a session of his court at or near the courthouse on the first Monday of each month. He is judge of the juvenile court also, and thus makes disposition of delinquent boys and girls who are brought before him. He disburses the pension fund provided by the state for Confederate veterans. In those counties which have supplemented the state pension for Confederate veterans he also disburses the county supplement. The greater part of his compensation comes from fees, but the county usually appropriates to the support of his office and in some cases to his salary.

Magistrates. Magistrates are not so numerous in South Carolina as in some other states. The constitution states that a sufficient number shall be appointed in each county by the governor with the advice and consent of the senate. In the rural areas one magistrate to each township seems to have been the rule heretofore, but the present tendency in some counties is to reduce the number. Despite the constitutional provision concerning their appointment, the custom has grown up to have them nominated in the primary and then commissioned by the governor. Their names do not appear on the tickets for the general election.

The jurisdiction of the magistrates does not differ greatly from that possessed by such officers elsewhere. In criminal cases it is exclusive if the punishment does not exceed a fine of $100 or imprisonment for 30 days. The magistrates have concurrent jurisdiction with the court of general sessions in cases of riot, assault and battery, and larceny. They also sit as examining or committing courts.[34]

In civil cases their jurisdiction does not extend over cases in which the value of property or the amount claimed exceeds $100;

[33] *Ibid.,* Vol. 1, secs. 166 and 167.
[34] *Ibid.,* Vol. 3, sec. 2243.

neither does it extend to cases in which title to real estate is in question nor to cases in chancery.

All magistrates receive salaries in lieu of fees in criminal cases, but they are paid in fees for civil work.

The law requires monthly reports to the county treasurer and auditor from all magistrates, but the law is ignored in many instances.

Constables. The constitution provides that the magistrates may each appoint a constable. This plan is still followed in numerous counties, but in others there is a tendency to reduce the number. In most cases where there is a rural police force of as many as three officers the number of constables has been reduced. In some counties in which a rural police force has been established two or more constables have been appointed by the legislative delegation to serve in the larger centers of the county. As in case of the magistrates, the constables are paid small salaries in lieu of fees for work in criminal cases.

Jurors. The jurors are important local officials in the administration of justice, but they seldom justify the popular faith that is placed in them. They may be useful in reflecting popular attitudes towards crime, but they do not guarantee that criminals will be brought into the courts nor that punishment will be meted out to them when they are brought to trial.

The jury list is prepared by the jury commission, which is composed of the county auditor, the county treasurer, and the clerk of the court. The list is made up of qualified electors of good moral character between the ages of twenty-one and sixty-five. It is prepared usually in December of each year, though in Newberry County it is prepared in July. Ten to twenty days before the first day of each week of any term of court thirty-six jurors are drawn publicly. However, in several counties, when the term of court is two or more weeks, no petit jurors may serve more than one week. In Marlboro and Clarendon counties thirty-six jurors are drawn for each week. In certain counties jurors drawn for the second week may be held over.

The constitution provides that all persons charged with an offense shall have the right to demand and obtain a trial by jury. The jury in all cases in all courts inferior to the circuit court consists of six men. The grand jury of each county consists of eighteen men, and twelve of these must agree on a matter before it can be submitted to the court. The petit jury consists of twelve men, all of whom must agree to a verdict in order to render the same.[35]

In addition to determining what shall be submitted to the court, but doubtless a result of this function, the grand jury is given some other important duties. It can not intelligently perform some of these. The foreman of the grand jury is required to be present at the annual settlement between the county auditor and the county treasurer. The annual reports, required by law of several county officials, are required to be submitted to the grand jury by the circuit judge, and the records of all county officials are subject to examination by it. In several counties the grand jury is authorized to hire auditors to make periodic audits of all county affairs. Unfortunately, in some instances, after the audit is made it serves for little else than a source of confusion.

The sheriff. A third constitutional county officer is the sheriff. He must be elected by popular vote for a term of four years. Perhaps no other county official is known so familiarly by the average citizen. In case of a vacancy in the office, the governor of the state fills it. In the interim the clerk of the court may take charge until the coroner arrives or until the appointment is made. The law requires the sheriff to make a written monthly report to the treasurer and auditor showing the amount of money collected by him on account of licenses, fines, penalties, and forfeitures.[36] In practice he reports when he gets ready. He is subject to heavy penalty if he purchases tax executions.

The sheriff is the executive officer of the circuit court. He may be authorized to perform the duties of the bailiff or constable to magistrates in his county. He has one or more deputies. In some instances he appoints them himself; again they are appointed by the delegation or upon its recommendation. Almost invariably he has a clerk, who may be a combination deputy and bookkeeper, or merely a full-time or part-time bookkeeper.

In thirty-three counties of the state the sheriff is delinquent tax collector also. There is a tendency to take the duties of collecting delinquent taxes from him. Undoubtedly it should be done. Law

---

[35] South Carolina Constitution of 1895. Art. V, sec. 22.
[36] Code, 1922, Vol. 3, sec. 2087.

enforcement and the collection of taxes should not be combined in one office. But the present plan of appointing a separate official to collect delinquent taxes serves to increase the number of county officials, to reduce the compensation of the sheriff in some counties to a figure that is entirely too low, and to increase the cost of collection without actually getting any more of such taxes collected than under the old plan.

The sheriff may appoint or help to appoint the rural police of his county, and in some instances they are subject to his regulations and supervision.

Rural police. Twenty-two counties of the state have rural police. In five of those counties there are police commissions which appoint or recommend the appointment of the police. The method of appointment and control, as has already been pointed out, varies much. A competent police force for every county to patrol the highways and the rural districts is an excellent thing. Perhaps all counties in the state will eventually establish such a force. But one can see no reason for rural police and deputy sheriffs both in the same county; neither for police commissions nor for the numerous methods of appointment and control. All law enforcing officials of the county should be under one head and subject to his control.

Coroner. The fourth constitutional county officer is the coroner. He remains in many state constitutions as a monument to resistance to change in the matter of the abolition of political office. It is a difficult thing to abolish a constitutional or other office, unless one or more are created to take its place.

The coroner must be elected by popular vote every four years. His duties are those generally performed by coroners elsewhere. In some states, aside from the fact that his name helps to clutter up the county ballot and that he is voted for as a matter of course, his election is of little consequence. He gets nothing unless he holds an inquest, and he may not hold one during his term. Here the story is different. Whether he has little or much to do he gets a salary. His salary ranges from $100 per year in each of the counties of Berkeley, Georgetown, and McCormick to $3,600 in Charleston County. In the last named county he has a deputy on a salary of $2,000 per year. In several of the counties appropriations are made for travel expense for the coroner in addition to his salary.

County judges and solicitors. The law provides that county courts may be established on petition of one-third of the registered electors of a county, asking for an election to be held on the matter, provided a majority vote is cast in favor of the court. The petition asking for the election must be filed with the clerk of the circuit court.

The jurisdiction of the county court extends over all criminal cases, except those for murder, manslaughter, rape, attempt to rape, arson, common law burglary, bribery, and perjury. In criminal cases and special proceedings, both at law and equity, it has jurisdiction where the value of the property or the amount claimed does not exceed $1,000. It may hear and determine appeals from judgments rendered by magistrates, but it may not try an action involving the title to real estate.[37]

Where these courts are established the criminal jurisdiction of the magistrates is abolished, except that they may issue warrants and hold preliminary examinations. Their civil jurisdiction is limited to cases and proceedings in which the amount involved does not exceed $25.00.

The county judge must be a resident attorney at law. He is elected by popular vote for a term of four years. Upon the establishment of the court the first county solicitor is appointed by the governor on the recommendation of the county legislative delegation. After the first term, he is elected by popular vote. He must also be a resident attorney of his county.[38] Such are the provisions of the general law.

County courts have been established in Florence, Greenville, Orangeburg, and Richland counties. They were created by special acts, and the jurisdiction conferred upon them is greater than that given in the general law. The manner of selecting judges and solicitors is also changed.

COUNTY ELECTION OFFICIALS

The board of registration. Every county has a board of registration consisting of three members appointed by the governor with the advice and consent of the senate. There is at least one

[37] Code, 1922, Vol. I, secs. 72-74.
[38] *Ibid.*, sec. 81.

exception to this plan. In Pickens County the board is elected by popular vote. The term of office is two years. The board enrolls the names of the qualified electors on the registration books, which are public records and subject to inspection by any citizen of the county. The voting precincts are fixed by the General Assembly. Each parish or township may be a voting place. The same is true of each city ward.

Election commissioners. The counties have two sets of election commissioners, one for state and county officials, and one for federal officials. Both sets are appointed by the governor of the state. Each set of commissioners appoints three managers of election for each polling place. The managers make returns to the commissioners by whom they were appointed. The commissioners make up the county boards of canvassers.[39] Thus each county has two boards of canvassers in every general election.

COUNTY HEALTH, CONSERVATION, AND DEVELOPMENT OFFICIALS

The last group of officials operating within the county may be listed as health, conservation, and development officials. They consist of health officers, game wardens, and farm and home demonstration agents. They are separate and distinct from each other.

County health boards and departments. Fifteen counties have health boards and departments, while eleven others have health nurses. The health boards are set up by special acts. In Cherokee County the health board consists of the county superintendent of schools, the president of the county federation of women's clubs or a duly elected or appointed member of the federation, and a resident of the county appointed by the legislative delegation. In Spartanburg County the board consists of five members, three of whom are appointed by the governor upon the recommendation of the legislative delegation. The other two members are ex-officio. They are the superintendent of schools and a member of the county board of commissioners.

These boards of health establish health departments. Each health department is in charge of a physician appointed by the county board of health upon the nomination of the state board of

[39] Code, 1922, Vol. 3, secs. 234 and 244.

health. The health departments consist of a staff of three or more persons. They are paid in part out of local funds.

In some counties with health departments there are no boards of health. In Darlington County the county board of directors appoints the county health officer upon the recommendation of the county medical association and the state board of health. In Fairfield County the health officer is chosen by the county board on the recommendation of the legislative delegation and the state board of health. Health nurses may be provided by special act, as in certain townships in York County, and a special levy made out of the proceeds of which to pay her salary.

Game wardens. Each county has one or more game wardens. These officials are appointed by the governor upon the recommendation of the county legislative delegations. There are, however, some exceptions. In Cherokee County the game warden is nominated in the primary, then recommended and appointed.[40] The same is true in York County.

Farm and home demonstration agents. Under a recent act of the General Assembly every county in the state must have a farm and home demonstration agent. These agents are now paid in full out of federal and state funds, and they are placed in the counties by the extension forces of the state of South Carolina, subject to the confirmation of the respective county legislative delegations.[41]

The present policy has some advantages over the old plan. It relieves the agents from anxiety about their jobs, and provides for the continuation of this very important work regardless of local whims.

SUMMARY

An attempt to portray the county government machinery as it exists in the state is difficult, for it is characterized by remarkable complexity and variety in detail. It is as completely free from responsible headship as any government is ever likely to be. It illustrates how extensively some state officials, the county legislative delegations, "meddle" in county affairs.

The county officials are grouped roughly into six groups. In the first group there is some centralization of authority in the county board of commissioners or in the supervisor. This group

---

[40] Acts and Joint Resolutions, 1930, Act No. 922.
[41] Acts and Joint Resolutions, 1929, Act No. 600.

has to do with the county roads in the main, though in many counties it also has charge of the care of the poor. The funds used by this department come from the finance department, but it is not responsible to the latter. When it expends all its funds, it goes to the delegation for more or for authority to create a temporary deficit.

The second group consists of numerous individuals, all of whom are virtually elected by the people. The more important ones, the treasurer, the auditor, and the boards of assessors may exhibit various degrees of coöperative effort, but they are virtually coördinate officials among themselves, and they are subject to no effective control elsewhere within the county or without.

The third group is made up of the county school officials. In this group the county board of education, including the county superintendent, and the district trustees, are practically two coordinate bodies. Thus authority in school affairs is divided. Nor are the school officials responsible to any other county authority. When they want something they turn to the legislative delegation.

The fourth group, composed of the court and law enforcement officials, represents more lack of organization and cohesion than any other group. The four constitutional officers are found in this group. They are elected by the people and are responsible to them alone. The minor officials in this group are subject to continual manipulation by the legislative delegations.

The group of election officials represents three separate and distinct sets: the board of registration, the election commissioners and precinct managers for state and county offices, and the election commissioners and precinct managers for federal offices. The precinct election managers, the township boards of assessors, the school district trustees, and the township magistrate and constable make up a rather large number of district officials.

The sixth and last group is made up of three sets of wholly separate officials. They are responsible almost entirely to state officials, if we include the legislative delegations as such.

These groups, or parts of them, touch at various points. In case they receive any compensation most of them get it or a part of it from the county treasury. Their claims in most cases are approved by the county board. The groups, except the first, are headless in themselves, nor are they responsible as groups to a single head.   There are, however, interlocking features between the groups.   For instance, the sheriff may be delinquent tax collector.   Until recently in Barnwell County the county superintendent of schools was also the county auditor.   The county board of commissioners may appoint the rural police and direct their work.   The county commissioners may be the county board of assessment and equalization as in Charleston County.   And the school district trustees may be the district boards of assessors, as in Darlington County.

However, above all the groups exists the county legislative delegation, apparently watching jealously every county or local official and his every power, and even seeking additional control over him. At each succeeding annual meeting of the General Assembly it is likely to add to the confusion already existing in county and district affairs.

CHAPTER IV

THE COUNTY THE UNIT OF LOCAL GOVERNMENT
AND THE AGENT OF THE STATE

Whether we look at the county as the unit of local government or as the agency of the state, the problem of area arises. The area does not determine whether the governmental organization shall be headless and irresponsible or not, but it is an important factor in determining what civic services the organization may provide and how adequately they may be supported financially. Thus it helps to shape the local governmental machinery.

Heretofore, historical factors, natural barriers, and lack of ready means of rapid transportation and communication have been the main factors in shaping county boundaries. Forces of habit and custom, feelings of local pride and attachment, but most of all perhaps the influence of local officials and county-seat towns tend to perpetuate existing units. However, consolidations of counties have already been made, and the drift of economic forces will doubtless accelerate the movement. The determination of the optimum area for the performance of recognized local civic functions must wait on many facts. Whatever other characteristics it may have, there can be little doubt that it must be somewhat elastic in order to meet the demands of a rapidly changing civilization. The county as it exists at present rarely approximates it. Let us now examine the county areas as they are found in the state.

The county as a geographical area. The total area of the state is 30,989 square miles. This area is divided into forty-six counties, which range in size from Cherokee with 373 square miles to Berkeley with 1,238 square miles. The following table places them in nine groups.

COUNTY GROUPS ON BASIS OF AREA

Area in Square Miles	No. of Counties
300-399	4
400-499	6
500-599	11
600-699	8

700-799	8
800-899	3
900-999	1
1000-1099	0
1100-1199	4
1200-1299	1
Total	46

Though there is a wide variation in area, thirty-seven of the forty-six counties fall below 800 square miles each. The average area is approximately 674 square miles. As a rule the counties are too small, but the average size is greater than that of the counties in North Carolina, Virginia, Georgia, Mississippi or Tennessee.

There are in the state no great natural barriers separating one region from another. Its northwestern boundary barely reaches the Blue Ridge. The Santee and Pee Dee river systems cross the state, but they present no great obstacles to transportation and communication with the present extensive development of the state and county highway systems. The most difficult situation is to be found in the coastal plain, where the numerous rivers and estuaries are frequently bordered by extensive swamps and marsh lands. However, many isolated sections of the lower coastal area are now very largely depopulated.

Despite great differences in natural resources, taken as a whole, there is much uniformity among the counties. There are many types of soils in the state, ranging from the very fertile loams found in the coastal plain counties to the white sands in the counties of the sand hill region. But the counties with the poor soils generally have compensating advantages in climate, or it may be in mineral, in timber, or in water power resources.

An examination of a map of the state reveals many county lines which follow natural boundaries. Many more of them do not. In a few instances there are evidences of the influence of local politics. The area comprising the counties of Hampton, Jasper, and Beaufort must have been divided in a very difficult manner. McCormick County has a long, handle-like projection extending southeastwardly between Edgefield County and the Savannah River. Bamberg County has a narrow wedge-like area projecting five or six miles into Colleton County, and the County of Charleston is a very irregular creation. However, the law now

TABLE II

County	Area in Square Miles	Population 1930	Density Per Square Mile
Abbeville	510	23,113	45.3
Aiken	1100	47,407	43.1
Allendale	435	13,289	30.5
Anderson	758	81,018	106.9
Bamberg	375	19,408	51.7
Barnwell	522	21,220	40.6
Beaufort	702	21,802	31.0
Berkeley	1238	23,546	19.0
Calhoun	391	16,639	42.5
Charleston	888	99,658	112.2
Cherokee	373	32,138	86.0
Chester	592	31,694	53.5
Chesterfield	837	34,336	41.0
Clarendon	704	30,132	42.8
Colleton	1126	23,912	21.2
Darlington	605	41,424	68.4
Dillon	405	25,733	63.5
Dorchester	613	25,320	41.3
Edgefield	524	19,326	36.8
Fairfield	705	23,295	33.0
Florence	699	61,028	87.3
Georgetown	828	21,724	26.2
Greenville	761	117,004	153.7
Greenwood	473	36,065	76.2
Hampton	513	17,243	33.6
Horry	1158	38,294	33.0
Jasper	596	9,989	16.7
Kershaw	673	31,925	47.4
Lancaster	515	27,981	54.3
Laurens	690	42,096	61.0
Lee	407	24,096	59.2
Lexington	779	33,889	43.5
Marion	529	27,221	51.4
Marlboro	519	31,677	61.0
McCormick	379	11,638	30.7
Newberry	601	32,452	54.0
Oconee	650	33,355	51.3
Orangeburg	1131	63,850	56.4
Pickens	529	30,589	57.8
Richland	751	86,215	114.8
Saluda	435	18,148	41.7
Spartanburg	765	116,270	151.9
Sumter	574	45,887	79.9
Union	492	30,915	62.8
Williamsburg	927	34,914	37.6
York	651	53,396	82.0
	30,989	1,732,567	55.9

provides that the General Assembly shall not create a new county the greatest length of which shall be more than four times its least central width, nor shall it reduce an old county to such a form.

Population. The most important element in the problem of area is that of population. Table II shows the total population per county for 1930 and the density per square mile. On the basis of density the counties are grouped as follows:

COUNTY GROUPS ON BASIS OF POPULATION

Density per Square Mile	*No. of Counties*
Under 20 Persons	2
20-39	10
40-59	18
60-79	7
80-99	4
100-119	3
120-139	0
140-159	2
Total	46

The range in density of population is quite wide. Berkeley County, the largest county in the state, lying in the coastal plain, has four families per square mile, while Greenville County in the Piedmont section has approximately thirty families to the square mile. If we eliminate the eight counties each of which contains a town of 10,000 or more inhabitants, very few of the remaining counties have above sixty persons to the square mile. Cherokee, the smallest county in the state, has the greatest density in this group, eighty-six persons per square mile.

Density of population has an important bearing on local civic affairs apart from that of financial support. As a rule, the more widely scattered the population, the more likely is one to find local authority decentralized and other evidences of rank individualism. Of course there are exceptions. Educational and historical influences may be the counteracting factors. On the other hand, it is possible for density of population to become too great, but such a condition is exceedingly remote from South Carolina counties.

Industries, including agriculture. Table III shows the industrial establishments in each county in 1929, the average number of wage earners employed for the year, and the value of the products of these establishments. The table also shows the number of farms per county in 1930, the estimated number of persons employed on them, and the total value of farm products.

The industrial establishments are to be found in the main in the Piedmont section of the state, though there are exceptions. In the coastal plain the counties of Charleston, Florence, and Darlington have important industries. In seventeen counties of the state fewer than one thousand persons per county are employed in industrial establishments. The Piedmont also excels in the number of farms, though the counties of Colleton, Orangeburg, Dorchester, Sumter, Williamsburg, Clarendon, Florence, Darlington, Marion, Dillon, and Marlboro comprise a fine agricultural region with numerous farms. Only five counties in the state excel Horry in

TABLE III

COUNTY	INDUSTRIES			FARMS		
	No. of Establishments 1929	Wage Earners Average No. for the Year	Value of Products	No. of Farms 1930	No. of Persons Employed	Value of All Farm Products (1929)
Abbeville.....	16	1,076	$ 3,769,636	3,403	6,125	$ 2,721,786
Aiken........	26	2,996	9,486,974	3,682	6,627	3,869,860
Allendale.....	18	369	750,192	1,019	1,834	1,318,196
Anderson.....	54	8,090	29,510,090	8,200	14,760	8,580,167
Bamberg.....	22	369	1,185,402	1,992	3,585	2,311,595
Barnwell.....	19	262	667,772	2,375	4,275	2,940,271
Beaufort.....	16	591	802,662	2,012	3,621	2,035,210
Berkeley.....	18	720	1,467,542	2,183	3,929	1,451,748
Calhoun......	28	170	408,565	2,466	4,438	2,622,617
Charleston....	89	5,270	32,574,467	1,957	3,522	3,699,438
Cherokee.....	25	3,557	10,075,808	3,258	5,764	3,903,672
Chester......	20	2,811	9,991,134	3,047	5,484	2,870,206
Chesterfield...	35	598	2,166,600	3,555	6,399	3,657,910
Clarendon....	21	851	1,467,010	4,256	7,660	3,452,058
Colleton.....	35	879	1,297,249	3,091	5,563	2,229,821
Darlington...	36	1,738	7,160,783	3,531	6,355	3,808,610
Dillon.......	11	633	2,585,293	3,066	5,518	4,805,185
Dorchester....	15	602	1,199,027	1,862	3,351	1,436,973
Edgefield.....	25	386	1,981,460	2,724	4,903	2,554,598
Fairfield......	*	*	*	2,269	4,084	1,806,965
Florence......	30	1,544	7,972,914	5,642	10,155	6,737,886
Georgetown...	13	2,172	2,696,253	1,045	1,881	757,147
Greenville....	113	15,975	57,887,553	7,079	12,742	7,684,528
Greenwood...	48	4,346	17,492,409	3,084	5,551	2,644,436
Hampton.....	35	1,068	1,585,025	1,403	2,525	1,497,316
Horry........	13	987	1,626,278	5,283	9,509	6,770,745
Jasper.......	14	805	893,429	940	1,692	633,977
Kershaw....	39	751	2,630,788	3,067	5,520	2,527,265
Lancaster....	39	2,722	9,854,172	2,778	5,000	2,334,552
Laurens......	25	3,458	10,810,491	4,464	8,035	4,948,077
Lee..........	15	210	1,109,941	2,688	4,838	2,709,024
Lexington....	81	1,346	4,954,294	3,295	5,931	3,081,560
Marion......	22	1,305	3,089,978	2,565	4,617	3,604,134
Marlboro.....	*	*	*	3,410	6,138	4,652,164
McCormick...	29	288	705,221	1,813	3,263	1,425,235
Newberry....	64	2,986	11,275,069	3,334	6,001	3,244,707
Oconee......	32	1,929	6,412,829	4,438	7,988	3,456,979
Orangeburg...	34	1,227	3,328,577	7,329	13,192	8,451,224
Pickens......	26	3,577	10,680,609	3,696	6,652	3,591,482
Richland.....	116	4,580	21,552,903	2,787	5,016	2,446,104
Saluda......	*	*	*	2,987	5,376	2,751,163
Spartanburg..	99	12,265	46,613,101	8,556	15,400	11,098,688
Sumter.......	50	1,906	5,367,051	3,937	7,086	3,693,374
Union........	35	3,534	13,621,175	2,538	4,568	2,536,359
Williamsburg.	*	*	*	4,659	8,386	4,366,819
York........	51	4,973	16,624,437	5,168	9,302	4,863,210
* 4 Combined.	106	2,678	8,007,298	.....	.....	....
Total.....	1,658	108,600	$385,339,461	157,933	284,161	$164,585,091

number of farms. In five counties in this group the number of farms was greater in 1930 than in 1925.

However, in twenty counties of the state there are fewer than three thousand farms each, and in each of fourteen of these the number of persons employed in industrial establishments is less than one thousand. In some cases the industries operate only in certain seasons. Nearly one-half the counties in the state may be thought of as two-legged stools, to borrow a figure from Dr. E. C. Branson. To have stable and vigorous economic life, each county needs another leg, at least, industry. One step on the way towards

TABLE IV

COUNTY	Total Taxable Property 1930	Total County and School Levy 1929-30	Approximate County-wide Levy—Mills	Fines and Licenses 1929-30	Total Disbursements 1929-30	Per Cent of Assessed Valuation
Abbeville.....	$ 4,891,038	$ 262,362.73	53	$ 1,302.40	$ 780,460.86	16
Aiken........	11,757,690	531,653.67	45	17,050.57	1,443,482.92	12
Allendale....	2,624,593	169,354.41	64	368.75	226,242.26	8
Anderson.....	20,141,900	979,579.33	48	18,207.37	2,178,556.03	11
Bamberg.....	3,519,590	134,788.20	38	1,123.96	305,650.07	9
Barnwell.....	4,362,590	257,330.65	58	1,192.62	494,880.53	11
Beaufort.....	4,019,630	219,448.50	54	5,687.24	333,121.54	8
Berkeley.....	4,170,816	245,212.93	59	1,907.26	554,185.41	13
Calhoun......	2,986,790	113,381.30	40	1,098.64	230,184.57	8
Charleston....	36,672,180	1,099,798.80	30	27,036.39	1,590,983.29	4
Cherokee.....	9,275,692	439,323.79	47	13,481.18	816,651.67	9
Chester......	10,492,624	388,329.85	37	17,715.25	784,590.63	7
Chesterfield...	5,136,760	420,242.39	82	9,244.10	594,164.84	11
Clarendon....	3,501,870	220,384.24	63	1,527.80	385,276.14	11
Colleton.....	4,552,805	304,305.41	67	1,268.25	795,966.70	17
Darlington...	9,161,303	482,694.58	53	3,886.60	946,216.18	10
Dillon.......	5,015,210	279,686.02	56	5,095.37	622,641.69	12
Dorchester....	4,094,132	215,499.29	52	1,109.60	832,634.28	20
Edgefield.....	3,734,350	179,011.23	48	1,206.90	531,650.37	14
Fairfield.....	7,928,895	319,699.12	40	2,841.85	576,726.66	7
Florence.....	11,962,915	612,209.37	51	4,225.25	1,386,567.47	12
Georgetown ..	4,102,870	198,739.31	48	14,243.06	555,666.16	13
Greenville....	32,767,915	1,644,394.88	50	67,632.12	3,736,616.81	10
Greenwood...	9,997,253	440,722.47	44	7,861.02	949,226.04	10
Hampton.....	3,682,667	196,615.05	53	1,016.50	341,209.59	9
Horry........	4,256,351	342,701.49	80	13,983.97	1,010,476.08	23
Jasper.......	3,430,411	139,739.16	41	....	211,978.23	6
Kershaw.....	7,525,919	298,631.99	40	5,054.00	1,031,620.68	14
Lancaster....	5,412,905	276,397.39	51	5,153.15	1,177,325.74	22
Laurens......	9,336,239	519,814.70	56	6,639.75	1,587,129.12	17
Lee..........	4,347,402	246,630.24	57	2,305.34	371,893.47	9
Lexington....	7,261,701	383,559.21	53	7,224.35	832,669.02	11
Marion......	4,774,120	115,230.81	49	1,406.00	289,328.88	12
Marlboro.....	6,207,390	297,369.04	62	4,016.70	839,161.44	17
McCormick...	2,328,044	342,888.48	55	5,381.80	631,505.24	10
Newberry....	9,403,340	567,119.90	60	4,197.09	1,133,779.94	12
Oconee.......	6,173,320	408,272.90	66	3,851.50	1,112,041.81	18
Orangeburg...	11,803,120	728,748.55	60	12,521.93	1,219,623.04	10
Pickens......	7,295,984	386,516.11	53	13,261.87	1,256,978.85	17
Richland.....	29,737,940	1,325,634.92	45	11,453.66	2,258,544.13	8
Saluda.......	2,791,176	160,316.76	57	1,609.25	419,696.88	15
Spartanburg..	37,348,062	2,021,116.12	54	25,016.83	4,805,796.39	13
Sumter.......	8,438,862	605,984.04	72	5,789.10	873,696.97	10
Union........	8,375,110	457,064.37	55	2,839.98	1,348,417.51	16
Williamsburg.	5,197,730	264,967.80	51	2,101.00	662,963.15	13
York........	13,390,921	631,902.95	47	15,217.00	1,393,948.98	10
	$415,390,125	$20,875,374.45	50	$371,804.32	$46,462,128.14	11

securing adequate economic support would be to increase the size of the counties by reducing the number.

Financial adequacy. It is difficult to determine the approximate true wealth of the counties of the state. The National Industrial Conference Board reports the estimated true wealth of the state as a whole for 1929 as $2,763,000,000. Table IV shows the total assessed valuations of the counties of the state on January 1, 1930, as shown on the complete abstracts filed by the county auditors with the comptroller general of the state. The sum total of the property of the state assessed for taxation is $415,390,125. If the 1929 figures of the National Industrial Conference Board are approximately correct for 1930, only about fifteen per cent of the true wealth of the state is assessed for taxation. But what may be true of the state as a whole can not be said to be true of each county. In the Report of the Joint Committee on Revenue and Taxation, appointed by the General Assembly in 1920, it was estimated that the property of the state assessed for taxation that year represented about 33⅓ per cent of its true value. The assessed valuation at present doubtless does not represent more than twenty to twenty-five per cent of the true value.

In 1920 the average ratio of the assessed value of real estate to its sale value varied greatly from county to county. In parcels under $1,000 in value the assessed value ranged from 20.2 to 39.4 per cent, while that of parcels over $10,000 in value ranged from 7.8 to 38.5 per cent. The larger the land holding the greater the tendency to get it on the tax books at a lower percentage of its actual value. There were great variations not only from county to county, but also within the same county. What was true in 1920 is no less true today. But the difference is that intangibles, which are not on the tax books, have increased rapidly, while the percentage of the true value of tangible property has been constantly reduced.

The assessed valuations for 1930 range from $2,328,044 in McCormick County to $37,384,062 in Spartanburg County. In the following table the counties are placed in eight groups.

COUNTY GROUPS ON BASIS OF ASSESSED VALUATION

Assessed Valuations	*No. of Counties*
Under $5,000,000	19
$ 5,000,000- 9,999,000	17

10,000,000-14,999,000	....	5
15,000,000-19,999,000	....	0
20,000,000-24,999,000	....	1
25,000,000-29,999,000	....	1
30,000,000-34,999,000	....	1
35,000,000-39,999,000	....	2
Total	....	46

ASSESSED VALUATIONS OF SOUTH CAROLINA COUNTIES 1930

LEGEND
ASSESSED VALUATIONS

UNDER $5,000,000
$5,000,000 - 9,999,000
$10,000,000 - 14,999,000
$20,000,000 - 24,999,000
$25,000,000 - 29,999,000
$30,000,000 - 34,999,000
$35,000,000 - 39,999,000

Forty-one of the forty-six counties of the state have less than $15,000,000 each of property assessed for taxation. The tax burden of the counties can not be increased very much. If all property were assessed at its true value, the rate of taxation could be lowered and the burden more equitably placed. Even in that event it appears that a number of counties in the state would not have sufficient economic resources from which to draw support for those civic services which should be found in every county.

The total tax levy for county and school purposes for the year 1929-30 is also given in Table IV, and the approximate rate of levy on a county-wide basis. Rates range from 30 mills in Charleston County to 82 mills in Chesterfield County, but if the property in both counties were assessed at the same ratio of its true value the differences in rates might be less, or they might be even more.

The table also shows receipts by county of fines and licenses for 1929-30, and total disbursements for the same year. These disbursements include borrowed money, whether on note or bond sales, receipts from miscellaneous sources, and all receipts for whatever purpose from the state. The disbursements represent from four to twenty-three per cent of the assessed valuations of the respective counties. But whether some of the counties are expending too much can not be definitely stated. It would be necessary to know what they are receiving for their expenditures in order to answer that question. There can be no doubt, however, that there are great differences in tax burdens and in the number and quality of services rendered to the taxpayers; and doubtless some counties carrying the heaviest burdens are getting least for their money.

County services. In the main county services in the rural counties are confined to roads, schools, courts and law enforcement, and the care of the poor. A number of counties have health departments, while others have only a county health nurse. Organized departments of public welfare are not to be found. County-wide library services are to be found in only a few counties.

There are no standards by which these services can be compared. Road systems vary widely in mileage. Methods of construction and maintenance differ. There are no standardized specifications for county highways and bridges, there is no uniform method of purchasing supplies and machinery. The road work may be done under expert guidance or not. If a county is spending a large sum each year on its roads, it may be indulging in waste or it may be making a good investment.

In the matter of schools there is perhaps more uniformity. All white schools are at least seven months in length. Many of them run for nine months. Teachers differ widely in preparation for their work. School buildings and equipments show still greater inequalities. In no case can it be said that all the white children of a county have the same educational opportunities.

The cost of courts and law enforcement varies greatly. Increased costs are to be expected where population is dense or where it is concentrated in industrial villages and in cities. But these differences may be due in part to different attitudes toward law enforcement or to relative differences in the incidence of law violation.

The care of the poor is somewhat different. With the exception of the county of Greenville and perhaps one or two others, the method of poor relief is practically uniform throughout the state. Where the county homes exist differences will be found in operating costs. The purchasing policy is an important factor in those cases, other things being equal. Where only out-relief is given, the sum is limited and the method of granting it practically uniform. The counties could not do much less for the poor and do anything at all. No exact basis of comparison can now be had for such functions as the counties perform. Perhaps none can ever be worked out, but there seems to be no good reason for such marked differences as now exist.

THE COUNTY AS THE AGENCY OF THE STATE

The unit of representation in the General Assembly. The county is the unit of representation in the General Assembly, as has already been stated. The basis of representation in the state senate is territory, the county. Each county has one senator. The basis in the house is population, though that is modified to the extent that each county regardless of population has one representative.

The unit for the administration of justice. It is on the unit of the county that the fourteen judicial districts of the state are formed. The judges of these district courts are chosen by the General Assembly, and the solicitors are elected in each district by popular vote. Courts are held within each county, and the clerks and sheriffs are chosen by the respective counties.

The unit for the assessment and collection of taxes. The state still levies an ad valorem tax. The county is the unit for the levy and collection of this tax. The fiscal machinery of the county functions for the district, the county, and the state.

The unit for the conduct of general elections. The county is the unit for holding elections for county, state, and federal officials, as well as for the registration of qualified voters. The county election commissioners are the boards of canvassers and as such make returns to the state board.

The unit for the distribution of state aid for schools. The county is the unit for the distribution of state aid to the schools. Table V shows the receipts which came from the state both for schools and highways in 1929-30. The state returns to the counties fifty per cent of the amount received by the state game warden from the sale of hunting and fishing licenses within the county. About half the counties of the state get something from this source. State aid proper is for the purpose of paying teachers' salaries for the six months' term. There are two state-wide levies for schools, the constitutional three-mill levy and the 6-0-1 four-mill levy. If the latter does not produce sufficient funds to pay the salaries of the teachers employed for six months, the state contributes the balance from other sources. The law specifies the salary schedule and the basis of apportioning the four-mill levy. Aid is given to all counties. Since no attempt is made to equalize assessments for the purpose of distributing state aid, the lower the assessment the more money the county gets from the state. This law contributes its influence to the already strong tendency to reduce assessments each year. Furthermore, it affords no more assistance relatively to the poor rural county than to the rich urban county. It treats all counties alike regardless of differences in their needs.

The unit for highway aid. The county is the unit also for state highway aid. The sums listed in Table V as coming from the state to the counties as highway aid are not all necessarily for that purpose. The insurance commissions or fees returned to the counties are to be thought of rather as for general county purposes instead of for roads. The gasoline tax returned to the counties is for the purpose of helping to maintain the county highway systems. At present the sum returned is one cent per gallon estimated on the basis of the number of registered motor vehicles in the respective counties.

The figures in the column under the heading "Highway Aid" represent payments coming from the State Highway Department on account of reimbursement agreements. From time to time the General Assembly specifies what roads shall be a part of the state highway system. Heretofore counties have gone ahead under agreement with the State Highway Department and have con-

TABLE V
STATE AID FOR SCHOOLS AND HIGHWAYS

COUNTY	SCHOOLS		HIGHWAYS		
	From State Game Warden 1929-30	State Aid 1929-30	Gas Tax 1929-30	Insurance License 1929-30	Highway Aid 1929-30
Abbeville	$ 601.94	$ 62,845.00	$ 12,423.06	$ 1,541.06	$ 42,946.12
Aiken		94,570.24	37,322.29	3,806.48	127,326.07
Allendale		21,751.00	6,259.87	1,154.16	1,442.77
Anderson	5,412.25	201,382.00	61,313.42	10,011.44	188,379.88
Bamberg	1,155.10	36,804.00	9,246.33	1,504.63	38,696.56
Barnwell		40,113.00	11,773.63	1,407.16	29,391.51
Beaufort	1,173.20	14,409.26	33,592.96	1,221.87	17,216.22
Berkeley		55,799.00	8,852.86	609.00	25,176.07
Calhoun		19,808.00	8,377.79	862.69	9,704.26
Charleston		19,585.00	88,354.12	25,282.77	164,229.84
Cherokee	1,291.45	64,136.00	19,814.70		65,359.51
Chester	1,224.60	50,579.00	19,580.16	4,070.50	115,219.50
Chesterfield		129,430.00	17,948.75	1,861.27	20,924.55
Clarendon	1,714.22	59,188.00	10,540.22	1,253.70	
Colleton	4,454.10	74,309.75	13,729.62	1,162.17	88,208.02
Darlington		76,751.00	25,009.32	4,469.79	17,764.81
Dillon		62,923.00	13,311.79	867.50	37,073.38
Dorchester		35,974.00	12,993.48	1,130.00	117,789.67
Edgefield		43,240.00	11,741.82	1,185.61	32,742.49
Fairfield		21,437.00	11,407.65	1,248.75	74,939.51
Florence		173,607.75	41,432.60	8,300.54	162,603.63
Georgetown	2,113.27	36,117.00	10,925.78	1,807.69	85,805.11
Greenville	7,000.00	351,517.00	114,332.40	20,264.74	180,854.41
Greenwood	1,725.80	59,972.00	27,895.77	6,112.51	120,335.39
Hampton	1,000.00	42,088.00	10,918.83	1,405.81	9,224.98
Horry		187,409.00	18,802.25	1,499.75	38,625.93
Jasper		15,306.26	4,864.21	414.78	14,244.00
Kershaw	796.09	66,226.50	19,137.66	2,504.33	149,098.24
Lancaster		91,230.00	15,684.56	2,098.49	47,732.18
Laurens	2,557.39	91,669.00	26,688.40	3,714.21	133,277.02
Lee		40,546.00	10,092.58	1,287.78	6,986.25
Lexington	3,747.62	138,164.53	34,102.12	2,382.62	124,563.42
McCormick	520.00	23.161.00	5,399.44	528.48	30,472.48
Marion	100.00	71,822.00	14,866.94	2,536.56	93,094.88
Marlboro		46,404.00	18,018.81	2,846.75	
Newberry		83,703.00	27,575.79	3,088.38	88,840.85
Oconee		148.790.24	20,107.70	794.26	103,077.46
Orangeburg		130,450.00	41,025.02	4,885.51	93,663.61
Pickens	649.58	128,013.00	23,576.30	1,880.11	65,803.39
Richland		76,371.85	216,911.39	21,317.64	165,401.67
Saluda		64,939.16	13,453.73	865.82	44,618.12
Spartanburg	3,389.57	280,834.00	166,504.23	15,611.92	125,793.05
Sumter		54,692.00	28,195.94	6,015.64	294,600.54
Union	1,027.47	64,709.00	17,732.51	1,805.45	104,246.30
Williamsburg	1,486.60	70,051.00	11,546.44	1,218.45	52,806.13
York		107,059.00	36,785.13	6,636.58	162,275.72
Totals	$43,140.25	$3,722,827.54	$1,410,170.37	$186,475.49	$3,712,575.50

structed some of these roads by county bond issues. Now the Department has taken the roads over and is reimbursing the counties for the money spent on them. The method of selecting the roads which are to be taken into the state highway system appears to have a considerable element of politics in it. The state distribution of the gasoline tax favors the counties with the greatest number of motor vehicles, which perhaps is as it should be. The other highway aid depends upon numerous factors.

STATE CONTROL OVER COUNTY AFFAIRS

There is no effective state control over county affairs despite numerous provisions in the constitution and the statutes. The constitution provides that whenever it is brought to the attention of the governor by affidavit that any officer who has the custody of public or trust funds is probably guilty of embezzlement or the appropriation of such funds to private use, he must direct his immediate prosecution by the proper official. If a true bill is found, the governor suspends the officer and appoints another in his stead until a verdict is rendered in the case. If the officer is convicted, the office is declared vacant and the vacancy is filled as may be provided by law.[1] It also provides that for willful neglect of duty, or other reasonable cause, that is not sufficient ground for impeachment, the governor may remove any executive or judicial officer on address of two-thirds of each house of the General Assembly. The cause for removal must be stated, the officer given a hearing, and the vote taken and entered on the journal.[2] This provision appears to cover all officials from the governor down.

There are numerous provisions in the code with reference to control over county officials by the state. The State Tax Commission is required to direct proceedings and actions against assessment and taxation officials for failure to comply with the laws, and to report them to the proper authority for removal. It may require the attorney general and the solicitors to assist in bringing actions against such officials.[3] The attorney general and the solicitors are required annually at such times as they may deem expedient to examine the condition of the offices of the clerk of the court, the

[1] South Carolina Constitution of 1895, Art. IV, sec. 22.
[2] Ibid., Art. XV, sec. 4.
[3] Code, 1922, Vol. 3, sec. 365.

sheriff, and the register of mesne conveyances, and report the same to the circuit court and the General Assembly.[4]

The comptroller general is directed to take action to compel defaulting treasurers to comply with the duty imposed upon them. The attorney general and the solicitors shall conduct the legal proceedings.[5] And the state treasurer may cause defaulting county treasurers to be committed to jail by warrant issued by himself. The defaulting treasurer must remain in custody until he has rendered full account and paid over the taxes due.[6] The state treasurer must report the names of defaulting county treasurers to the General Assembly at its annual meeting and the means he has used against them.

It is the duty of the comptroller general to prescribe the system of bookkeeping to be used in the offices of the board of county commissioners, the county auditor, the county treasurer, and the school board. He must examine the books and report to the General Assembly.[7] The county auditor may be suspended and removed by the governor by and with the advice and consent of the senate.[8]

Other provisions of the law might be given, but enough has been said to show the nature of state control over county affairs and officials. Executive or administrative control is almost wholly lacking. Legislative and judicial control is provided for, but both are ineffective. The governor or other executive and administrative officials may institute proceedings and make reports, but they have very little means with which to gather facts upon which to make reports or to institute proceedings. The attorney general and the district solicitors may not be competent to pass on the condition of county offices, should they examine them, and they are not provided with funds with which to have expert examinations made. The private citizen is not likely to be sufficiently interested in or capable of securing the facts upon which to make an affidavit to the governor or to bring cause before the General Assembly.

It is useless to pass laws requiring officials to do this or that, and then leave them without the means for carrying out the laws. But one of the worst features of the system is that whatever con-

[4] *Ibid.*, sec. 813.
[5] *Ibid.*, sec. 848.
[6] *Ibid.*, sec. 863.
[7] *Ibid.*, sec. 539.
[8] *Ibid.*, sec. 434.

trol the executive and administrative officials of the state attempt to exercise must be subjected to the approval of an infallible legislature, or to the slow procedure of the courts. The legislature will be guided in the main by the wishes of the county legislative delegation concerned. Local politics enters here and justice probably departs. The courts move slowly, after actions are instituted, and they punish only after conviction of criminal action. That rarely restores wasted or stolen public funds.

A statement from Dr. Wallace on this problem of control seems adequately to summarize the situation in the state.

The outstanding characteristic of American state government is that the people through the legislature enact laws and then leave them to be enforced or neglected by a body of county officials generally responsible, *short of criminal action punishable by the courts,* only to the people of their own counties.[9]

He illustrates the lack of state executive control by some incidents: during a bitter industrial dispute some years ago the sheriff of a certain county refused to serve the process of the magistrate's court. When the governor telegraphed him to enforce the law, he wired back that if the governor did not like the way the law was being enforced he could enforce it himself. In another instance a county auditor refused to add the prescribed penalties to delinquent taxes. The comptroller general instructed him to add them. He replied that it had never been done in that county and that he would not do it.[10]

In neither case did the state executive concerned do anything, nor perhaps could he. The governor might have sent the state militia to perform the work the sheriff refused to do. The comptroller general might have reported the defiant auditor to the State Tax Commission or to the governor. The former might have asked the attorney general or the district solicitor to institute proceedings against the auditor in the courts. The latter might have suspended the auditor with the advice and consent of the senate, if it had been in session.

Local government in any responsible sense has never existed in the state and does not now exist. The General Assembly con-

[9] Wallace, *op. cit.,* p. 43.
[10] *Ibid.,* pp. 42-43.

trols both state and local affairs, there being no sharp line of demarcation between them. However, locally chosen officials perform the functions assigned to them by the legislature very largely as they will to do.

CHAPTER V
COUNTY ADMINISTRATION

When we come to the actual administration of county affairs, we find in a large measure what is logically to be expected under the existing system of county government machinery. As we have already seen, it is characterized by lack of responsible headship, by lack of uniformity in structure, and by constant change in the details of the structure and in delegated authority. As a result, efficiency and economy in administration are as varied as the organizations themselves. By virtue of the power of the county legislative delegation, or despite that power, county government is too local, and the tendency in that direction shows little, if any, evidence of subsidence as yet. If to these things we add the fact of habitual and universal disregard of the laws governing the administration of county affairs, we may readily understand something of the chaotic condition that exists in them in general. We shall consider first the administration of county fiscal affairs.

FISCAL ADMINISTRATION

The county finance officials with their general powers and duties are discussed in Chapter III. The administration of county fiscal affairs, however, involves the whole machinery of county government. The county finance officials make up the very heart of the county government system, and as such they furnish life-blood to the whole system.

The first steps in fiscal administration have to do with the assessment of property for taxation and the fixing of the tax rates. The provisions in the state constitution concerning taxation are not unlike those generally found in American state constitutions. No taxes may be levied without the consent of the people or their representatives lawfully assembled. All property must be taxed in proportion to its value, as that is ascertained by an assessment. And the General Assembly is required to provide by law for a uniform and equal rate of assessment and taxation, though it may impose a capitation tax and provide for a graduated tax on incomes and a graduated license on occupations and business. Only the products of mines may be taxed. No tax may be levied except in pursuance of a law, which shall distinctly state the object of the same. Exemptions include all county, township, and municipal property used exclusively for public purposes and not for revenue, and the property of all schools, colleges, and institutions of learning, all charitable institutions, public libraries, churches, parsonages, and burying grounds.

Corporate authorities of counties and their subdivisions, of cities, towns, and villages may be given authority to assess and collect taxes for corporate purposes. The public debt of the state and its subdivisions is limited, as has already been pointed out, but the limit may be and frequently has been raised by constitutional amendment. Finally, the constitution specifies a three-mill levy on all taxable property of the respective counties and a capitation tax of $1.00 on all males between the ages of 21 and 60 to be laid by the governing authorities of the counties for the support of the schools.[1]

THE ASSESSMENT OF PROPERTY

The assessment machinery. The county officials whose duties are related to the assessment of property have been given already, but it may be well to look at the whole assessment structure including state as well as local officials. The process of tax listing or assessing begins with the taxpayer himself. Above him are to be found the county auditor, the district boards of assessors, the county board of equalization, the state tax commission, and the board of review. To these we may add the comptroller general of the state. The final authority in the state is in the board of review, a board composed of a chairman and six other members, one from each congressional district, appointed by the governor with the advice and consent of the senate.

The compensation of local assessment officials. In 1929 the counties of the state were divided into ten classes and the salaries of the county auditors and treasurers were fixed for each class. The salaries of these officials are the same for any class, and the state pays two-thirds of them. They range from $2,000 each in Class H counties to $5,400 each in the single Class AA county of Spartanburg. The treasurer is not an assessment official, but the

---

[1] South Carolina Constitution of 1895, Art. X, secs. 1-13; Art. XI, sec. 6.

auditor is. The latter is required to give corporate surety bond in the sum of $5,000. The premium on the bond is paid out of county funds.

The chairman of the district board of assessors is paid $2.00 per day for his work, and the same compensation is allowed the other members of his board. The chairmen of the local boards make up the county board of equalization. As members of the latter board, they are allowed $3.00 per day and five cents per mile for all necessary travel.

The compensation as given above is that provided in the general law. It is the minimum. There are many exceptions to be found due to the passage of special local acts. For instance, the members of the county board of equalization in Beaufort County receive $5.00 per day and six cents per mile for necessary travel. In the town of Saluda the members of the local board of assessors receive $3.00 per day. In Charleston County the members of the county board of assessment and equalization are paid $10.00 per day, though they may not be paid more than $1,500 each in one year. Also, they are allowed $3.00 per day for traveling expenses when out of the city or parish of their residence.

Tax listing and assessing. Property must be listed every year and real estate assessed every fourth year. The law requires every person of full age and of sound mind to list annually for taxation all personal property, including moneys, credits, investments in bonds, stocks, joint stock companies, or otherwise owned and controlled by him, whether in or out of the state, and to file a return thereof, verified by his oath, between the first day of January and the 20th day of February, with the county auditor. Every fourth year this return must include the real estate sold or transferred since the last listing of property and to whom transferred. The property to be returned is that on hand January 1, except in case of agricultural products. The farmer is allowed to return his agricultural products on hand the preceding August first.

Personal property is defined to include all things other than real estate which have any pecuniary value. The term "money" is defined to include coin, bank bills or notes authorized to be circulated as money, whether in possession or on deposit subject to draft on demand. "Credits" are defined to mean all legal debts, claims, and demands, however payable, less outstanding obligations of the taxpayer.[2]

The penalty for failure to make return or to subscribe to the oath required is an addition of fifty per cent to the value of the property charged against the taxpayer for the previous year. The oath required is that all property is returned and that it is returned at its full value.

The county auditor may and sometimes does assist the taxpayer in listing his property. In certain counties of the state the auditor visits convenient places in the county to receive returns, and in some instances actually fills out many of the lists himself. Such is the case in Colleton County. However, the lists are not always in the hands of the county auditor by February 20, as required by law, but how promptly they come in depends to a great extent on his efforts.

The law requires that the auditor make an alphabetical list of the taxpayers in each taxing district or township and present it to the chairman of the board of assessors for his guidance in canvassing his district. This canvass he must make following February 20. The list may or may not be prepared, and the canvass is in many cases merely perfunctory. In some counties when February 20 comes the auditor collects the tax returns which are in, arranges them alphabetically by district, and turns them over to the chairmen of the respective district boards for their attention. In other cases the auditor invites the boards to his office and they with him go over the returns to discover, if possible, whether any taxpayers have failed to make returns and whether any valuations should be changed. The chairmen of the district boards may be paid for five days, the other members for only three days, except when real estate is assessed. Then they also may be paid for five days. In cities and towns the boards of assessors get compensation for more time, since they have more work to do. The chairmen of the boards of assessors, as members of the county board of equalization, receive compensation for five days, except when real estate is assessed. Then they may be paid for ten days. Special local acts, however, have made many exceptions to the general law.

The work of listing and assessing property by district should be complete by the first Tuesday in March or soon afterwards.

[2] Code, 1922, Vol. 3, sec. 341.

Then the auditor notifies all taxpayers whose valuations have been raised $100 or more by the district boards. The county board of equalization meets on the fourth Tuesday in March. The taxpayers whose valuations have been raised $100 or more may appear before the board and protest against the raises. The board passes on these protests, but the latter may be taken up to the State Tax Commission, if the decision of the county board is unsatisfactory. The county board may also equalize between districts or townships. It may raise assessments or reduce them, but the aggregate must not be less than that of the county auditor. Since it is composed of the chairmen of the district and special boards, where these exist, and of the district assessors where the boards do not exist, frequently its principal work as a board of equalization is confined to hearing protests, if any.

Methods and standards of valuation. The tax system of the state is very defective. One gathers the idea in observing its operations that under it the chief purpose of each county, district, and individual is to keep just as much property off the tax books as possible. And this object is to be attained either by not listing property at all or by listing it at the lowest possible proportion of its true value. Inequalities between individuals, districts, and counties are very great. Methods of assessing are not scientific and standards of valuation do not exist. Local officials have no uniform method of determining the value of taxable property. Records of land sales, tax maps, insurance carried on buildings and personal property, as a rule are not available for the use of these officials. Those in one county have no very definite information about what is being done in the other counties. Since no real efforts are made to determine the actual value of property and to assess it uniformly, the race is on to escape taxation as far as possible.

The following table made from the tax records of six counties gives evidence of what is being done throughout the state in the assessment of land in the country.

LAND ASSESSMENTS, SIX COUNTIES

County	Approximate Land Area	Acres Listed 1929	Acres Listed 1924	Average Value per Acre 1930	Average Value per Acre 1929	Average Value per Acre 1924
Aiken	704,000	669,134	670,071	$4.10	$4.02	$4.20
Colleton	720,640	611,359	621,874	2.90	2.90	2.88
Darlington	387,200	341,492	350,404	7.70	9.54	9.80

Fairfield	451,840	443,750	450,249	2.66	3.60	3.90
Laurens	441,600	440,254	440,689	5.84	7.00	7.00
Williamsburg	556,800	570,580	575,704	3.84	4.10	4.10

The exact land area of the counties is not known definitely. If it were, there could be no reason for the differences in the number of acres listed from year to year, if the assessing officials did their work with care. The carelessness of the assessing officials along with the fact that the exact land area of the counties is not known account for these differences, and in nearly every instance the number of acres listed falls short of the approximate land area as reported by the United States Department of Agriculture. Allowances, however, should be made for the lots listed in cities and towns.

The average value per acre listed varies widely also. The counties of Darlington, Colleton, and Williamsburg have large areas of swamp lands, especially the latter two; otherwise their soils are very much of the same type. Aiken County lies largely within the sand-hill region. Fairfield and Laurens are both in the Piedmont. If $2.66 per acre on the average represents about twenty per cent of the true value of land in Fairfield County, then land in Laurens on the average must be more than twice as valuable or else it is listed at more than forty per cent of its true value. Differences among the coastal plain counties are great also, while the average value in Aiken lies between the extremes in both the Piedmont and coastal plain counties. Many factors enter into the determining of the true value of this one class of property alone. Under the present system of assessment it is not possible to assess lands equitably. The facts on which to make the attempt are not available, but a start might be made. The general tendency therefore is to list land at a gradually decreasing ratio of its true value. The same general tendency is to be found in the assessment of other classes of real estate and also in personal property.

The following table shows what is happening in one class of personal property alone, household furniture.

HOUSEHOLD FURNITURE LISTED, FIVE COUNTIES

County	1929	1922
Colleton	$112,855	$202,095
Darlington	243,530	285,785
Fairfield	114,640	195,595
Laurens	248,375	252,565
Williamsburg	151,540	182,090

The same tendency may be seen in practically all personalty, except automobiles, but lack of carefully kept records makes it impossible to illustrate some classes. Intangibles have virtually disappeared from the tax books. Money, for instance, was found listed for taxation in only one of the six counties surveyed, and the sum in that case was just $8,950.

The amount of property appearing on the tax duplicates in some instances is larger than it should be because of duplications. Such duplications are due in the main to careless work of the auditor and the assessors. In rare instances they may be caused by carelessness on the part of the taxpayer himself. He may have some one else list his property, or he may not always sign his name exactly the same way on the tax returns. The greatest source of such duplications, however, is the failure of the auditor to keep a careful record of transfers of property. This applies to real estate especially. The duplications bring in no revenues. The carelessness of the tax listing and assessing officials undoubtedly is responsible for another and more serious matter, the escape of much tangible property from taxation. But the amount of duplication is hard to determine in any case from the records, since such items are charged off and may be included in abatements and in nulla bona items along with many others.

The State Tax Commission assesses the property of merchants and corporations. Occasionally it takes a hand in the work of the county assessing officials. One instance was found in Fairfield County in 1930. The county tax assessing authorities gathered the idea from some source that a certain other county in the state was assessing its land at a much smaller ratio of its true value than was Fairfield. Since 1930 was the year for reassessing land, the officials thereupon proceeded to reduce the average value of $3.60 per acre to $2.28. After looking into the matter the State Tax Commission ordered a sixteen and two-thirds per cent increase, which brought the average value up to $2.66 per acre.

The county tax assessing officials are instructed also to assess livestock so that each class will average a certain sum per head. In some instances all animals of one kind are put on the tax returns at the average value regardless of the worth of the individual animal. Usually, however, an effort is made to list each at such a uniform ratio of its true worth as will produce the average value required for the group as a whole. The county auditors are furnished also with a guide for assessing automobiles and with a list of those registered within their respective counties, but the guides and the lists are both frequently put to no use.

The fifty per cent penalty provided by law for neglect or refusal to make returns of property for taxation is never imposed. Those who do not list in many cases have their names and property carried forward from the previous year's record. This custom may be also a source of errors in the tax records.

Tax levies. Before the tax records can be completed the auditor must have the state, county, and district tax levies. The state still makes use of the ad valorem tax. The comptroller general furnishes the auditor with the state levy. For 1930 it was five mills. It has not been above five and a quarter mills in the last five years. The county supply bill, or appropriation bill, usually fixes the levy for ordinary county purposes, though it may authorize the auditor or the county board to fix it. The county-wide levies for schools are fixed by the constitution, by general law, and by special laws. The county auditor is usually authorized to fix the levies for county bonds. The school district levies for bonds or notes are required to be fixed by the auditor, or by "the county officers charged with the assessment and collection of taxes." District levies for school maintenance are fixed by special act on popular demand. In Aiken County the school district levies are required to be fixed in a joint meeting of the county board of commissioners, the county superintendent of schools, and the district trustees.

While the ratio of the assessed value of property to its true value has been decreasing constantly, tax rates have been rising steadily. This statement does not apply to the state levy. It is small and has varied very little within the last few years. It usually produces slightly above $2,000,000 annually.

The county levies may be put into two classes, county-wide levies and district levies. The county-wide levies are not uniform throughout the state, except in the case of the two state-wide levies for schools. They are the constitutional three-mill levy and the 6-0-1 four-mill levy. The proceeds of these levies, however, are retained in the respective counties. To these levies we may add also the poll levy of $1.00. The 6-0-1 four-mill levy is provided for by a general law. Under this law the schools for whites are provided with a minimum term of seven months, if the district provides maintenance for the seventh month. The name 6-0-1 is due to the original purpose of the bill, which was that the state should provide for a term of six months, the county nothing, and the district one month. If the four-mill levy is not sufficient to pay teachers' salaries for the six-month term, the state provides the additional sum necessary from other sources.

Each county has its levy for ordinary county purposes, but these levies vary also from county to county. The following table gives the 1929 county-wide levies of the six counties surveyed.

COUNTY-WIDE LEVIES IN MILLS, SIX COUNTIES

County	Ordinary County	Roads	County Bonds	School Bonds	School	School N.	Total
Fairfield	9	—	6	¾	7	½	23¼
Darlington	11	—	2½	—	7½	—	21
Williamsburg	5¼	7	6	—	17	—	35¼
Colleton	18	2	4½	—	14½	1½	40½
Aiken	19½	—	3	—	7½	—	30
Laurens	5½	14½	5	—	8	—	33

The levies listed under "Roads" might be included under "Ordinary County," since the latter levy frequently includes the total county levy for road maintenance and construction. If we combine these two groups of levies in the table, we find a range from nine mills in Fairfield County to twenty mills in Laurens County. Of the levy in the latter county four and one-half mills were taken from the county road bond levy and added to the road maintenance and construction levy. It does not so appear in the printed lists of the county levies, but a provision in the 1930 county appropriation bill directs the county auditor to make the change.

Only one of the six counties surveyed had a levy for school bonds, but this fact is not to be taken as an indication of the absence of school bonds. They are numerous, but as a rule they are district bonds and not county-wide bonds. The large levies for schools found in Williamsburg and Colleton counties are due to the fact that the six-months school term is supplemented by the county. All white schools in these counties have terms of either eight or nine months each. These counties have taken a step in the direction of the county as a unit in the matter of school maintenance.

District levies are numerous and in many cases very large. In

the rural districts they are confined almost wholly to levies for
school purposes and they serve to show, as regards school affairs,
that county government is "too local" for the best results. The
following table shows the lowest and the highest district rates for
1929 found in six counties.

DISTRICT LEVIES, SIX COUNTIES

County	Lowest Rate	Highest Rate
Fairfield	7 mills	23¼ mills
Darlington	3	34
Williamsburg	1	30
Colleton	2	43½
Aiken	1	31
Laurens	3	25

These rates include levies for school maintenance, school bonds,
and school notes, where they exist. Several districts in Williamsburg County do not have district levies at all. To find the total
rate of taxation in these districts it is necessary to add the county-
wide and state levies to the district levies. The foregoing tables
reveal great differences in tax levies among counties and among
districts in the same county. The levies are all on general property.

Capitation levies. There are three additional levies. The poll
levy of $1.00 on each male between the ages of 21 and 60, provided
for in the constitution, has already been mentioned. There is also
a capitation road tax levied by the counties on able-bodied males
between the ages of 21 and 55 years. Neither the age limits nor
the tax are uniform for all counties. The tax ranges from $1.00
in Newberry and some other counties to $10.00 in Saluda County.
Particularly in those counties where the tax is very high provision
is made for the payment of the tax by work on the public roads at
a certain price per day.

The dog tax. The general law of the state provides for a levy
of $1.25 on each dog. Twenty-five cents of this sum is to be re-
tained by the county treasurer on the payment of the tax, and the
remaining $1.00 is put into the school funds of the county. How-
ever, many special acts concerning the dog tax have been passed,
so that at the present time the tax is as low as 50 cents in some
counties, while in others it is $1.00. Where the tax has been re-
duced the treasurer gets no fee for collecting it.

The dog tax in some instances produces more trouble than
revenue. The owner of a dog is required by law to return his

dog just as he does his other property. He probably does not obey the law in every instance, for in one county at least the delinquent tax collector is authorized to make a census of the dogs not previously returned by their owners, for which he receives 25 cents each. But even the efforts of this official to get the dogs on the tax books apparently were not successful. The county legislative delegation authorized the county treasurer to borrow $4,500 with which to have a complete census of the dogs made. The greater part of this sum was paid out to nine citizens of the county for making the census. The revenue coming from the dog tax was not materially increased as a result of the new census of dogs.[3]

In a few counties all horse-drawn vehicles and auto-trailers are required to be registered and a license fee for each is charged. In Clarendon County the fees are collected by the county supervisor, who retains ten cents of each as his compensation. The remainder is turned over to the county treasurer, who places it to the credit of the school district from which it was collected. It is then known as the vehicle road and bridge maintenance fund.[4]

Tax sources. County tax revenues come from two sources, the general property tax and the capitation taxes. The general property tax is the chief source of district and county revenue. The capitation taxes produce relatively little revenue. In the counties surveyed the general property tax produced from about 55 per cent to nearly 70 per cent of the total county revenue. The proportion of revenue coming from each of the classes of levies varies much from county to county. In the six counties surveyed the revenue coming from district levies amounted to from 25 per cent to 106 per cent of that coming from county-wide levies. The highest ratio was found in Darlington County.

The preparation of the tax records. The work of listing and assessing taxes should be complete soon after the fourth Tuesday in March, for it is on that date, according to the law, that the county board of equalization meets to hear protests and to make such changes in valuations as it thinks necessary. When the board has completed its work, which may last for one or more days, the auditor is ready to begin the preparation of his tax duplicate. Before he can complete it, however, he must have the valuations

[3] See county government survey files of the Department of Rural Social Economics, The University of North Carolina.
[4] Code, 1922, Vol. 3, sec. 1279.

placed upon the merchants and corporations of his county. These come to him from the State Tax Commission by way of the comptroller general. He must also have the various tax levies.

The preparation of the tax duplicates and abstracts, particularly the former, is no small task. The tax returns or lists are arranged alphabetically by district and by township and are so entered upon the duplicate, and the amount of the tax for each levy, for each separate piece of real property, and for each taxpayer is calculated. If the county auditor and the district and county boards have done the listing and assessing promptly, the auditor is ready to begin work on his tax duplicates early in April. By the 30th of June, according to the law, his tax records should be complete, though the treasurer's duplicate must be turned over to him on or before September 30. But as a matter of fact they may not be complete on November 1. Auditors almost without exception reported that they were delayed more or less by the failure of the State Tax Commission to report promptly on the valuations of the local corporations. It does not seem probable, however that these delays would occur in all counties every year. The auditor's busy season begins with January 1 and lasts six or more months. He usually has one or more helpers in the preparation of his tax records, and he should have the bulk of his work done not later than the first of August. Frequently such is not the case. In Darlington County the 1930 records were incomplete at the close of August. The auditor reported some returns not yet in at the first of the same month. The tax levies were not decided upon definitely until the last days of the month. The Laurens County records were completed late in the fall, in the early days of November. The writing up of the tax receipts in the latter county was approaching completion at mid-December.

In most counties the auditor prepares an abridged form of his duplicate for the county treasurer. In one of the counties surveyed a special form of tax receipt has been substituted for the treasurer's duplicate. In addition to the lists or returns, which are required to be kept for a period of five years, and the tax duplicates, the auditor must prepare and keep a number of other records. He is required to prepare during the fiscal year a complete abstract of the tax duplicate, an abstract of realty, an abstract of personalty, an abstract of additional property, an abatement book and an abstract of abatements, an abstract of penalties, and an abstract of executions. In no case was the abatement book, which is required to be kept by the auditor for the guidance of the treasurer, found to be kept as required by law.

These abstracts are to be forwarded to the comptroller general, but copies of them should be kept and placed on file by the auditor. The complete abstract, and the abstracts of realty, personalty, and of additional assessments seem to be the only ones usually prepared. Copies of them may be found scattered around in the auditor's office or in that of the treasurer. In one county surveyed the auditor kept a copy of the complete abstract only, saying that the others were mere statistical information for which he had no use. In no case were the copies of the abstracts kept filed regularly nor did they extend back many years.

Nearly all county auditors need more adequate offices and office equipment, especially filing cabinets. If these things were supplied, tax records would doubtless be better kept. In general the preparation of the tax records and the preservation of them is in keeping with tax assessment methods and practices. The whole system tends to encourage indifference and carelessness. The office of county auditor is a very important one. If properly conducted, there is an almost infinite amount of monotonous detailed work to be done in it. It is a type of work which is hard and for which one is likely to get small credit. The average citizen does not appreciate the fact. He may not know the difference between a well-conducted and a poorly-conducted office. As a consequence, the average auditor may do little more than is absolutely necessary. But no system can be so bad as to obscure the good work of some officials, and a number of these are to be found. The work done by the auditors of Williamsburg and Colleton counties, especially the latter, is of a high order. The carefully kept alphabetical list of taxpayers and their property, with all transfers promptly recorded, is to be commended. The list is subject to constant revision.

Additional assessments. Omitted property is entered on the tax duplicates as additional assessments. But it is a rare thing to find additional lists or returns made out on regular forms. The law contains no specific provisions for additional returns, other than that the treasurer shall notify the auditor in case an individual against whom there is no tax charge desires to pay his taxes. With a capable and energetic county auditor and district boards of assessors wholly familiar with the persons and property in their districts there should be few additional assessments. Yet the number frequently is large. In one of the counties surveyed the county treasurer enters the additional assessments on his duplicate. Individuals come to pay their taxes. No tax charge against them is found. They are questioned about their property and its value. It is entered upon the treasurer's duplicate, the tax is calculated and paid. Later the auditor takes a copy from the treasurer's duplicate and enters it upon his own. Then he charges the treasurer with it. This instance illustrates a weakness that may be permitted to creep into the system. The auditor, a part of whose business it is to act as a check on the treasurer, fails to do so in such cases.

THE COLLECTION OF TAXES

The county treasurer, the tax collector. The county treasurer is the tax collector. He draws the same salary as the auditor of his county, and only one-third of it comes from the county. His bond is a corporate surety bond and ranges in amount from $20,000 to $50,000, though the former sum is the one most generally found. The premium is paid out of the county treasury. He may receive a small additional compensation from fees. In some counties he gets 25 cents for each tag sold to the owners of dogs. In all counties he receives a fee for issuing executions against delinquent taxes.

When he receives his tax duplicates from the auditor, he proceeds to write up his tax receipts. With few exceptions the receipts are prepared in duplicate. The original serves both as a receipt for the taxpayer, if he pays his taxes within the prescribed time, and as an execution, when properly filled out, if he allows his taxes to become delinquent. In Darlington County a special tax receipt, prepared in quadruplicate, is substituted for the form commonly used. This form has some advantages over the older and more common form. It dispenses with the necessity of the treasurer's duplicate; it furnishes a notice for mailing to the taxpayer, a receipt for him when he pays his taxes, a special form for execution, if he fails to pay within the required time, and a permanent record for the treasurer's office.

Unless exceptions have been made, the books of the treasurer's office are opened for the receipt of taxes on October 15. Frequently the tax receipts are not all written by that time, but taxes are received nevertheless. Few treasurers mail out notices of taxes due, unless requested to do so. In some counties an advertisement is carried in the county paper during the tax receiving period to the effect that taxes are now due and payable at the office of the county treasurer. In a few counties the treasurer may receive taxes at convenient places in the county after giving notice of the time and place at which he will do so.

Taxes may be paid between October 15 and January 1 of the following year without discount or penalty. A penalty of one per cent is charged in January, two per cent in February, and seven per cent in March. After March 15 executions are issued against those not paid on that date, unless the time for payment has been extended. In 1930 the time was extended by order of the comptroller general to May 1 with a one per cent penalty only. A joint resolution of both houses of the General Assembly directed the comptroller general to take this action.

The treasurer receives taxes. He can hardly be said to collect them. The taxpayers who are able to pay promptly and are accustomed to doing so pay him. As a rule, those in financial distress and those with little or no property pay the delinquent tax collector, if they pay at all. The delinquent tax collector may be the county sheriff or a special official appointed for the purpose of collecting delinquent taxes.

The approximate percentages of the 1929 levies collected by the respective treasurers of six counties are shown below.

PERCENTAGE 1929 LEVY COLLECTED BY
COUNTY TREASURER
SIX COUNTIES

County	Percentage
Aiken	85
Colleton	80
Darlington	73
Fairfield	90
Laurens	82
Williamsburg	60

The Darlington County treasurer mails out notices to the taxpayers. He also permits certain banks in the county to receive taxes. They notify him, giving the name of the taxpayer and the amount of taxes deposited to the credit of the county treasurer. Thereupon the treasurer mails a receipt to the taxpayer.

It is difficult to account for the differences in the percentages of the total levies of the various counties collected by the respective treasurers. The figures for Williamsburg County are very low. The situation in that county seems to be due in part to habit, for the economic condition of the county is no worse than that to be found in some of the other counties surveyed. Only Fairfield and Darlington out of the group of six have the special delinquent tax collectors. In the other four counties the sheriff collects the delinquent taxes. The percentage of the total levy finally collected is very high in both Williamsburg and Colleton counties. The sheriff in each of these counties seems to be an unusually good collector.

Tax settlements. According to the law, the annual settlements between the auditor and the treasurer may be had on or before the first day of May or at any other time the comptroller general may direct. At this settlement the auditor takes from the treasurer's duplicate a list of all taxes, assessments, and penalties which the treasurer has been unable to collect, noting the reasons assigned by the treasurer why they have not been collected. This list is called the delinquent list and it is required to be sworn to and signed by the treasurer before the auditor. The auditor is required to record the same in a book kept for the purpose and to transmit an abstract of it to the comptroller general. The delinquents in each district, city, town, and village are listed separately. The treasurer is given credit for the taxes, assessments, and penalties included in the list and stands charged with the remainder. But he may assign only the following reasons for failure to collect.

1. Sheriff returned execution with statement that sufficient property could not be found.
2. Property sold to sinking fund commission for lack of bidders.
3. Executions issued and in the hands of the sheriff.
4. Collection of taxes, assessments, and penalties enjoined by a competent court.[5]

Auditors rarely keep a book in which the delinquent taxpayers are listed. The delinquent tax collector does keep such a book in some instances.

[5] *Ibid.,* sec. 531.

The law also requires the auditor and treasurer annually to have a full and final settlement as to tax executions issued by the treasurer within twelve months after the expiration of the time allowed for the payment of taxes in any one year.[6] This provision of the law may be only perfunctorily observed or entirely ignored in many counties.

The compensation of the delinquent tax collector. The general law of the state provides certain fees and charges for the collection of delinquent taxes. For issuing each tax execution the treasurer receives $1.00 in case the tax is paid. The sheriff receives the following fees: for serving each execution $1.00; for each mile actually travelled in executing the process five cents; for advertising the sale, if necessary, 25 cents; for making sale and executing deed of conveyance and putting purchaser in possession $3.00; and in addition five per cent of the sum levied.[7]

These fees and charges do not apply to all counties, since many special local acts have been passed. Probably in every case where a special delinquent tax collector has been provided his compensation has been fixed by the act. Act No. 61, passed in 1927, provides for the appointment of a delinquent tax collector for Fairfield County. It states that he shall receive all the fees and allowances now allowed the sheriff for collecting tax executions. In addition he gets 25 cents for each dog listed for taxation, if the same has not been previously returned by the owner, and he receives such further compensation as may be determined by the county legislative delegation, to be paid out of county funds. This further compensation is $50 per month, though it does not appear as such in the county supply bill. In Williamsburg County a recent act has abolished the five per cent commission and reduced the $1.00 fees of the sheriff and treasurer to 50 cents each. In Darlington County the treasurer's fee of $1.00 has been divided between himself and the county auditor.

The work of the delinquent tax collector. The collection of delinquent taxes is one of the difficult problems of local government in the state. Present economic conditions add to the seriousness of it, as do the shifting farm tenants and textile employees. The amount of tax executions issued varies greatly from county to county, as well as the percentage of the total levy put into execu-

6 *Ibid.,* sec. 533.   7 *Ibid.,* sec. 521.

tion. If the work of the tax assessing officials is not done with care, the amount of the executions may be very much larger than it should be in fact. The result may be an excessive sum charged off as nulla bona. The percentage of the delinquent taxes finally collected varies greatly, depending upon the care with which the assessing machinery has functioned and also upon the skill and persistence of the tax collector. In the counties surveyed the tendency seems to be to give the delinquent taxpayer every consideration possible. Sales are made only as a last resort, when they are made at all. Many of those made are mere formalities by which the auditor bids off the lands for the forfeited land commission, and the taxpayer is given another year in which to pay without additional charge. The following table shows the tax executions outstanding in six counties on June 30, 1930.

TAX EXECUTIONS OUTSTANDING, JUNE 30, 1930
SIX COUNTIES

County	Amount
Fairfield	$161,976.88 (1920-29)
Darlington	465,040.29 (1920-29)
Williamsburg	145,742.66 (1924-29)
Colleton	60,360.32 (1929)
Aiken	217,057.07 (1926-29)
Laurens	143,024.81 (1926-29)

The delinquent tax situation is somewhat better in Williamsburg and Colleton counties than in the others given in the table. In Williamsburg the amount of executions outstanding for 1927 and previous years is very small, a little more than $4,600, most of which is against property tied up in bankruptcy proceedings. The situation in Colleton is not as good as the figures in the table indicate because of the custom of allowing the sheriff at the end of each fiscal year to charge off as nulla bona all tax executions in his hands for the previous year. However, he retains the tax executions after they have been charged off as nulla bona and continues to collect them. Such a policy is likely to prove injurious sooner or later to both sheriff and treasurer. This is another instance in which a system of checks and balances may fail to work. The delinquent tax situation in Darlington County is especially difficult. The six counties surveyed doubtless give a fair indication of the delinquent tax situation throughout the state.

According to the law, the delinquent tax collector is subject to the control of the comptroller general in making levies and sales,

in making returns, and in paying over money collected on executions. He is required to make return of all tax executions to the
treasurer within 90 days after the date of issue, designating such
as are nulla bona and such as have been collected by distress or
otherwise.[8] How well this provision of the law is observed may
be seen by reference to the foregoing table of tax executions
outstanding.

Sheriffs as a rule distribute the tax executions to their collectors. In some instances they probably never see them again.
Executions have been located in the sheriff's waste basket. They
have been and' are yet being handled very carelessly. Hundreds
and perhaps thousands of them have been lost. Rarely, if ever,
are the uncollected executions returned to the treasurer, and in
none of the counties surveyed is it customary for the collector to
prepare an abstract of nulla bona, as required by law. In some
cases executions are permitted to pile up for years, and then perhaps a very large sum will be charged off as nulla bona. Such an
instance was found in 1929 in Fairfield County. In that year
$90,000 was charged off the tax records as nulla bona. Part of
this sum, however, represented entries for the current year which
the auditor had been forced to charge off in order to change. In
some of the counties nulla bona items are charged off more frequently. The longer the executions are permitted to remain outstanding, the greater the chance that they will never be collected.
In fact, the law declares that taxes are presumed to have been paid
after ten years from the last date they could have been paid without penalty, if the state has not instituted judicial proceedings in
the meanwhile.[9]

Perhaps no other detail of county affairs is handled so loosely
as the collection of delinquent taxes. Many thousands of dollars
of revenue have been lost to the counties because of careless and
dilatory methods of collection. In several counties of the state the
collection of delinquent taxes has been taken out of the hands of
the sheriff and placed in those of an appointed official. But there
is much evidence to indicate that the change has brought about no
improvement. In some instances the counties have been put to
additional expense with no material increase in tax collections. Of
the six counties surveyed only two had the appointive delinquent

[8] Code, 1922, Vol. 3, sec. 527.   [9] *Ibid.*, sec. 529.

tax collector, and the showing of these counties is among the worst in the group.

The special delinquent tax collectors ordinarily do the collecting themselves. The sheriffs may collect themselves, or they may secure the assistance of the regular deputies. Frequently, however, they select temporary township or district deputies for the work. These officials make collections for the mileage allowance, while the sheriff gets the $1.00 fee and the five per cent commission where these are allowed. In a few counties still other officials get a hand in the collection of delinquent taxes. In some instances the executions against the poll and capitation road taxes, or a part of them, are turned over to the magistrates for collection. In Laurens County, for instance, about $3,000 of such executions have been so placed. Such a policy can scarcely be recommended in view of the poor esteem in which magistrates are already held. It seems quite obvious that a better method of collecting delinquent taxes is not to be had by increasing the number of collectors nor by seeking some more indirect and devious method of appointing them. To be sure, they should not be elected by popular vote. Perhaps one appointive official should be charged with the collection of all the taxes, whether delinquent or not, and the means should be provided by which he may be called promptly and definitely to account.

Tax adjustments. Tax adjustments may be made in three ways. The county auditor may make adjustments in the poll taxes, but he may not make any deductions from the valuation of any real estate, except on the written order of the comptroller general, made upon the basis of a written statement of the facts submitted to him.[10] Tax refunds are made by legislative enactment. The latter are to be found frequently in the county supply bills.

The county auditor on occasion may take matters into his own hands. In one instance a prominent minister came into the office of an auditor and complained to the clerk that the taxes on his real estate for the year had been increased rather than diminished, as he had been led to expect. A rather hasty checking of the number of acres, the value at which the property was listed, and the various levies on the property revealed no errors. However, the minister was informed shortly that if he would pay a certain amount it

10 *Ibid.*, sec. 459.

would be satisfactory. The sum named was considerably less than the tax charge. Later, in answer to an inquiry as to the proper authority to grant reductions in tax charges, the clerk gave the very confident answer that the county auditor had virtually complete authority in the matter. The law does not support his statement, but he may have had in mind actual practice rather than the provisions of the law, which he tried to locate without success.

Tax sales. The delinquent tax collectors sell real estate for taxes only as a last resort. Sales of personalty are also rare. In two of the counties surveyed no real estate has been sold for taxes very recently, or such was the case at the time of survey in the summer of 1930.

As a rule, land sales are made one or more years after the tax executions have been issued. In December, 1929, and in February, 1930, the sheriff of Laurens County sold lands for 1926 and 1927 taxes. In Williamsburg and Colleton counties tax sales are usually made each year. The greater amount of the real estate sold for taxes is bid in by the forfeited land commission, though there is always a considerable amount purchased by individuals. Most of that sold, regardless of the purchaser, is redeemed eventually by the owner or by some one for him. There are usually individuals at these tax sales on the "still hunt" for desirable tracts of land that may be sold, but under present economic conditions the number is not large.

No case was found in which a forfeited land commission had taken title to any real estate. In case of sales the sheriff may not make title until twelve months after the date of sale. The original owner then has six additional months within which he may redeem the property by paying the taxes, penalties, costs, and expenses of the sale together with eight per cent interest on the whole amount of the purchase price.[11] The sheriff's deed of conveyance is taken as *prima facie* evidence of a good title in the holder and that all requirements of the law have been duly complied with. No action for recovery of land sold by the sheriff under the provisions of the law or for the recovery of possession thereof can be maintained unless it is brought within two years from the date of sale.[12] Neither the laws nor popular attitude encourage the purchase by private individuals of lands sold for taxes.

[11] *Ibid.*, sec. 522.   [12] *Ibid.*, sec. 525.

When the forfeited land commission makes the purchase, the owner is given another year or more in which to pay his delinquent taxes, and he pays no charge for the privilege. Where no sales are made at all, one might take, as has been done in some instances, ten years in which to pay his taxes with no further charges than the usual penalties and the fees and commissions due the tax collector. The whole tax system discourages honesty and promptness in performing the most important civic duties, the listing of property for taxation and the payment of taxes.

THE CUSTODY AND DISBURSEMENT OF COUNTY FUNDS

Classes of funds. The county funds might be put into numerous classes. In the annual settlements between the county auditor and the county treasurer they appear in two general classes, county funds and school funds. Each of these classes may be subdivided into many classes. These subdivisions might be made on the basis of territory, as district or county-wide. This classification would apply particularly to school funds. In some counties the road funds may be classified on somewhat the same basis. Or, the funds may be classified according to the object or purpose for which they are to be expended. From the standpoint of custody, however, they may be put roughly into two classes, operating funds and sinking funds. The latter class will include only such funds as have been set aside to meet maturities of term bonds.

The custodian of county funds. The county treasurer is the custodian of all operating funds, and also in some counties of the sinking funds. But where he has custody of the sinking funds he exercises that authority not as treasurer of the county but as a member of the county ex-officio sinking fund commission. In this capacity he has the assistance and advice of the other members of the commission. They are the county auditor and the clerk of the circuit court. In some counties one of the other members of the commission has the custody of the sinking funds, or part of them. In some counties the district trustees are the custodians of the school sinking funds.

In a number of counties sinking fund commissions, the members of which are appointed by the governor on the recommendation of the respective county legislative delegations, have been set up to have charge of all sinking funds of the county and its sub-

divisions other than municipalities. These commissions are composed of three or more members, and they are required to have
corporate surety bonds. In Darlington County each member is
bonded in the sum of $20,000, in Cherokee County the bond is
$10,000, and in Greenville County, where the commission has some
ex-officio members, the appointive members are bonded in the sum
of $5,000 each.

Operating funds. Receipts from all sources and for all purposes are placed by the treasurer into one account, though it may
be carried in a number of banks. This appears to be the general
rule, though there have been and may be yet a few exceptions.
Collections of state revenue within the county are placed in the
same account. Separate funds generally, whether for a particular
area or for a particular object or purpose, are bookkeeping devices
only. If the treasurer is a diligent and careful bookkeeper, he distributes his collections and other receipts at least once each month
to the various funds. If he does not distribute them carefully, as
sometimes happens to be the case, one can readily imagine the
eventual resulting confusion.

The proceeds of tax levies for term bonds are required to be
placed in separate accounts to accumulate through interest earnings
and future accessions from the levies for the purpose of meeting
bond payments as they mature. In a few instances local laws have
been passed requiring receipts from other sources to be set apart
as sinking funds. Such is the case in Williamsburg County, where
sums recovered from broken banks are to be so used. As a rule,
however, collections from bond levies are deposited along with
other funds. Periodically they are distributed with more or less
care on the books of the treasurer, and sometime during the year
they may be transferred to the sinking fund accounts. All other
funds with very few exceptions are kept in one account by the
treasurer. Aiken County has a special contingent fund set up,
which is in the custody of the clerk of the county board of commissioners. Formerly in Darlington County the appropriation for
the dental clinic was paid over in a lump sum to the county superintendent of schools, who later disbursed it. In Cherokee County
the treasurer is instructed to pay over to the judge of probate the
sum of $2,500 to be used for the hospitalization of the indigent sick
and poverty-stricken persons. While there are doubtless many

such exceptions to be found in the state, the sum total of the funds so handled is probably not great, relatively speaking.

The treasurer usually divides the county funds among the banks of the county; if not among the banks of the county, certainly among the banks of the county seat. In Fairfield County the funds are divided among the banks of the county seat and when the county borrows money, as it does every year in anticipation of taxes, the banks furnish the money in a certain ratio to each other. In some counties such an arrangement is required by special act. In 1930 Act No. 636 was passed requiring the treasurer of Lee County to deposit all county and school funds in the various banks of the county proportionately to the amount of the capital stock and surplus of said banks, but each bank was required to furnish a surety bond ten per cent greater in amount than the sum of the money deposited with it. In Dorchester County the treasurer is required by special act to deposit county funds equally in three banks named in the act.

Formerly in Fairfield County the banks made bids for the custody of the county funds. The county has received a bonus of as much as $1,800 per year for the use of its funds, but under the new arrangement no bids are made. No interest is paid on average daily balances, nor is the county given more favorable rates than other large borrowers when it needs to borrow funds. Some of the county notes given the banks specify that they are to bear seven per cent interest after maturity. The banks neither furnish surety bonds nor pledge securities to cover county funds on deposit. This county is doubtless representative of a large number of counties in the state, but not all of them by any means.

In Williamsburg County banks handling county funds are required to pledge securities in amount sufficient to cover the funds, and the treasurer keeps the securities in the vault of a Charleston bank. In other counties the treasurer may keep such securities in his own safe. A number of counties has gone far enough to take such precautions as these. Bank failures and the consequent loss of funds may have been largely responsible for the change.

Still another group of counties may be represented by Aiken. This county not only requires corporate surety bonds for county funds deposited with the bank, but also receives two per cent on average daily balances. However, at the close of the fiscal year,

June 30, 1930, the amount of surety bonds given by the banks was only about one-half the sum of the deposits. The number of counties represented by Aiken is doubtless very small.

Many local laws concerning the custody of county funds have been passed. Probably these are not always observed. One cannot safely generalize other than to say that uniformity in the custody of county funds throughout the state scarcely exists. There is the fact, however, that county funds are divided widely among local banks and that a minimum number of separate accounts are carried. Mississippi counties represent a striking contrast in this matter as well as in others. In most cases one depository is chosen, securities are required to be pledged for funds in every case, and the number of separate accounts carried runs as high as 150 in some cases.

Sinking funds. If the treasurer is inclined to be careless or if he is overburdened with work, payments into sinking funds may not be promptly made, or they may be made in part only. Such happens to be the case now and then. Laurens County is an example. In 1930 no one knew how much the county sinking funds should be, but the sheets of the accountants who had made an audit of the county books indicated that the funds were perhaps somewhat more than one-half as great as they should have been. Such a condition, however, may not always be charged justly to the treasurer. A sufficient bond levy may not have been made in the first place. In the next place, a part of the bond levy, or the proceeds of the levy for a period, may have been diverted to other purposes by legislative act. Doubtless constitutional limitations should be placed upon the legislature in such matters.

The custody of sinking funds is characterized by very little more uniformity than that of operating funds. In Fairfield County the county auditor, as an ex-officio member of the county sinking fund commission, is the custodian of these funds. He divides them among four banks of the county. They draw four per cent interest annually, which rate is probably uniform throughout the state. No security of any kind is required to safeguard the funds.

In Darlington County until recently the county treasurer was custodian of the sinking funds. He had been authorized to invest the funds in securities. He had so invested a part of the funds when in 1930 a special sinking fund commission was set up. This commission, composed of three successful local business men, has been given complete authority to invest the sinking funds, to change the form of investment when it seems wise to do so, and to designate some bank in the state as fiscal agent for the prompt payment of interest coupons on county or district bonds and also the payment of the principal on maturity. The commission may invest in bonds of the United States, the state, the county or a political subdivision of it, in county tax anticipation notes, or in other sound interest bearing securities. But it may not deposit funds in a bank without an indemnity bond with personal or corporate surety.[13]

In Williamsburg, Colleton, and Aiken counties the treasurer is custodian of the sinking funds. In all three cases the funds are divided among two or more banks. In the first two counties the banks have pledged securities to cover the funds. In the last the funds are covered in part by surety bonds.

In Laurens County the situation is somewhat different. The clerk of the court is the custodian of the county sinking funds only, as distinct from the school sinking funds. He distributes these funds among four or five banks, but requires no security of any kind. He holds that since the county gets a high rate of interest and since the funds are widely distributed it can afford to carry its own risk.

In this county the district trustees are in reality the sinking fund commissions of their respective school districts. The county treasurer, however, holds the bank pass books for each district and sees that accrued interest and all deposits are entered upon them. The trustees select the bank or banks in which the funds are to be placed and have the authority to require that funds be changed from one bank to another or that they be divided among a number of banks. What is true of the district trustees of Laurens is true also of numerous other district trustees in the state.[14]

THE DISBURSEMENT OF COUNTY FUNDS

There is no effective state supervision over the expenditure of county funds. Neither is the expenditure centralized within the county nor subject to any effective local control. The county

[13] Acts and Joint Resolutions of the General Assembly, 1930, Act No. 738.
[14] Code, 1922, Vol. 3, sec. 2612.

appropriation bills frequently carry sections forbidding the county supervisor or the county board to over-expend appropriations, or at least requiring them to get the permission of the county legislative delegation before doing so. At any rate little attention is paid to such sections. In fact, the permission of the delegation to over-expend is not difficult to secure as a rule.

County disbursements may be placed roughly into two classes from the standpoint of actual practice. These are county disbursements and school disbursements.

County disbursements. County disbursements cover a wide field. They include everything except those for schools, and even there the line is not distinctly drawn. The constitution provides that the salary of the county superintendent of schools shall not be paid out of school funds. As a result, it is generally included in the county appropriation bill, though in some cases, as recently in Laurens County, the salary fixed in the appropriation bill is supplemented by a sum coming from the school funds. Again, in Darlington County all current borrowings whether for county or school purposes are made by the county board of directors, and until very recently no definite sum seems to have been allocated to the schools, though they used part of the borrowed funds.

The law requires that all accounts against the county must be presented to the county board and approved by it before they may be paid. Roughly speaking, that requirement may be said to be met. Claims are filed with the clerk to the county board. The law also requires that the claims be accompanied by an affidavit, but the law is not always complied with. The clerk audits the claims in some cases; in others he merely files the claims in the order of their presentation and holds them until the regular meeting of the board; then he submits them to the board. The board may take them up claim by claim, or a number of them may be approved by one motion. The board may refuse to approve some. When the claims are approved, the clerk draws warrants for them, and the warrants are signed by the supervisor or the chairman of the board and by two or more of the other members. They are also countersigned by the clerk. The warrants are numbered consecutively, and each claim is given a number corresponding to the warant issued in payment of it. When the claims are approved, they are entered on the claim ledger and then filed.

The warrants are drawn upon the treasurer, who issues checks for them. The appropriation against which a warrant is issued may be overdrawn, but if there is still a balance in the operating funds the treasurer may issue a check for the warrant and leave the problem of an overdraft in the account to the county board and the county legislative delegation. On the other hand, he may refuse to issue a check if the overdraft is large or if he wishes to have some provision made for taking care of the matter first.

As has already been noted, the disbursements in some cases may be made by indirect methods in which the details are left altogether to a particular individual or board. In such cases the county board does not pass upon the individual claims. The treasurer merely pays over a lump sum to another party, as directed in the appropriation bill, and thereupon his responsibility ends. The 1930 appropriation bill for Cherokee County instructed the treasurer of the county to pay over $2,500 to the judge of the probate court. The sum was to be expended on the order of the county health physician for the hospitalization of the indigent sick and also for poverty-stricken persons. The same bill also authorized the treasurer to pay over $600 to the local pension board to be distributed equally among the remaining Confederate soldiers in the county. A somewhat similar plan was in operation until recently in Darlington County, where the appropriation for the dental clinic and that for demonstration work was paid over to the county superintendent of schools to be expended by her. Examples of this sort are rather numerous.

In numerous cases the county legislative delegation undertakes to exercise some control over county disbursements. In Fairfield County the miscellaneous contingent fund of $4,000 for 1930 could be expended only on consent of the legislative delegation. The purchase of road machinery out of the proceeds of a bond issue made the same year was required to be approved by the senator and at least one-half of the county representatives. In Berkeley County for 1930 the appropriations for roads and bridges, the special contingent fund of $8,000, as well as certain other funds, could be expended on the direction of the legislative delegation only. The road and bridge fund set up was $25,000. This fund could be expended without the approval of the county highway commissioners. The treasurer was directed to pay all claims against the fund, if they were approved by a majority of the members of the county legislative delegation. In Chesterfield County the county board and clerk were forbidden to issue a warrant until the county attorney had endorsed on the claim in writing that it was a valid and legal obligation of the county. These examples are only a part of those that might be given. They illustrate the more common variations in the process of disbursing county funds, but not all of them.

In some cases no warrants are drawn on the treasurer by the county board in the payment of notes, bonds, and interest on the same. The treasurer makes such payments without the formality of a warrant. This practice is doubtless responsible largely for the fragmentary records of county bonds and notes to be found in the offices of some county boards.

School disbursements. The disbursement of school funds presents more uniformity than that of county funds. The trustees of the various districts have charge of the expenditure of the district school funds. Teachers and others who may have claims against the school funds draw up a warrant, which is signed by at least two of the trustees. The warrant is then taken to the county superintendent of schools, who must approve it before the treasurer may pay it. The greater part of the school funds are so paid out. In all counties some disbursements are made on the warrant of the county board of education countersigned by the county superintendent of schools. The so-called county board funds are disbursed in this manner, and payments on county-wide school bonds and interest, and on school notes, if the borrowing in the latter case has been done by the county board of education, are so made. In some counties there are special districts which have their own treasurers. The taxes collected within them and their proportion of state aid are disbursed by their own boards and treasurers.

County budgets. County budgets do not exist. That is, no comprehensive financial plan covering all departments of county government is anywhere attempted. The county appropriation bills which are set up annually and enacted into law by the General Assembly are in no true sense budgets. For instance, the Colleton County bill for 1930 makes appropriations to twelve classes of objects with numerous items in each class. These classes are

1. Roads and bridges
2. Salaries
3. County boards
4. Jail expenses
5. Jurors and witnesses
6. The county home, poor house and poor
7. Post mortems, inquests and lunacy
8. Public buildings
9. Printing, postage, and stationery
10. Miscellaneous contingent
11. Club and demonstration work
12. Tax refunds

From the total of the appropriations for all these classes of objects are deducted the estimated receipts from the capitation road tax, from fines and licenses, and from the state distribution of the gasoline taxes and the insurance fees. · A tax levy is then made sufficiently large to provide for the balance. Except in the counties having the larger cities little provision, as a rule, is made in the appropriation bills for debt service. If such an item does appear in the appropriation bill of the rural county, it is usually an appropriation to pay interest on notes already outstanding and on tax anticipation notes which will probably be issued later on in the year. The assumption seems to be that payments on bonds and bond interest will take care of themselves, since there are tax levies for them. The county appropriation bill has no relation to school affairs, except that it includes in nearly every instance the salary of the county superintendent of schools, or a part thereof, and it may include the salary of the assistant superintendent or of the attendance officer, where these officials are to be found. It also usually includes a small appropriation for the county board of education.

Recently laws have been passed for Aiken and certain other counties requiring a school budget to be set up. The budget is made by districts. Those examined were merely estimates for the requirements for teachers' salaries, for fuel, transportation, grounds and buildings, furniture and apparatus, debt service, etc. No attempt was made to consolidate the district estimates into a county estimate. Florence County and perhaps a few others have followed a different course. By a local act passed in 1930

Florence County appropriated the sum of $50,000 for thirteen items related to school affairs. This act covered only such funds as were disbursed by the county superintendent and the county board of education, but it did include the salary of the county superintendent of schools, which is usually an item in the county appropriation bill. No estimates or appropriations were set up for the various districts.

The bare beginnings of budget making are to be found in the counties, but there is no uniform method of procedure followed in the little that is being done.

County Debts and Borrowing Practices

County debts. County and district debts have grown to very large proportions in many cases within the last twenty years. The constitution placed a bonded debt limit of fifteen per cent of the assessed valuation on any area of the state. This limit has been raised to twenty per cent in numerous instances by constitutional amendment. Thus the people of the state settle local matters in which they can have little or no interest.

The exact amount of county and district debt in the state is not accurately known. The following table shows the debt on June 30, 1930, of the six counties surveyed.

GROSS AND NET DEBTS, JUNE 30, 1930
SIX COUNTIES

County	County Bonds		School Bonds		5 Notes	6 Other Forms	7 Total
	1 County	2 District	3 County	4 District			
Fairfield	$ 745,000	$50,000	$25,500	$222,000	$ 68,310	$40,000*	$1,150,810.00
Darlington	185,000	46,000	....	565,000	398,005	....	1,194,005.00
Williamsburg	199,000	....	....	186,700	146,420	9,247	541,367.00
Colleton	842,600	....	....	153,200	172,047	....	1,167,847.00
Aiken	1,768,350	....	....	273,300	315,000	....	2,356,650.00
Laurens	1,161,500	18,000	....	562,600	255,300	71,185	2,068,585.00

County	Reimbursements to come from State Highway Department 8	Sinking Funds 9	Total 10	Net Debt 11	Percent of Assessed Valuation 12
Fairfield	$ 474,820.00	$ 116,664.00	$ 591,484.00	$ 559,325.00	7.0
Darlington	74,699.00	331,595.00	406,294.00	787,710.00	8.6
Williamsburg	54,154.00	200,823.00	254,977.00	286,391.00	5.5
Colleton	548,681.00	160,789.00	709,470.00	458,376.00	10.0
Aiken	1,506,250.00	154,929.00	1,666,179.00	695,470.00	5.9
Laurens	393,403.00	258,670.00	652,073.00	1,416,511.00	15.0

* Estimated.

Each county had assets represented by sinking fund accumulations and reimbursement agreements with the State Highway Department to offset in part their bonded debts, as shown in the table.

The debt burden varies greatly from county to county, if the above table is a true indication of it. However, there is no sound basis upon which to make comparisons. The limitation in the constitution applies only to bonded debt, while the figures given in the table include debts of all types. Of the counties surveyed Laurens had the highest percentage of debt. Nevertheless, a constitutional amendment was proposed in 1930 to raise the bonded debt limit of the county to twenty per cent of the assessed valuation.

The bonded debts of the counties have been incurred principally for two purposes, roads and schools. Occasional issues for public buildings are found and much less frequently one is found for railroads. Issues called "Past Debt" bonds are rather numerous, but the debts for which they were issued were incurred in the main in the construction and maintenance of roads and bridges. The school bonds are principally district bonds, and as a result the interest rates are high, some of them ranging up to seven per cent. The earlier issues of both county and school bonds are term bonds. Terms range from ten to thirty years.

Borrowing practices. The counties can scarcely be said to have a borrowing policy. Borrowing practices vary. Many of the county road bond issues were submitted to a vote of the people. When issued the proceeds of the bonds were used on roads which have since been taken into the state highway system. Now the counties are being reimbursed in part at least for these bonds by the State Highway Department. Additional bonds however are being issued in a few instances on the strength of the reimbursement agreements on the authority of a local act of the General Assembly and without popular referendum. A case in point is to be found in an act of 1930. Act No. 972 authorized the supervisor of Fairfield County to issue $175,000 bonds for county highway purposes.

Appropriations for roads and bridges are as a rule over-expended. This happens with or without the consent of the county legislative delegation. Temporary loans are made to take care of the deficit. The next year the loan may have to be increased.

Eventually bonds may be issued to replace the notes. Sometimes however a small special levy may be made to take care of such notes.

Many of the appropriation bills authorize the county supervisor or the county board to borrow a certain sum in anticipation of taxes. Or, it may be a certain per cent of the sum estimated to come from the taxes. Such borrowing is done in every county. If delinquent taxes continue to pile up, as they have been doing in recent years, borrowing will probably become heavier each succeeding year. Over expenditures for highways and large accumulations of delinquent taxes have been two of the principal causes of increased county debts.

School borrowings are in the main district borrowings. Bond issues are authorized by popular vote in most cases. Occasionally they are authorized by legislative act only. The districts frequently borrow from the state sinking fund or from local banks on note. Such loans are authorized by local acts and special levies are generally authorized at the same time to retire the notes as they come due. District trustees have been known, however, to borrow on note on their own authority without any definite plan for repayment. Perhaps the most common cause of short-time borrowing by school districts is the practice of permitting the districts to overdraw their allotment of the school funds. In nearly every county surveyed some districts were found with such overdrafts. Others had balances, at least on the books. In one county, if the outstanding warrants had been paid, there would have been a considerable deficit in school funds; yet several districts in the county had balances on the books of the county superintendent.

Borrowing practices are haphazard, but generally the county legislative delegation determines them.

COUNTY PURCHASING

Generally speaking the counties have no purchasing policy. Practices vary from very haphazard methods by numerous individuals to centralized and business-like purchasing by one agent. Almost without exception county officials purchase their own office supplies. The purchasing of school supplies is done by both the county superintendent of schools and the district trustees, with the latter doing the bulk of it in many cases. Undoubtedly much money could be saved the schools over a period of years if the purchase of sites for school buildings, building materials, buses, fuel, and other items was handled by one agency in the county rather than by a dozen or perhaps three score.

But a more wasteful situation is found in the realm of ordinary county affairs, in the construction and maintenance of roads, in the handling of chaingangs, and in the management of poor homes and farms. This is not to say, however, that the men in charge of these matters, or at least any great number of them, are deliberately wasting money. Nevertheless, they are wasting it.

In Fairfield County at the time of the survey there were many officials making purchases of supplies. The county had no poor home, but it had a chaingang and numerous road gangs in its road construction and maintenance organization. The superintendent of the chaingang purchased nearly all supplies for the chaingang; the road gang foreman made purchases of repairs for road machinery and of gas and oil. All these purchases were made in what appeared to be a very generous manner. The county warehouse gave ample evidence of the results of careless purchasing with its large and unused supply of blades for road scraping machines and its stock of cup grease and disinfectants. Generous quantities of supplies were purchased with little or no regard for price. But there were other purchasers than the superintendent of the chaingang and the five road gang foremen. The county supervisor made purchases also, some of which had to be made with the consent of the county legislative delegation or a part of it. In the last place, a recent law required the county board to make purchases of all supplies on the lowest competent bid. Thus, all told, about fourteen individuals had hands in purchasing supplies for road and bridge construction and maintenance and for the road working organizations. The board of county commissioners, but recently re-established, was not at the time doing much of the purchasing. Most of it was being done by the county supervisor, the superintendent of the chaingang, and the road gang foreman.

In Laurens County the purchasing was done in somewhat the same manner, despite a provision in the appropriation bill that the supervisor should advertise for competitive bids for the purchase of all supplies used by the county and that he should accept the lowest bid made by a responsible bidder. However, there were not so many purchasers as in Fairfield County. The county supervisor made most of the purchases of supplies other than those for the poor home and farm. The latter were made by the superintendent. Both men bought on bid or not just as they preferred.

In the other counties surveyed purchasing was done in a more business-like way. In Williamsburg and Colleton counties the county supervisors did the purchasing and with much better results. Williamsburg operated no poor home and farm. Colleton did. It was under the direction of the supervisor, and he purchased the supplies for it as well as those for the use of the road working organizations. In Aiken County the county board of commissioners had virtually made the clerk to the board the county purchasing agent. The clerk had had considerable experience in managing a general store. An examination of the well-kept county warehouse and of the bills for supplies gave evidence of the use of business-like methods of purchasing. The best purchasing policy found in operation, however, was that in Darlington County. In that county the board of directors, composed of five successful business and professional men and farmers, purchased all supplies, including office supplies, on competitive bid for cash after fifteen days' notice. The actual negotiations for the purchase of all supplies for road work and for the road working organizations were made by the county highway engineer. Because of his knowledge of road machinery and the cost of repairs, the engineer was able to keep the cost of these items at a minimum. The county operated no poor home and farm. It was very difficult to secure data on which to make definite comparisons of the results of the purchasing policies of the counties. However, the gas and oil bill of Darlington County for the fiscal year 1929-30 was not as much as $2,000 in excess of that of Fairfield County for the same period. Yet Darlington operated ten trucks and eleven tractors, three of which were very large ones, against four tractors and four trucks operated by Fairfield.

COUNTY BOOKKEEPING

County bookkeeping in general is not uniform; it is fragmentary, unsystematic. It is characterized by the same defects as the county government organization itself. However, a department of county bookkeeping here and there is being improved. The whole system needs to be reorganized, but to secure the best results the county government organization also should be reorganized. Certain details of county bookkeeping have been treated briefly in the sections on tax records and also in that on the disbursement of county and school funds.

The law states that the comptroller general shall prescribe the system of bookkeeping to be used in the offices of the county commissioners, the county treasurer, the county auditor and the school commissioners, so that the same shall be uniform. In making visits to witness settlements between treasurers and auditors of the respective counties he is expected to examine the books and report the results to the General Assembly.[15] In the counties surveyed the forms found in the offices of the auditors and the county superintendents of schools were uniform, though they were not kept in a uniform manner. Dr. Wallace quotes from a letter from a comptroller general of the state, one paragraph of which in reference to the system of bookkeeping says, "Whether this has been uniform throughout the state I am not in position to say."[16] The author of the letter should not be judged too harshly; he has been given no effective means of control over the bookkeeping system of the counties.

Certain forms and ledgers are probably uniform throughout the state. These include the tax returns, the auditor's duplicate, the treasurer's duplicate, the various forms of abstracts, tax receipts in most of the counties, and a ledger used by the county superintendent of schools. Perhaps the list might be extended. Methods of keeping these records vary more than the forms themselves. In one case an auditor was using the treasurer's tax duplicate, which is an abridged form of his own. In one county a special form of tax receipt had been adopted, an excellent change, which made the use of the treasurer's duplicate unnecessary. Two treasurers were found who had designed ledgers of their own, both of which seemed to be improvements over the one in general use for the same purpose. Ledgers in the offices of the county boards ranged all the way from the modern loose-leaf type to an old single-entry type. There were many other differences in the types of records found. In no case was there found a complete system of

[15] *Ibid.*, sec. 539.
[16] Wallace, *op. cit.*, p. 97.

fiscal records. Perhaps the most unsatisfactory records are those of bonded debts, especially those of bonded debts of school districts. In the counties surveyed, with the possible exception of two, there was some question about these records. It was a bond lost, though not paid; or the list of bonds was not complete; or some detail about the rate or the date of the serial payments was lacking. In one instance in order to get a complete list of county and school bonds the writer had to examine the records in the offices of the treasurer, the clerk of the court, the superintendent of schools, and the county attorney.

The records in the offices of the county boards at the time of the survey were generally being kept with care, considering the variety of forms used. The most modern forms were found in Darlington and Aiken counties. To reconcile exactly the fiscal records of the county superintendent of schools with those of the county treasurer is a difficult thing in some counties. Because of the peculiarities of the system, errors easily creep in. In some cases they are of long standing and thus mar records that are being kept with great care at the present time. The school records were being kept with meticulous care in Williamsburg County. Those of the auditors were excellently kept in Williamsburg and Colleton counties, especially in the latter. The most important records are those of the treasurer. Carelessness by the treasurer in bookkeeping results in the utmost confusion in county affairs. In Williamsburg County the records of the treasurer were kept promptly and carefully. In many counties the work of the treasurer is postponed as long as possible and thus it piles up. Later when it is done in haste it is not done well. The prompt distribution of tax collections at definite periods to the various districts and funds, an arduous task at best, is a most important matter. In one instance the treasurer never distributed actual collections. He merely credited the various funds and districts with the amount of the tax levy for each, less a certain per cent. Such a plan saves an immense amount of work, but it brings about untold confusion in county fiscal affairs. Probably in no case are the records of tax executions kept with care.

The work of the treasurer and auditor could be greatly diminished if the counties should consent to abolish their school districts as taxing districts and to make the county the unit of school support, as it should be. The consolidation of the county bookkeeping in one office would eliminate part of it and doubtless guarantee that what was done would be more accurately done.

The fiscal year. A matter that would help to simplify county bookkeeping in a measure would be the adoption of a single fiscal year. Under the existing system the county has two fiscal years. One of them runs from January 1 to December 31; the other from July 1 to June 30. The county appropriation bill is made out for the first fiscal year; the annual settlement between the treasurer and auditor is on the basis of the second.

The time for assessing and collecting local taxes could not be changed to advantage, but at some opportune time it seems that a somewhat larger tax levy might be made and the expenditure of its proceeds spread over a period of eighteen months rather than twelve. In such a manner the county appropriation year could be made to correspond with the annual settlement year and the counties put more nearly upon a cash operating basis.

County audits. Most, if not all, of the counties of the state have their books audited periodically by outside accountants. There is a general law authorizing the grand jury to hire the accountants. This law may be superseded in some instances by special acts.

The cost of these audits varies greatly, and the forms in which the reports come back to the county officials are never uniform. Unfortunately, the comptroller general of the state is not given sufficient funds and an adequate staff with which to do this work for the counties.

Audits had been made in the six counties surveyed, and doubtless these present a fair sample of those made throughout the state.

COUNTY AUDITS, SIX COUNTIES

County	Accountant Chosen by Whom	Period Covered by Audit	Cost of Audit
Fairfield	Grand Jury	1925-29	$1,800
Laurens	Grand Jury	Annual	1,681
Colleton	Grand Jury	1924-30	3,000
Darlington	Grand Jury	Annual	750
Aiken	Grand Jury	Annual	475
Williamsburg	Grand Jury	Annual	—

Though the Fairfield audit covered a four-year period, each year's operations were shown separately. The Darlington audit was much more in detail. The accountant employed in the latter county was also engaged in attempting to segregate the nulla bona tax executions and in making a survey of the Darlington school district. For these tasks he was given additional compensation amounting to $950 and $500 respectively.

The cost of the audit for Williamsburg, as shown in the table, is for the year 1928. The cost of the audit for each of the last two years has been much less, and the reports are very brief. The cost of the Colleton County audit was approximately $3,000. It is a consolidated report for a six-year period. The cost of the Laurens County audit does not appear as a separate item in either the county appropriation bill or in the county disbursements. The last one made in the latter county was the most thorough found, except those in Darlington County. Only in Darlington County did the accountant attempt to audit the sinking funds and fund requirements. No more significant details could have been omitted.

It is not to be supposed that the intricacies of modern accounting systems may be revealed as if by magic to the common citizen of the county. However, the writer can not get away from the conviction that accounting technicalities may be used, whether by design or not, for the confusion of this citizen rather than for his enlightenment. In no report examined so far has there been found a serious attempt to state the essential facts concerning the financial condition of the county so that the citizen of average intelligence could understand them without a great deal of assistance. Technique is essential in these modern times, but it is hardly a holy mystery; and it ought not to be used to make confusion worse confounded.

Highway Administration

The State Highway System. On December 31, 1929, the state highway system consisted of 5,981.2 miles. These roads were classified as follows:

Roads in State Highway System

	Miles
Hard surface	1,346.05
Surface treatment	329.90
Soft surface	3,331.35
Unimproved	973.90
Total	5,981.20

Of this total, 3,178.2 miles were federal aid roads. The number of miles actually maintained by means of state and federal funds was only 5,645.55, and these were by no means equally divided among the forty-six counties. The lowest mileage was to be found in Allendale County with 58 miles and the highest in Orangeburg with 278.8 miles.

The State Highway Department was established in 1917. It comprised seven members, one from each of the seven congressional districts, appointed by the governor by and with the advice and consent of the senate. It was seven years later, however, that a state system of roads was provided for and the highway department began to be one of the most important in the state government. Act No. 731, passed in 1924, to provide for a state system of roads, specified by counties the roads which were to be taken into the state system, and the type of surface for each road, but the sections of roads so listed did not make up the entire mileage in the state system, according to the act.[17] Future additions to the system were to be made by the legislature with the approval of the State Highway Commission. It is the purpose of the State Highway Department eventually to hardsurface all roads now in the system as well as those to be added in the future.

The act required that the construction of the roads in the system be carried on simultaneously in all judicial districts of the state. Maintenance and construction funds came from federal aid, from the gasoline tax, from the license tax on motor vehicles and motor vehicle dealers, and from a state levy for highways. The annual state levy was abolished in 1925. The State Highway Commission was authorized to reimburse counties for funds expended on the construction of roads taken into the state system, though the average cost for hardsurface roads for which reimbursement might be made should not exceed in any one year $30,000 per mile. Additions have been made to the system from year to year.

In 1926 an act was passed authorizing the proper county officials to issue negotiable bonds from time to time for the purpose of raising moneys to pay the cost of constructing highways embraced in the state highway system in the respective counties. These issues could be made only when based upon reimbursement

[17] Acts and Joint Resolutions, 1924, p. 1193 ff.

agreements with the State Highway Department. By agreement the State Highway Department might construct the highways. The act declared each county to be an incorporated road district, and the bonds might be issued either in the name of the county or the road district. Two or more counties, by the action of the senator and at least one-half the representatives from each, might form themselves into a road district, which should be a separate and distinct corporate entity.[18]   The act did not apply, however, to fourteen counties of the state.

In the same year Act No. 756 was passed creating the Coastal Highway District embracing six counties extending across the coastal plain of the state from the North Carolina line to the Savannah River, except that Berkeley and Charleston counties were not included. This district was created for the purpose of completing the coastal highway across the eastern end of the state. The creation of these corporate road districts with their reimbursement agreements with the State Highway Department eliminated the need of submitting the issue of bonds to popular vote. Beginning thus with the conversion of the county into a separate corporate body for the purpose of building roads, the principle was put to further use in the creation of the Coastal Highway District in 1926. Within a few years the counties and districts were burdened with road bonds. Then the application of virtually the same principle to the state was made in 1929, when the $65,000,000 road bond issue was authorized by the General Assembly and later declared constitutional by the supreme court of the state sitting *en banc.* Such in brief is the development of the state highway system. The construction of hardsurfaced roads is now progressing rapidly in each judicial circuit of the state, and the completion of the present program should find the state with an excellent system of roads.

Local roads. The system of local roads is quite large according to estimate. The following table shows the local roads in each of the six counties surveyed as estimated by local road officials.

LOCAL ROADS, SIX COUNTIES

County	No. of Miles in Road System
Fairfield	650
Darlington	1,200

[18] Acts and Joint Resolutions, 1926, Act No. 559.

Williamsburg 900
Colleton 1,200
Aiken 1,300
Laurens 1,600

The figures for each county in the state are not available, but the total for all counties, as estimated by the United States Bureau of Public Roads, is 51,697 miles. The maintenance and expansion of these systems of local roads places a heavy burden on the counties.

The powers of county boards over roads. The provisions of the law concerning the powers of the county supervisor or the county boards of commissioners over roads are very general and brief. These officials have general jurisdiction over all public highways, roads, bridges, and ferries. They may obtain rights of way for public roads by gift or purchase, or they may condemn the lands therefor and assess the damages and compensation.[19] They have the same jurisdiction over water courses. Frequently, however, the county appropriation bill sets forth specifically what roads shall be constructed or improved and maintained and just how it shall be done. Thus the county legislative delegation may with or without the assistance of the county supervisor or county board actually exercise jurisdiction over the county roads, while the supervisor, where he exists, is generally in charge of the actual construction and maintenance of all or a part of the particular system in question. A few provisions of the law taken from the 1930 county appropriation bills will illustrate the restrictions placed upon the local road officials by the respective legislative delegations.

In Abbeville County the supervisor was forbidden to open any new road or roads unless they were approved by the legislative delegation. The board of directors of Beaufort County was directed to purchase a suitable tractor with plow attached, two motor trucks, and other machinery for use in constructing and maintaining county roads, but the cost of same might not be more than $7,500. The supervisor and commissioners of Cherokee County were required to keep the cross-country roads in good condition by using a section of the chaingang, and they were especially reminded of their duty to maintain the rural mail routes. The board of directors of Chester County was authorized to use $400

[19] Code, 1922, Vol. 3, secs. 1059 and 2907.

from the appropriation for roads and bridges and a like amount from the Baton Rouge Township road fund to make any change in the public road leading from No. 91 towards Patrick and Steadman. Three provisions were added, however, the final one stating that the whole matter was left to the discretion of the board and that the purpose of the section was merely to authorize the use of the funds. In Chesterfield County the supervisor of roads was required to divide the county into three divisions and to keep at least one maintenance crew in each division. The foreman of each crew was required to report daily on the work done. Also, $5,000 was set apart to be used exclusively for construction or improvement of cross-country roads during the months of July and August in such communities as will furnish work or material on a fifty-fifty basis. The board of Lancaster County was directed, among other matters relating to roads, to work and maintain the road or street known as Mill Street or Brooklyn Avenue, which leads from state highway No. 26 to the property line of the Lancaster Cotton Mills, and to topsoil and maintain in good order the Chesterfield road from the old Gills Creek Church place to the Tradesville Turnoff, passing through Dixie, Dwight, and Wild Cat.

FINANCING LOCAL ROAD WORK

Local road work is supported in the main from three sources, county ad valorem levies, capitation road taxes, and the state distribution of the gasoline tax. Borrowing on note or bond for road work is also resorted to. However, most of the roads constructed out of the proceeds of bond sales have been or will be taken into the state highway system.

Ad valorem road taxes. A specific road levy may be and frequently is set up in the county appropriation bill, or it may be set up by those authorized in the bill to do so. More often such is not the case, but rather a levy for ordinary county purposes is made, which includes roads, the support of the poor, salaries of county officials, and other items. The greater part of the local road funds comes from this source.

The capitation road tax. The counties of the state still levy the capitation road tax. It ranges in amount from $1.00 to $10.00 on each able-bodied man between certain ages. This levy brings in a considerable amount of revenue or is productive of a considerable amount of more or less valuable work on the public roads by local citizens in many counties. The following table shows the capitation levy for 1929-30 in five of the six counties surveyed.

CAPITATION ROAD LEVY, 1929-30
Five Counties

County	Amount
Aiken	$ 4,970
Colleton	9,336
Darlington	18,846
Laurens	6,934
Williamsburg	9,962

The higher the capitation road levy, the more of it may be paid with work instead of cash, or such appears to be the rule. This tax must be used in the district or township in which it is collected.

The state distribution of the gasoline tax. Table V in Chapter IV shows the receipts coming to the counties for the fiscal year 1929-30 from the gasoline tax distributed by the state. This fund is distributed on the basis of the number of registered motor vehicles in the county. The state now distributes the equivalent of one cent per gallon of the gasoline tax to the counties to assist in the maintenance of their road systems. The county receives from local officials certain fees and fines and from the state its share of the tax on insurance premiums, but these funds are not necessarily for the support of roads, since they are put into ordinary county funds and may be disbursed for salaries and other purposes.

Road Construction and Maintenance

Road working organizations. Road working organizations present a remarkable variety. In the six counties surveyed the best found was in Darlington County. There the county board of directors selects the highway engineer and the superintendent of the chaingang, but the latter is subject to the directions of the engineer. There are eight road maintenance gangs consisting of a tractor driver and a helper each, a mule oufit, and a bridge crew. The engineer selects the foremen of all the road and bridge gangs. All of them including the superintendent of the chaingang are responsible to him. The crews are well supplied with modern road machinery. In the summer of 1930 the organization was doubtless one of the best in the state. The organizations in Williamsburg and Colleton counties were very much of the same type as in Darlington County, except that the supervisor in each of these took the place of the highway engineer. These supervisors were handicapped for lack of funds to employ more road gangs and to purchase more modern road machinery.

In Aiken County there was a different road working organization. The county was divided into three districts and the chaingang into three sections. Each of the three members of the county board had charge of the roads in his district and had a section of the chaingang with a superintendent over it with which to build and maintain his roads. One of the districts had a maintenance gang in addition to its chaingang.

The organizations in Fairfield and Laurens counties were loose and ineffective. In the former the county supervisor had charge of some of the road work. His son was superintendent of the chaingang and took more or less freedom in the details of directing its work. The county was divided into four road districts with a gang for each district and two extra ones. The foremen had been chosen by the supervisor, but they too exercised a great deal of freedom. There was a highway engineer also, who was hampered on the one hand by the supervisor and on the other by the road foremen. In Laurens County the supervisor was in charge of the chaingang, which was divided into two sections. He had jurisdiction, however, over only a part of the road work. The county appropriation bill required that the top soiling of the roads be let on contract, and the two county commissioners were paid a small sum each to inspect the work.

These cases represent the types of road working organizations most commonly found in the state. There is, however, one other type found in several counties. It is that in which there is found the township road supervisors. This type of organization was doubtless quite common in earlier days, and one would expect to find it in the less progressive counties. But such is not necessarily the case. In Spartanburg County there is the township supervisor nominated in the primary, then recommended by the county legislative delegation and appointed by the governor. He has charge of certain township roads and of bridges under a certain length. In a few counties the county board is composed of the township commissioners. The road working organizations in the state vary all the way from a highly centralized, carefully directed and supervised organization to those virtually headless and therefore indifferently handled. The latter are adapted especially, though not intentionally, to the waste of road funds.

Compensation of road officials. The compensation of the more important road officials employed in the six counties surveyed is shown in the following table.

COMPENSATION OF COUNTY ROAD OFFICIALS
SIX COUNTIES

County	County Supervisor	County Commissioners	County Engineer	Road Gang Foremen
Fairfield	$1,800	—	$3,150	Up to $140 per month each
Darlington	—	—	3,300	$110-130 per month
Williamsburg	2,700	—	—	$75 per month
Colleton	2,700	—	—	$100 per month
Aiken	—	$900 each	—	—
Laurens	1,800	200 each	—	—

The salary of the supervisor in each case shown in the table includes $300 for expenses. The table does not include the superintendents of county chaingangs, who might be included. The range of supervisors' salaries for the state as a whole is from $1,300 to $4,000 per year. In Aiken County the county board of commissioners has charge of the roads. Each of the three commissioners receives $900 per year, but this salary is in full compensation for all duties including those concerning roads. In a number of counties the salary is considerably smaller.

The salary of county engineer runs as high as $4,000 per year. In Cherokee County the board of county commissioners is made up of the township commissioners, and each commissioner is paid $100 per year. In Spartanburg County each township has a road supervisor, and he is paid $400 per year plus fifty cents per mile for all mileage in excess of 100 miles. The county has a highway commission also, each member of which receives $400 per year.

Methods of road administration. Methods of road and bridge construction and maintenance vary from county to county, depending largely upon the type of road working organization and on resources for road work. The best methods found in the six counties surveyed were those used in Darlington County. The county is not large. Its area is 605 square miles. The local road system consists of about 1,200 miles. The true wealth of the county is probably about $40,000,000, though its assessed valuation is only slightly more than $9,000,000. Aside from considerable areas of swamp lands, its soils are well adapted to the advantageous use of modern road machinery. Mixtures of sand and clay may be secured without excessive expense. All road work was under the direction of the county engineer at the time of the survey. There was a small bridge crew engaged constantly in the construction and maintenance of bridges. The county owned a pile driver for the use of the crew. In the construction of new roads the mule outfit and the chaingang were used where the heavier machinery could not be used to advantage, and at such work as could not be done with the use of tractors. Each of the eight maintenance gangs had about 150 miles of road to keep in repair. All new roads were being constructed and old ones widened to a uniform width of forty feet. The engineer reported the average cost of new construction at $700 per mile, and the average maintenance cost at $30 per mile per year.

All supplies were bought in quantities at close prices for cash. Gasoline and oil were distributed regularly from the storage tanks in Hartsville to the various units at their places of work. The road organization, the purchasing policy, the planning and supervision of the work were all businesslike. The results in evidence could hardly have been obtained otherwise.

Methods in use in Williamsburg and Colleton counties were similar. But in those counties swamps were somewhat more numerous and more extensive and road funds less adequate to the needs. In Colleton County the road system was much larger. In each county the supervisor was in charge of all road work. Each had a chaingang and a small number of maintenance crews. Each also had one or more temporary crews hired to construct roads. The larger bridges to be built in both counties were let on contract.

Methods of road construction and maintenance in Aiken County were similar to those found frequently in Mississippi counties, except in one particular. The purchase of road machinery and supplies was made on much the same policy as that used in Darlington County. The county was divided into three road districts, and each of the county commissioners had charge of one district. The chaingang was divided into three sections, so that each commissioner had his own chaingang with its superintendent.

One district had one maintenance crew in addition to its chaingang. However, the county in common with several others in the state made an appropriation for certain mail roads, and the funds so appropriated were expended under the direction of the rural mail carriers.

Methods found in use in Fairfield and Laurens counties were perhaps as ineffective as could be found in the state. In Laurens County a considerable part of the road work was done by the county chaingang. This organization was divided into two sections with a superintendent over each. The supervisor directed their work. There was included in the 1930 county appropriation bill an item of $9,000 to be expended on cross-country roads, $1,000 to each of the townships. An appropriation was made also for certain rural mail roads to be expended under the direction of the rural mail carriers. Certain roads were designated for topsoiling and an appropriation was made for each. This work had to be done by contract and the two county commissioners were authorized and paid to inspect it. Perhaps from one-half to two-thirds of the road funds was expended under the direction of numerous individuals and officials other than the county supervisor. However democratic the method may be, there can be little doubt but that it will prove to have been very wasteful in the end.

Methods in Fairfield were different, but no better. The county had both the supervisor and the engineer. One of these officials should have had charge of all road work in the county, but neither did have. The county was divided into four districts. In addition to the chaingang there were five road gangs, one for each district and one floating gang. The 1930 legislature established the sixth gang for the purpose of maintaining the permanent roads of the county. Despite the existence of the chaingang, the road gangs, the supervisor, and the engineer, road building was on occasion contracted. In one or more instances the contractor was permitted to do his own engineering. The road working organizations were not welded into one with a responsible head. Purchases of materials and supplies were made by numerous officials with little regard for prices.

In many counties the capitation road tax must be expended in the district or township in which it is collected. Where the township road supervisor exists this tax is literally so expended. In

other cases it may not be. In some counties sums in addition
to the capitation road tax are appropriated for township roads and
bridges. In Spartanburg County a large sum is appropriated each
year for certain roads and for bridges under twelve feet in length.
The county board apportions this sum to the townships according
to their mileage, and the township road supervisors expend the
funds.

School Administration

As indicated in Part I, the development of a public school system in the state was a very slow process. The state system had
its beginning in the act of 1811, but because of serious handicaps
it had made no great progress when the War Between the States
began. The constitution of 1868 provided the machinery for a
state system of schools and directed the legislature to levy taxes
for their support. However, certain radical provisions of the constitution ruined what otherwise might have been an excellent piece
of work. It was required that all schools supported in whole or
in part by public funds should be open to the children and youth
of the state without regard to race or color. And the provision
that the local school commissioners be chosen by popular vote,
under the conditions then existing, was a sure guarantee that they
would be as wasteful and incompetent as they soon proved themselves to be. After ten years the responsible people of the state
came into power again. Under the leadership of Superintendent
Hugh S. Thompson rapid progress began to be made after 1878,
and today the schools for white children are probably on a par
with those of any other southern state.

The county system of schools existing in the state is classified
as a weak system by educators. That is, school authority is divided between the district trustees and the county superintendent
of schools. It is the product of the coalescence of two antago-
nistic forces to be found operating in almost every phase of local
government in the state. On the one hand, there is the strong
tradition of legislative control of all local as well as general affairs; on the other, the demands of a large democratic element
which is characterized by its excessive individualism of the frontier
type. The power of the tradition is evidenced by the great number
of local laws passed each year by the General Assembly dealing in
many instances with the minutest details of district affairs; the

strength and spirit of popular demand by the constitutional limitations on the size of school districts and by the election by popular vote of the county superintendents of schools. There is a growing tendency also to choose district trustees by the same method.

School districts. The constitutional limitations on the size of school districts have been removed in at least four counties by means of constitutional amendments. In these counties the districts may be changed by the respective county boards of education. In those in which the limitations have not been removed new districts may be created, or consolidations of existing districts may be made, within the limitations, only on petition of one-third of the qualified electors within the area concerned. Despite this provision, however, the legislature sets up new districts on occasion. For instance, district No. 3½ was established in Berkeley in 1930 by Act No. 890. Every school district is declared to be a body politic and corporate, and it is also a division of the county for taxation for all school purposes.

Despite the numerous school districts in the state, there appear to be three classes only. The first class consists of districts which have been operating schools under special acts for many years. Examples of this type are found in the city of Charleston and the town of Winnsboro. Such districts select their own trustees or part of them and operate more or less independently of the county system, though they may make statistical reports to the county superintendent of schools.

The second class of districts is very numerous. The district of this class is the one ordinarily thought of when the term district is used. It is limited in area, except in certain counties, by the constitution which created it. In general it is so small in area that it lacks sufficient population and wealth adequately to support more than a small elementary school. According to the Sixty-first Annual Report of the State Superintendent of Education there were 1,790 white schools in the state in 1929. Of these 370 were one-teacher, 510 two-teacher, and 270 three-teacher schools. Of the 2,348 Negro schools only 210 had more than three teachers.

The third type of district is called a high school district. Such a district is formed by creating a separate corporate organization out of two or more districts for the purpose of establishing and

TABLE VI
PUBLIC SCHOOL ENROLLMENT, PER PUPIL INVESTMENT IN
SCHOOL PROPERTY, AND PER PUPIL DISBURSEMENTS.
ENROLLMENT BASIS—RACES SEPARATE

County	Enrollment		Investment in School Property per Pupil Enrolled		Per Capita Disbursements Enrollment Basis	
	White 1928-29	Negro 1928-29	White 1928-29	Negro 1928-29	White 1928-29	Negro 1928-29
Abbeville............	3,305	3,552	$123.00	$15.00	$45.16	$4.64
Aiken...............	6,621	6,038	135.00	23.00	43.45	7.58
Allendale...........	1,070	2,555	219.00	16.00	74.87	5.21
Anderson............	14,997	5,945	117.00	20.00	40.55	6.58
Bamberg............	1,908	3,684	163.00	19.00	67.79	5.40
Barnwell............	2,244	3,407	154.00	18.00	124.29	5.85
Beaufort............	1,187	3,295	228.00	22.00	111.81	7.23
Berkeley............	2,244	4,464	113.00	13.00	80.35	6.29
Calhoun............	1,116	3,470	189.00	10.00	70.06	3.75
Charleston..........	9,258	10,226	224.00	55.00	84.15	16.03
Cherokee...........	5,787	2,391	147.00	20.00	44.93	8.37
Chester.............	4,142	4,999	171.00	18.00	78.22	6.99
Chesterfield.........	6,616	3,883	112.00	17.00	55.10	6.21
Clarendon..........	2,560	5,398	105.00	5.00	54.60	4.46
Colleton............	3,377	3,914	100.00	7.00	53.75	6.58
Darlington..........	5,237	6,130	134.00	29.00	64.43	7.95
Dillon..............	3,425	3,678	175.00	28.00	59.62	7.05
Dorchester..........	2,414	2,735	113.00	9.00	52.71	6.26
Edgefield...........	1,947	3,820	120.00	15.00	46.23	5.46
Fairfield............	1,947	4,834	174.00	12.00	109.41	5.73
Florence............	9,708	8,070	206.00	31.00	53.53	7.67
Georgetown.........	2,244	3,198	121.00	9.00	52.50	9.46
Greenville..........	23,743	7,922	127.00	30.00	56.93	10.98
Greenwood..........	5,166	4,407	145.00	17.00	47.34	7.44
Hampton............	2,372	2,546	117.00	10.00	57.27	4.94
Horry..............	8,347	2,729	70.00	19.00	66.10	10.37
Jasper..............	980	1,774	159.00	8.00	82.05	5.17
Kershaw............	4,044	5,480	125.00	13.00	59.13	6.39
Lancaster...........	5,108	3,538	131.00	32.00	47.30	7.56
Laurens............	5,552	5,580	135.00	17.00	62.80	5.80
Lee................	2,406	4,681	204.00	7.00	57.67	3.89
Lexington...........	7,523	2,854	106.00	13.00	39.21	10.73
Marion.............	3,410	3,792	197.00	31.00	59.71	10.46
Marlboro...........	3,618	4,756	256.00	22.00	70.40	14.99
McCormick..........	1,073	2,442	147.00	5.00	77.18	4.77
Newberry...........	4,899	4,890	195.00	25.00	71.67	8.58
Oconee.............	7,469	1,992	84.00	28.00	47.65	8.55
Orangeburg.........	6,889	10,436	144.00	17.00	59.11	5.56
Pickens............	7,797	1,467	92.00	28.00	39.40	12.53
Richland............	9,902	9,481	229.00	48.00	68.87	13.43
Saluda.............	2,936	2,652	71.00	16.00	40.05	8.23
Spartanburg.........	22,670	8,381	147.00	32.00	76.30	9.15
Sumter.............	3,828	9,095	126.00	8.00	60.71	5.66
Union..............	4,670	4,106	117.00	26.00	53.58	7.05
Williamsburg........	3,088	6,990	112.00	7.00	70.16	5.61
York...............	7,838	6,132	128.00	19.00	52.80	8.44
State..............	248,682	217,809	$143.00	$21.00	$60.06	$7.89

operating a high school. The original districts do not lose their identity. The courts have held that this district is not limited to forty-nine square miles in area.[20] As a rule, the high school district boards of trustees are composed of the chairmen of the trustees of the districts included in the high school district, and they are vested with the power to do all things necessary to the establishment and maintenance of a high school.

The total number of districts in the state in 1929 was 1816. Per county they ranged in number from eight in Beaufort to ninety-four in Spartanburg County. Not every district has a white school however.

Types of schools. The system of schools is an eleven-grade system with a seven-four division; that is, seven grades are in the elementary school and four in the high school. There seems to be no distinct classification of schools other than that of elementary and high schools. Consolidations may be made within districts, but these rarely produce large schools unless the rural population is unusually dense or unless there is a consolidation of such rural schools as may exist with a town or city system within the district. Pupils may be sent from one district to a school in another under a coöperative arrangement between the trustees of the districts concerned. The high school districts, which are created by special act of the legislature, are established for the purpose of organizing and maintaining high schools only.

High schools receiving state aid must operate not less than 180 days, though four holidays may be granted by the trustees and included in this number. The elementary schools in the high school districts must run the same number of days. All schools doing high school work are not diploma or standard high schools. The standardization of elementary schools has made far less headway than that of the high schools.

The average number of days per county in 1929 in which the white schools operated ranged from 153 to 180 days. The shortest terms for rural schools were found in Cherokee County, where they averaged 145 days. In Charleston, Fairfield, and Jasper counties the term for rural schools for the same year was 180 days each.

Transportation. Transportation is making considerable head-

[20] General School Law of South Carolina, 1929, p. 63.

way in the state. The sparse white population makes it very expensive in many districts. The constitutional limitations on the size of districts is slowly being removed by constitutional amendments. The creation of high school districts makes necessary the transportation of high school pupils. The transfer of pupils from one district to another under agreement between the trustees also calls for transportation. In the year 1928-29 the total number of pupils transported in the state, with the reports from four counties missing, was 29,054. The total average cost per pupil ranged from $15.87 in Lee County to $77.74 in Fairfield County.

Administration in six counties, 1929-30. Until 1930 there had been no provision for a school census in the state for a long period. As a result school officials had no very definite ideas of the number of pupils of school age not enrolled in the public schools. In one of the counties surveyed the county superintendent estimated that there were 400 white and 600 Negro pupils not enrolled. This was the only estimate found.

The following table shows the number of school districts, and the number of schools and the value of school property by race in the six counties surveyed.

NUMBER OF SCHOOLS AND VALUE OF SCHOOL PROPERTY
SIX COUNTIES

County	No. of Districts	No. of Schools White	Negro	Value of School Property White	Negro
Fairfield	34	15	80	$338,745	$ 58,715
Darlington	27	25	39	702,700	177,465
Williamsburg	52	30	81	338,075	53,925
Colleton	43	45	67	306,920	28,792
Aiken	59	52	81	846,492	114,617
Laurens	41	37	61	726,020	97,344

The next table presents the figures for enrollment, average daily attendance, and number of pupils transported.

ENROLLMENT, ATTENDANCE AND TRANSPORTATION
SIX COUNTIES

County	WHITES No. Enrolled	Percentage in A.D.A.	No. Transported	NEGROES No. Enrolled	Percentage in A.D.A.
Fairfield	1947*	80.0*	698*	4834*	75.8*
Darlington	5112	79.0	1275	6039	73.1
Williamsburg	3015	75.7	1150	7644	68.1
Colleton	3288	74.1	770	4043	73.3
Aiken	6826	69.4	2535	6619	68.2
Laurens	5541	78.0	802	4662	66.6

* Winnsboro schools not included.

The number of pupils enrolled is doubtless much less than the number of school age. The ratio of pupils in average daily attendance is low, and in this respect the whites do not make much better showing than the Negroes.

School finances. School finances come from local sources and from state aid. Since 1878 the state has levied the constitutional three-mill tax for schools. This levy is collected in the county and retained there. The county superintendent apportions it to the districts on the basis of the number of pupils enrolled. The 6-0-1 four-mill levy is also state-wide. It is collected and retained in the respective counties and distributed by the county superintendent on basis of the number of teachers employed. If it is insufficient to pay the salaries of all teachers for six months, the state contributes the remainder from other sources. From the state to the counties comes also fifty per cent of the sums received by the state game warden from the sale of hunting and fishing licenses within the respective counties. However, many of the counties receive little or nothing from this source. Those counties which do receive something from this source place it in the county board fund, which may be used to assist weak schools or to encourage the erection and improvement of school buildings. The state appropriates also to vocational education in agriculture, in industries, and in home economics. It also gives aid for school buildings under certain conditions.

Sources of local school finances. Since the three and four-mill levies for schools are collected and retained in the respective counties, it may be said that financial support for the schools comes in the main from local sources. The general property tax provides the greater part of the funds. Other sources are the poll tax, the dog tax, certain fees and fines, and local contributions. The following table gives the local school revenues of five of the six counties surveyed.

SCHOOL REVENUES, 1929-30
FIVE COUNTIES

| County | From General Property Tax | | Polls | Dogs | Non-tax | Total |
	County-wide	District				
Darlington	$77,349.27	$228,821.38	$8,288.00	$2,152.00	$24,600.00	$341,210.65
Williamsburg ..	98,369.53	46,361.70	5,616.07	2,737.03	2,917.05	156,002.08
Colleton	76,207.25	72,719.75	4,438.00	874.00	4,996.89	159,235.89
Aiken	89,948.63	147,793.73	7,318.00	2,046.00	7,492.81	254,599.17
Laurens	68,537.60	183,229.18	6,812.00	1,970.25	9,133.12	269,682.15

The following table shows the percentages of local revenues coming from the various sources:

PERCENTAGES OF LOCAL REVENUES BY SOURCE, 1929-30
FIVE COUNTIES

County	From General Property Tax	Other Sources	Total	From District General Property Tax
Darlington	89.7	10.3	100	67.0
Williamsburg	92.7	7.3	100	29.7
Colleton	93.5	6.5	100	45.6
Aiken	93.3	6.7	100	58.0
Laurens	93.3	6.7	100	67.2

State aid for teachers' salaries coming to these counties ranged from eighteen per cent of all school funds in Darlington County to about thirty per cent in Colleton and Williamsburg. This variation is due in the main to differences in density of population, to consolidations, and perhaps to differences in the percentages of the true wealth assessed for taxation. Where there are many small schools the ratio of teachers to pupils is usually higher than in town and consolidated schools. These tables show also that some counties are much further along towards county-wide financial support for schools than are others. For instance, only 29.7 per cent of local school revenues comes from district levies on general property in Williamsburg County, whereas in Laurens 67.2 per cent comes from the districts.

The next table shows the annual per pupil cost for 1929-30 of both instruction and transportation in the white schools and of instruction in the Negro schools. The six counties surveyed are all included in the table, and the figures are on the basis of enrollment.

INSTRUCTION AND TRANSPORTATION COSTS, 1929-30
SIX COUNTIES

County	White Schools Instruction	White Schools Transportation	Negro Schools Instruction
Fairfield	$28.29*	$24.70*	$5.17*
Darlington	38.82	14.93	7.01
Williamsburg	41.13	26.40	5.18
Colleton	40.20	26.31	5.68
Aiken	33.19	13.24	4.51
Laurens	36.31	56.68	6.63

* Winnsboro schools not included.

Cost of instruction includes teachers' salaries only. The table shows wide variations in costs of both instruction and transportation. Figures for all counties in the state would doubtless show still greater differences. No Negro pupils are transported, and the per pupil cost of instruction is very low indeed. For white schools the variations of both types of costs are much greater within the respective counties than among the counties themselves. The following table gives the highest and lowest costs within each of the same counties.

RANGE OF PER PUPIL COSTS OF TEACHERS'
SALARIES AND TRANSPORTATION
WITHIN EACH OF SIX COUNTIES

County	Teachers' Salaries		Transportation	
	Highest	Lowest	Highest	Lowest
Fairfield	$94.73	$29.03	$51.00	$19.95
Darlington	57.80	20.54	44.76	7.15
Williamsburg	66.00	23.22	—	—
Colleton	165.00	27.23	76.10	7.51
Aiken	68.00	20.00	—	—
Laurens	57.06	20.73	109.00	13.08

The table indicates that costs in some districts are excessive. The teaching and transportation services rendered these districts are of no higher quality than those where costs are lowest; in fact, in some cases they may be of poorer quality. Whether the funds come from district or county-wide sources, the costs are too great. But they can not well be reduced until population has had time to regroup about the town, village, and other consolidated schools. Wide areas with sparse population mean small schools, numerous teachers with high per pupil costs, if the teachers are paid well, or high transportation costs. The abolition of all school districts, except for temporary designations by the county board of education, and the gradual elimination of all district tax levies would doubtless help to hasten the time when costs could be materially reduced or the quality of services greatly improved.

In many of the counties efforts are made to assist the weak schools to some extent. In Fairfield County there is a four-mill levy which is placed in the county board fund and apportioned by the superintendent and the county board of education among the schools of the county for assistance in paying transportation costs and teachers' salaries for terms beyond the six months. The districts must levy a special three-mill tax in order to share in the fund. In Colleton and Aiken counties there is a half-mill levy in each for the county board fund. To these funds are added such sums as come from the state game warden.[21]   In Darlington a half-mill levy is made for high schools.   Laurens County has a county-wide levy of two mills for paying the salaries of high school teachers in certain districts for the time for which they are not paid by the state.   The county also has a one-mill levy for the help of weak schools.   Colleton and Williamsburg counties have county unit levies of thirteen and ten mills respectively for paying teachers' salaries for the term beyond the six months.   Parts of these levies are used for paying transportation costs.   Colleton also levies a three-mill tax for the purpose of paying a per capita tuition fee to the various high schools in the county.   The proceeds of this levy are apportioned to the various high schools by the county superintendent on the basis of their enrollment.

The compulsory attendance law.   The state legislature passed a compulsory attendance law in 1915.   It provides that children between the ages of eight and fourteen years must attend some school or be sent to a competent tutor, subject to the approval of the county superintendent of schools, for four months or eighty days, unless the term of the school is less than eighty days.[22] However, if a majority of the qualified electors residing in any school district request the attendance of the pupils throughout the full term, the county board must order such attendance.   Pupils adjudged completely unfit physically, mentally, or morally are exempt from the provisions of the law, as well as those living two and one-half miles from a school, or two miles, if under twelve years of age.   But if the pupil lives within one mile of a school wagon or bus route he is not exempt.[23]

As a rule, the enforcement of the law is left to the district trustees.   The law requires the parents of children of compulsory age to report them to the chairman of the board of trustees.   The trustees determine when the compulsory period shall begin.   Trustees of one or more districts may nominate an attendance officer to the county superintendent, or to the district superintendent, if a special district.   It is the duty of this attendance officer to take a census of the children of compulsory age during July and August

[21] Total receipts from sale of hunting and fishing licenses, 1928-29: N. C., $188,-819.50, S. C., $142,026.00.   Figures taken from the 1931 Yearbook of Agriculture, United States Department of Agriculture.

[22] *Code*, 1922, Vol. 3, sec. 2739.

[23] *Ibid.*, secs. 2740-42.

of each year and to report them to the trustees and superintendent in question. On the other hand, the county board of education with the approval of the county superintendent and the county legislative delegation may employ a county attendance officer. The county attendance officer may excuse any absence. He has the right also to visit any places of employment to see if any child of compulsory age is being employed.[24]

Violation of the law by a parent is a misdemeanor. Upon conviction the parent may be fined from $5 to $10 or be imprisoned from five to ten days. Reports of unexcused absences are required to be turned over to the rural police or the nearest constable. The officer apprehends the parent of the child concerned and carries him before the nearest magistrate for the trial.[25]

Little attention is paid to the compulsory law in most counties. Of the six counties surveyed only one had an attendance officer, and she gave only part-time to the work. In the other five the trustees were the enforcement officials. So far as could be discovered nothing was done about the law in those counties. In fact, the lack of an accurate census of school children makes it impossible to enforce the law. The General Assembly has recently passed an act requiring the teachers to make a complete census of the children in their districts. Thus it may be that a start is being made towards the enforcement of the law.

Leaving the enforcement of the compulsory law in the hands of the trustees really leaves it up to the people themselves. What they do with it shows unmistakably how much value they place upon education. Until the school census of 1930 is complete, one can not tell how many white children of compulsory age are not attending school, but the number is doubtless large for the state taken as a whole.

Teachers, qualifications, salaries, homes. Very few white teachers in the counties surveyed held other than first grade certificates. These certificates however are not necessarily an indication of the possession of a bachelor's degree in education, or its equivalent. But the teachers are rapidly becoming better trained.

Salaries actually paid to white teachers were found to range from $90 to $183 per month. These figures were for teachers

[24] *Ibid.*, secs. 2744-47.
[25] *Ibid.*, secs. 2748 and 2751.

holding first grade certificates. In one county only was an elementary teacher found who received more than $100 per month. The larger salaries are paid to the high school teachers. Some districts supplement the state schedule of salaries, but the supplementary salaries go to the high school teachers, coaches, and administrative officials. This is not an uncommon state of affairs.

As a rule, homes for the teachers do not exist. In a few cases the principal has a home near the school building, but he may have built it himself. These necessary adjuncts to the rural school are slow in coming. The enrichment of rural life awaits the development of fit country schools, and fit country schools must be more than mere buildings. Teachers qualified by natural aptitudes and adequate training and rooted in the community are the prime essentials.

Supervision. Supervision of teaching, particularly in the rural schools, hardly exists. Very few counties in the state employ supervisors of elementary schools. In the six counties surveyed only one was found, and she gave part-time to attendance work. In some counties the county superintendent attempts to do some supervision, but when he is competent to do so his other duties make it almost impossible for him to plan the work and carry it out in such a manner as to be of real value to the teachers. Teachers properly trained and selected doubtless need no supervisor, but the value of a competent and tactful supervisor in a system of schools containing many young and inadequately trained and carelessly chosen teachers can not be overestimated. County systems frequently have considerable numbers of just such teachers.

County libraries. County libraries are to be found in only a few counties. Public libraries are to be found in most of the county seat towns. These are supported in part by public funds. There are a few public libraries supported by one or more school districts. An instance is the library at Darlington. A two-mill tax is levied on the property of the Darlington school district for the support of the library. The library attempts to serve the schools of the county through the teachers.

Of the six counties surveyed only Laurens had a county library, and it had been established only very recently. It is housed in a well-lighted room on the second floor of the Laurens city hall.

Though it was only a few months old at the time of the survey and though the appropriation for its support was small, it contained from 3,000 to 4,000 volumes, many of which were in constant use. The library has a number of sub-stations out in the county. Each is in charge of a teacher or other responsible person. Books are carried to and from the library to these sub-stations by private individuals who are interested in bringing the services of the library to the various rural communities. Books are being added to the library by purchase and gift. The librarian is capable and enthusiastic, and the library gives promise of becoming a permanent agency for the diffusion of knowledge throughout the county.

THE ADMINISTRATION OF JUSTICE

The machinery for the maintenance of peace and the administration of justice in the state does not differ materially from that to be found generally in the states of the American Union, and the same may be said of the results obtained on the whole.

At the head of the judicial system of the state is the supreme court consisting of a chief justice and four associates chosen by joint *viva voce* ballot of the General Assembly for terms of eight years each. The judges of the circuit courts are chosen in the same manner, but for shorter terms. A unique provision of the constitution concerning the supreme court is that which authorizes it to call to its assistance the circuit judges in passing on questions involving constitutional law. It is doubtless but a modification of the early custom of the circuit judges to sit *en banc* for revision of errors and to hear appeals. Our interest lies however in the local administration of justice, and so we shall begin with the courts which are found nearest the people.

The justices of the peace. The manner of choosing magistrates and their jurisdiction have already been given. They serve for two years each. The number to be found in the state is too large undoubtedly, but it is very small when compared with that found in North Carolina, where the average is about thirty to the county and where magistrates are chosen in abundance by three methods. In South Carolina the tendency seems to be to reduce the number, and the tendency is a good one, for it should result eventually in attracting to the office men with better training.

The magistrates are paid salaries in lieu of fees in criminal cases. For civil cases and commercial work they may charge fees. The following table shows the range of salaries paid to magistrates and constables. These represent the highest and lowest found in the state.

SALARIES OF MAGISTRATES AND CONSTABLES

County	Salary of Magistrates		Salary of Constables	
	Highest	Lowest	Highest	Lowest
Abbeville ....$	500	$125	$180	$125
Calhoun	550	150	400	100
Charleston	1,800	500	900	250
Cherokee	900	600	—	—
Chesterfield	600	120	—	—
Clarendon	500	100	50	50
Edgefield	350	75	—	—

Each magistrate may appoint one constable, but he does not always do so. In some counties two or more constables are appointed by local act to serve the magistrates. In other cases the rural police may serve them.

The law requires the magistrates to make monthly reports to the county auditor and treasurer of fines, penalties, and forfeitures collected. In many cases the law is not complied with. In a few instances in the counties surveyed magistrates were found who had not accounted for all funds. In one case the sum was $720. Some of the dockets examined were very carelessly kept. In the counties in which periodic audits were made by outside auditors, the latter frequently complained that the magistrates did not readily submit their dockets for examination. In a few instances the dockets were not sent in at all.

Those magistrates located in the larger towns usually have office rent paid out of county funds, unless they are located in the county courthouse.

As already indicated constables may be appointed by the magistrates and also by legislative act. However, there is still another method of appointing them. The governor may appoint on recommendation of the county legislative delegation. Chester County has one so appointed whose special duty it is to enforce the prohibition law. He has all the powers now conferred on sheriffs and other peace officers.

The following table was prepared from the dockets of the magistrates at Darlington and Laurens. The record of cases of the Darlington magistrate covered the period from July first, 1929, to July first, 1930; that of the Laurens magistrate covered the period from October first, 1930, to December tenth, 1930. The latter magistrate had taken office on October first. His record includes the cases bound over to the higher courts.

A RECORD FROM THE DOCKETS OF TWO MAGISTRATES

Cause	Town of Darlington			Town of Laurens	
	No. Cases	Found Guilty	Bond Forfeited	No. Cases	Guilty or Bound Over
Disorderly conduct..............	1	1	..	5	5
Operating car without license....	5	1	4	..	..
Breaking quarantine...........	1	1	..	..	..
Carrying concealed weapons.....	4	3	1	2	2
Drunk and disorderly..........	9	9	..	4	4
Petit larceny.................	10	10	..	5	5
Receiving stolen goods..........	2	2	..	..	..
Assault and battery...........	3	3	..	3	3
Trespass.....................	4	4	..	..	..
Injury to property............	1	1	..	..	..
Violation of prohibition law.....	1	1	..	8	8
Malicious mischief.............	3	3	..	..	..
Reckless driving..............	..	..	..	4	4
Issuing worthless checks........	..	..	..	8	8
Despoiling property under lien...	..	..	..	4	4
Breach of trust with fraudulent intent.....................	..	..	..	2	2
Non-support..................	..	..	..	1	1
Grand larceny................	..	..	..	4	4
Housebreaking and larceny......	..	..	..	5	5
Murder......................	..	..	..	1	1
Obtaining goods under false pretence..................	..	..	..	3	3
Vagrancy....................	..	..	..	4	4
Arson and housebreaking.......	..	..	..	1	1
Cruelty to animals............	..	..	..	1	1
	44	39	5	66	66

The large number of cases which came before the Laurens magistrate in such a short time is accounted for in part by him by the fact that many cases are brought before him from the rural townships in addition to those coming from his own. The table gives some indication of what is happening in two county seat towns, one in the coastal plain and the other in the Piedmont. But it does not tell of course how many petty crimes are committed and not brought into the magistrate courts.

The court of probate. With a single exception there is a separate court of probate with its elective judge in every county. The probate judge is the successor to the district ordinary of the earlier days. Originally the governor exercised the jurisdiction of ordinary for the whole province.

The law requires that the court meet on the first Monday of each month and continue in session as long as may be necessary. The compensation of the judges of probate varies considerably from county to county. It is materially increased in case the judge combines other official duties with those of probate. In some counties the judge of probate is also the master in equity, and he may receive more compensation in that capacity than as judge of probate. In the six counties surveyed the appropriations for the judge of probate or for his office ranged from $100 in Colleton County to $1,500 in Darlington County. These appropriations however are not always for salary. They may be made for clerical help or for office supplies. In some counties the probate judge issues marriage licenses. Such is the case in Colleton County. The probate judge receives the county's share of the state pension fund for Confederate veterans from the state treasurer and distributes it to the veterans. He receives small fees for this work. For instance, the Laurens County appropriation bill for 1930 provides that the judge of probate shall receive twenty-five cents for paying out pension claims and the same sum for indexing them. The fees for this work are not necessarily uniform.

Administrators appointed by the judge of probate are required to give bond for double the amount of personal property to be administered by them. Administration may continue indefinitely. Annual returns are required by law. One judge reported difficulty in having the law complied with. Another reported no difficulty whatever in securing prompt reports from administrators and guardians. He attributed his success in the matter to the fact that he required corporate surety bonds in all cases. As a rule, the judges of probate hold no large amounts of trust funds in their own keeping, frequently none at all. In some cases such funds as they hold are limited to those belonging to estates of the value of $500 or less each. The bond of the probate judge is usually fixed at $5,000. It must be a corporate surety bond and the premium is paid out of the county treasury. The probate judge is the juvenile judge also and as such he commits delinquent boys and girls to the institutions provided by the state for their training.

The coroner's court. The coroner still exists in the state, as elsewhere, by virtue of a hoary tradition and by virtue of his being embedded in the masonry of the state constitution. His powers and duties are not materially different from those of coroners elsewhere in the United States. He is perhaps called upon to perform his duties no more often here than elsewhere, but whether that be a fact or not he is given the dignity of a stated and regular salary.

The county court. Municipal courts exist in the towns and cities. In a very few counties the county court has been established. In perhaps two instances its jurisdiction extends to a part of the county only. No county court had been established in any of the counties surveyed.

The various local acts creating the county courts may differ in some details from each other, and they do differ materially from the general law concerning the establishment of the county courts. The act creating the Orangeburg County Court may be taken as an example to show the general structure and jurisdiction of this class of courts. The qualified voters of the county pass upon the establishment of the court before it is created. In the case of Orangeburg County the judge is appointed for a four-year term by the governor on the recommendation of the Orangeburg County Bar Association. He is paid a salary of $3,000 per year. The first county solicitor was appointed in the same manner to serve until the next general election. Then and afterwards he must be elected by popular vote. His term is four years, and his salary was fixed at $1,200 per year.

The jurisdiction of the court follows: (a) The court has concurrent jurisdiction with the court of common pleas in all civil cases and special proceedings, both in law and equity, in which the amount involved does not exceed $3,000, and in all other civil cases and special proceedings, both in law and equity, in which there is no money demanded, or in which the right involved can not be fixed by monetary value. (b) It has concurrent jurisdiction with the court of general sessions in all criminal cases, except murder, manslaughter, rape or attempted rape, arson, common law burglary, bribery, perjury, and forgery; and concurrent jurisdiction with the magistrates courts in all criminal cases within their jurisdiction. (c) The court also has concurrent jurisdiction with the court of common pleas and general sessions, respectively, to hear and determine all appeals in civil cases and criminal cases, respectively, from judgments rendered from the magistrates courts and all other inferior courts; and the proceedings on such appeals shall be the same as now provided for appeals in such cases from the magistrates courts to the courts of common pleas and general sessions respectively. Procedure for the trial of cases in the county court is the same as that in the circuit court, unless that in the latter is inconsistent with the act establishing the county court. The jury for the trial of cases in the county court consists of six. The judge may designate certain weeks for jury trials. The appeals from the county court are to the supreme court, and the procedure is the same as that which governs appeals from the circuit courts. The clerk of the circuit court is ex-officio clerk of the county court, and the grand jury serving the court of general sessions constitutes the grand jury of the county court.[26]

Municipal courts. The law provides for the establishment of municipal courts in two classes of cities: those having a population of 20,000 and not exceeding 50,000, and those having a population between 2,000 and 20,000.

The municipal court has jurisdiction to try and determine all cases arising under the ordinance of the city in which it is established, and generally has such judicial powers and duties as are now conferred upon the mayor of such city by charter or by laws of the state. Furthermore, it has all such powers, duties, and jurisdiction in criminal cases as are conferred by law upon magistrates appointed and commissioned for the county in which it is established, except that it does not have authority to appoint a magistrate's constable.

The court has jurisdiction over and power to investigate the condition of incorrigible and destitute children under seventeen years of age. Decisions in such cases must be filed with the circuit court clerk among the records of the court of general sessions. The child has the right to appeal from the decision of the municipal court to the city council or to the judge of the circuit court.

The law provides also that the municipal court shall be held by a recorder who shall be chosen by the mayor and aldermen of the

[26] Acts and Joint Resolutions, 1925, Act No. 114.

city. His term of office is four years, and his salary, which is fixed by the mayor and aldermen, may not be increased or diminished during his continuance in office.[26a] However, Act No. 577 passed in 1928 gives the mayor and aldermen the power to fix the recorder's term by ordinance for less than four years. And by Act No. 117 passed in 1923 the second class of cities was enlarged to include those with a population as small as 1,500.

The intendants or mayors of the cities and towns that are chartered, or that may be chartered, have all the powers and authority of magistrates in criminal cases within the corporate limits, and police jurisdiction of their respective cities and towns. They may try without jury, unless the accused demands one. In case a jury is demanded the chief of police, or the marshal, or such officer as the intendant or mayor may appoint, shall act as constable to prepare the jury list. The complainant, or some officer designated by the mayor, is authorized to make the challenges. The jury consists of six men. Punishments in municipal courts may not exceed a fine of $100 or imprisonment for more than 30 days.

The defendant has the right of appeal to the city or town council, provided he gives notice within twenty-four hours after sentence has been passed, and enters into bond to appear at the time specified and to abide the sentence of the council. But in cities of over 5,000 inhabitants, incorporated under Art. V, chapter 51, of the Civil Code, the appellant may pay the fine imposed under protest and appeal without giving bond. The aldermen sit as a court, with the mayor presiding. And a majority of the aldermen is necessary to reverse the judgment of the mayor.

The defendant may appeal from the decision of the mayor or council to the court of general sessions. But the appeal does not stay execution of sentence, unless the applicant gives bond, approved by the mayor, to abide the judgment of the court of general sessions. This appeal is heard upon the report of the presiding officer of the trial below and upon the testimony reported by him. These provisions do not apply, however, to the city of Charleston. The jury in municipal court consists of six men. Any party has the right to have the testimony given at such a trial taken down by a stenographer appointed by the recorder, provided he first tender or pay charges for the same.

[26a] *Criminal Code, 1922,* Chap. III, secs. 49-52.

The chief of police of the cities in which a municipal court is established must attend the sessions of the court, and execute all orders of the court and all duties in connection with it as may be prescribed by the ordinances of the city. He is invested with the same powers and duties as those of the magistrate's constable.[26b] Act No. 127 passed in 1923 provides that in towns and cities of less than 5,000 population the mayor and aldermen shall be the jury commission for the municipal court.

There are exceptions to the provisions of the general law. The municipal court established in Spartanburg is presided over by a judge, who is appointed by the governor upon the recommendation of a majority of the legislative delegation of Spartanburg County. He holds office for a term of two years, and his salary is fixed in the Act establishing the court. This court has jurisdiction over all juvenile delinquents, and the judge holds juvenile court separate from the sessions of the municipal court.[26c]

In the city of Charleston three city courts have been established. The civil and criminal court of Charleston has jurisdiction over certain territory outside the city. It has the same jurisdiction as was formerly provided for the judicial magistrate's court in the city. In civil actions it has jurisdiction in cases where the amount sued for, or the value of the property claimed, exclusive of costs, does not exceed $500. But its jurisdiction does not extend to cases where the title to real estate is in question, nor to cases in chancery. It has concurrent jurisdiction with the court of common pleas in matters within its own jurisdiction.

The presiding judge must be a resident attorney. His term is four years, and he is chosen in the same manner as the probate judge of the county. In the absence of the recorder he is authorized to preside over the recorder's courts of the city.

All summons and other processes of this court are issued exclusively by one of the ministerial magistrates in the jurisdiction, except in cases wherein the amount sued for, or the value of the property claimed, exceeds $100.

Jury trials may be held on certain weeks, provided demand is made for the same in advance. The jury consists of six men, as is the case in other municipal courts. The judge of the court has

[26b] Ibid., secs. 60, 55, 54.
[26c] Ibid., secs. 52a, 51a.

authority to appoint a clerk. Appeal from this court is allowed as in the case of the ordinary magistrate's court.[26d]

Acts were passed in 1923 and 1924 providing that this court be abolished in case a county court was established in Charleston County.

The city court and the police court are presided over by the recorder, who is appointed by the city council and holds his commission during good behavior.

The jurisdiction of the city court is limited to the trial of causes arising under the ordinances of the city. Jury trial may be had in this court on demand. The right of appeal in this court is to the supreme court.

The recorder also holds the police court. This court has jurisdiction over all offenses committed within the limits of the city, which may be subject to a fine not exceeding $100, or imprisonment not exceeding 30 days. Trial by jury may be had on demand in this court.[26e]

The circuit courts. The state is divided into fourteen judicial districts or circuits. Each circuit is composed of several counties. There are two courts called the courts of general sessions and of common pleas. The court of general sessions, or the criminal court, sits three times each year in each county, while the court of common pleas, or civil court, sits twice. These courts are two branches of the same court. The judges are chosen by joint *viva voce* ballot of the two houses of the General Assembly for a period of four years each. Solicitors are chosen in each district by popular vote for terms of the same length as those of the judges.

To be eligible for the supreme or circuit court bench an individual must be a citizen of the United States and of the state, must have attained the age of twenty-six years, and must have been a resident of the state for five years next preceding his election.

Jurisdiction. The court of common pleas has original jurisdiction, subject to appeal to the supreme court, to issue such writs or orders of injunction, mandamus, habeas corpus, and such other writs as may be necessary to carry its power into full effect. It has full jurisdiction in all civil cases. It has appellate jurisdiction in all cases within the jurisdiction of inferior courts, except those from which appeals may be made directly to the supreme court.

[26d] *Civil Code, 1922,* Chapter VI, secs. 233-236, 240, 242.
[26e] *Ibid.,* Chapter VII, secs. 245-247, 256, 261, 264.

The court of general sessions has jurisdiction in all criminal cases, except those cases in which exclusive jurisdiction has been given to inferior courts, and in these it has appellate jurisdiction. It has concurrent jurisdiction with, as well as appellate jurisdiction from, the inferior courts in all cases of riot, assault and battery, and larceny.[27]   Though these courts are state courts, they meet in the counties, and aside from the judges and solicitors, they are conducted by officials chosen by the county.

The clerk of the circuit courts.   The clerk of the circuit courts has many powers and duties. Some of these are not related directly to the work of the courts. He keeps the records of the courts of general sessions and common pleas. In a number of counties he is in charge of the county courthouse. Where the county court exists, he is as a rule ex-officio clerk of it. Except in the counties of Charleston, Greenville, and Spartanburg he is register of mesne conveyances for his county. As such he records deeds, marriage settlements, conveyances, renunciations of dower, mortgages, and crop liens. In some counties he issues marriage licenses. He is required to keep a record of all county bonds, a task he frequently forgets, of mercantile establishments, and of physicians in his county. He receives reports from the registers of vital statistics and transmits them to the state board of health. In a few counties he is master in equity. He is also a member of the jury commission, the county sinking fund commission, if it is an ex-officio body, and of the forfeited land commission.

The clerk's compensation comes almost entirely from fees. These are not uniform throughout the state. In the counties surveyed the appropriation bill in each case contained an appropriation for the clerk's salary or for his office. These ranged from $350 to $1,200. However, the sums so appropriated were usually not sufficient to purchase office supplies and pay the clerical help employed.

The master in equity.   The duties of the master in equity, who may be elected or appointed, include attendance upon the sittings of the court of common pleas in the hearing of any causes in which he may have acted officially; to make all such sales as the court may order him to make in granting equitable relief and to execute all proper conveyances. In causes praying equitable re-

[27] South Carolina Constitution of 1895, Art. V, secs. 15 and 18.

lief he hears motions and makes orders thereon, extends the time
to answer or demur, grants leave to amend pleadings and to make
new parties, appoints guardians *ad litem* for infants, and makes
all orders necessary for the service publications of absent defendants. He has power also to make orders of reference in matters
of account, reserving all the equities of the parties, and may grant
all such orders of an interlocutory character as may be necessary
to prepare such causes for hearing on merit.[28]   He may also exercise certain powers which are generally exercised by the clerk of
the court or the probate judge. His compensation is principally
in fees.

The juries. The juries are selected in the usual familiar manner. Jurors must be qualified electors and men of good moral
character between the ages of 21 and 65. One compartment of the
jury box is called the tales box. This box contains the names of
eligibles living within five miles of the court, and it is drawn upon
in cases of emergency. The grand jury is authorized among its
various duties to employ an expert accountant to audit the books
of the county officials,[29] and this duty it performs in most counties.

The compensation of jurors is $3.00 per day and five cents for
each mile travelled. In the magistrate courts jurors get fifty
cents for each case and mileage.[30]

The sheriff. The sheriff of the county exercises powers not
unlike those of sheriffs in counties of the other states. The law
gives him authority to appoint one or more deputies to be approved
by the judge of the circuit court. In actual practice, however,
his deputies are not always appointed by himself. The legislature
or the legislative delegation may step in and appoint one or more
deputies and prescribe their duties, so that the sheriff is relieved
from responsibility in the matter. A case in point was to be
found in Laurens County in 1930.

He is required by law to keep a writ book in which he records
all writs, citations, subpoenas, injunctions, warrants, etc., issued
to him; an execution book; and a sale book. In many cases these
books are very carelessly kept, if kept at all. There are many
laws on the statute books concerning breach of duty on the part
of the sheriff, forbidding him to purchase property sold officially

[28] Code, 1922, Vol. 3, secs. 2229 and 2233.
[29] Code, 1922, Vol. I, sec. 566.
[30] *Ibid.*, sec. 573.

or to trade in tax executions, requiring monthly statements, and the proper handling of tax executions. Many of these laws are entirely ignored. Perhaps no other single county official throughout the country so completely follows his own will as the sheriff.

However, in some of the counties surveyed he was very active and effective within the limitations placed upon him both in law enforcement and as a delinquent tax collector. In others he did little, leaving the law enforcement to the rural police and the collection of delinquent taxes to the delinquent tax collector. In such cases a deputy or a rural policeman might be employed to keep the jail and the office of sheriff abolished. Where the collection of delinquent taxes has been taken from him or where the fees for making such collections have been reduced, the compensation of the office has been reduced to such an extent that it is inadequate in some cases. But by the appointment by special act of the legislature of special deputies and rural police forces, with which the sheriff may or may not have anything whatever to do, he has been reduced to little more than a deputy or rural policeman himself. Thus the dignity, the responsibility, and the compensation of the office, one or all in part, may have been removed. The sheriff, if he is to be retained, should be so chosen that he can be called to account, but he ought not to be stripped of his dignity or his power or of adequate pay.

Rural police. The duties of the rural police may be prescribed by the local act creating them or by the sheriff of the county. Their duties may be confined largely to patrolling the highways, as in Aiken County, or they may be required to patrol the rural districts instead. The latter should be one of their duties in every instance. As has already been seen, they are chosen by various methods, their duties differ from county to county, and they are not responsible to the same person. In fact, they may not be definitely responsible to anyone. Such a condition tends to create a spirit of indifference and to make them less effective than they would be if they were uniformly appointed and controlled and made a part of a state-wide organization which might build up a reputation for courage and general effectiveness in maintaining the peace and enforcing the law. Perhaps few states present a more heterogeneous array of law enforcing officials, or one so completely headless. There are the sheriff, the sheriff's deputies and the special deputies, game wardens, the rural police, the magistrate's constables and the special constables. At the top of the group may be placed the governor's constables and the state highway patrol. These numerous officials need to be included in one organization with a competent and responsible head, and thus converted into an effective machine for the enforcement of law.

The salaries of the circuit judges and the solicitors are paid by the state. The salaries of other court and law enforcement officials are borne by the counties. To these items may be added certain court costs and jail expenses. The following table gives the various salaries and costs pertaining to the courts and law enforcement in the six counties surveyed. The number of deputies, rural police, and magistrates and constables is also given.

SALARIES AND COSTS PERTAINING TO THE COURTS AND LAW ENFORCEMENT

SIX COUNTIES

County	Court Costs	Jail Expense	Sheriff Salary	Deputies No.	Deputies Salary
Fairfield	$2,330.85	$1,513.55	$1,500.00	2	$2,400.00
Darlington	3,379.90	2,463.72	2,500.00	1	1,200.00
Williamsburg	2,745.45	744.40	2,300.00	1	1,200.00
Colleton	1,701.36	1,557.94	1,500.00	2	1,860.00
Aiken	9,698.96	7,298.65	3,349.95	3	6,800.00
Laurens	6,174.40	2,444.36	1,800.00	1	1,500.00

County	Rural Police No.	Rural Police Salary	Mag. and C. No.	Mag. and C. Salary	Cost of Court	Total
Fairfield	2	$3,600.00	28	$2,330.85	$ 350.00	$14,025.25
Darlington	3	6,300.00	5	3,350.00	500.00	19,693.62
Williamsburg	..	....	16	3,450.00	450.00	10,889.85
Colleton	..	....	18	4,190.34	600.00	11,409.64
Aiken	2	4,702.00	36	6,511.51	1,200.00	39,561.07
Laurens	6	9,594.72	12	3,310.50	400.00	25,223.98

This table shows a remarkable range in the number of court and law enforcement officials, and in costs. Taken with the following table it gives an interesting look into the operations of the courts of these six counties. The following table is made from the records of the courts of general sessions for a period of one year. In four of the counties there were three terms each, and in the other two there were four terms each.

RECORD OF CASES, COURTS OF GENERAL SESSIONS, 1929-30
SIX COUNTIES

County	No. Cases	Found Guilty	Not Guilty	Con- tinued	Placed on Cont. Docket	Nol Pros	Sentence Sus- pended
Fairfield	49	34	6	—	—	4	4
Darlington	148	41	11	48	33	8	—
Williamsburg	56	24	2	24	2	2	—
Colleton	86	31	14	25	3	8	—
Aiken	137	103	21	—	—	13	—
Laurens	124	54	2	40	7	19	—

County	Mistrial	Sent Back to Magistrate	Absconded	Sent to Reform- atory	Dis- missed
Fairfield	—	—	—	1	—
Darlington	2	4	1	—	—
Williamsburg	—	—	2	—	—
Colleton	—	—	2	—	3
Aiken	—	—	—	—	—
Laurens	1	—	—	—	1

The range in the number of cases coming before the courts is remarkable. But no data are on hand on which to attempt an explanation. However, the absence of rural police may account for the smaller numbers coming before the courts in Colleton and Williamsburg counties. But Fairfield with an even smaller number has a small rural police force. Fairfield, Colleton and Williamsburg are almost wholly rural, while Darlington, Aiken, and Laurens have thriving towns and considerable industries. But the disposition of the cases is perhaps of more interest than the number. In four of the counties a great many cases are continued, and in one quite a large number was placed on the contingent docket. On being asked why so many cases were placed on the contingent docket, an attorney replied on one occasion that it was a good place for them to rest until they were forgotten. These records reflect at least in some measure popular attitudes towards crime and its punishment. The number of cases includes many duplications, since all that were continued have been counted each time. Some of the cases in the list have been continued as many as six times. Many factors enter into the problem of crime and its detection and punishment. These tables suggest an interesting and what might prove to be a very profitable study.

HEALTH ADMINISTRATION

It may be said that twenty-three counties in the state maintain health departments, but in each of ten of these there is only a health nurse. In some of the latter counties the activities of the nurse are limited to certain districts only, in which case the districts served support her work. Still other counties make appropriations for clinics of various kinds, but more often for dental clinics for school children, and to hospitals. Appropriations for the support of health units for 1930 range all the way from $5,000 in Fairfield County to $21,330 in Charleston County. But the greatest health program carried on by a single county is that of Spartanburg County, where considerably more than $100,000 was appropriated.

The health units are supported in part by state and other funds. The state appropriation for 1930 for field directors and county personnel was only $39,500.

The methods of establishing health units and their composition have already been described. In some counties they have been established and then shortly afterwards abolished. Such was the case in Colleton County. In other counties the necessity for and the value of public health services are not yet understood, but the fact that more than half of the counties of the state are contributing to some form of public health work indicates a growing interest in the matter. Perhaps the methods of public health officials are sometimes not understood, and again perhaps one may not actually give much service. An editor of one of the leading dailies appeared skeptical about the work of the health departments, and asked for facts that would prove their worth.

In the six counties surveyed only three were supporting health units. These were Fairfield, Darlington, and Aiken. The work in Darlington was at a standstill at the time of the survey on account of the fact that the health officer had recently resigned, and his successor had not yet taken up his work. The staff of the Fairfield unit was composed of the health officer, the nurse, and a stenographer. Through the efforts of this unit it was claimed that malaria had been virtually eliminated from the county. The same claim was made for typhoid, except in one area in which it seemed impossible to get the coöperation of the people in protecting their wells from surface drainage. The value of an adequately staffed health unit for all counties, but especially for those in which there are large numbers of tenants of both races with the consequent low standards of living, can hardly be overestimated.

And the need of these units is perhaps even greater in the coastal plain area than in the upper Piedmont because of the wide prevalence of malaria.

The health unit of Aiken had the largest staff and was the most liberally supported of those found in the six counties surveyed. The staff consisted of the health officer, nurse, sanitary inspector, and stenographer. The work of this unit was excellent. In the matter of health education the annual report of the unit for 1929 contains the following: Twenty-five educational talks were made by members of the unit to audiences aggregating more than 3,000 people; more than one hundred educational articles on health were published; and five health exhibits were held at community fairs or exhibits and more than 2,000 pieces of literature concerning health facts and conditions were distributed.

In the control of communicable diseases the health department gave almost 10,000 doses of anti-typhoid vaccine. Half of these doses and the assistance of four sanitary inspectors were furnished by the federal government. This work was made necessary by the flooding of the Savannah River and the Horse Creek valley sections of the county. Over 1,500 doses of toxin-anti-toxin were administered also.

In sanitation, with the assistance of the federal sanitary inspectors, the report for the year 1929 shows over 2,000 private premises, 411 public places, and 326 food handling establishments inspected and sanitated. More than 500 other unsanitary conditions or premises were remedied.

Despite emergency conditions the health nurse kept control and supervision of sixty-three mid-wives and met with them regularly for required courses of instruction. She also arranged for a number of small tonsil-adenoid clinics during the year, and continued the transportation of children with orthopedic defects to Columbia. She is planning nutrition classes in the principal schools of the county, and more than 500 children have been weighed and measured preparatory to this work.

The health department was also undertaking to check the great increase of pellagra in the county by making surveys to determine the number of cases and by holding clinics for the disease. As far as possible each case was interviewed, advised as to diet, and hygiene, and if possible placed under the watch care of the family physician. Brewer's yeast was secured through the state board of health at the cost of $1.25 for five pounds. Through the help of charitable organizations yeast was furnished free to many individuals. The department alone had more than one hundred cases of pellagra under its supervision.

Where the health nurse only is employed, appropriations range from $1,250 to $3,000. The higher figures invariably include travel expense, office rent, and perhaps other items.

Clinics. About one-half the counties of the state make appropriations for one or more clinics. The one most frequently found is the dental clinic for school children. Appropriations may be made for such a clinic when no other support for public health is given, as in the case of Lee County. Other types of clinics are those for persons suffering with tuberculosis and venereal diseases. As a rule, the clinics are held under the direction of the county health department, where it exists. In some cases the dental clinics are held under the direction of legislative delegation or the county superintendent of schools.

Hospitals. County hospitals exist in a few counties. They are to be found in Aiken, Anderson, Charleston, Spartanburg, and perhaps others. Appropriations for 1930 for the maintenance of these hospitals range from $5,000 to $73,000. Numerous other counties make appropriations to private hospitals for assistance in the hospitalization of indigent citizens. Still other counties, singly or jointly, are preparing to build tubercular or other hospitals. Recently Darlington and Florence counties have been authorized to establish a tubercular hospital and are proceeding to do so. Charleston County maintains a hospital and in addition a camp for tubercular sufferers.

County physicians. As we have already seen, the county physician is to be found in every county. In fact, a few counties have two. Each physician is paid a salary, and the salary except in the more populous counties does not generally amount to more than $200 to $600. The highest salaries are those paid in Spartanburg and Richland counties. The sum is $900. Richland County has two physicians whose combined salaries are $1,800.

The county physician hardly deserves to be included along with the county health officers. His duties are confined to attendance on the inmates of the poor home, the jail, and the chaingang. His work in many instances appears to be as nearly perfunctory as medical work can be. In the writer's opinion it is doubtful if the services the county physician renders justify his selection regularly with an annual salary, even though the latter is small.

CORRECTIONS AND CHARITIES

County jails. Every county has its jail, and the jail is frequently an institution about which the citizen does not wish to know too much. Intimate knowledge of it, if he is inclined to be sensitive, may make him slightly uncomfortable. Perhaps at some future time the state will take over all penal institutions and the county jail will give way to the district prison operated by the state under expert direction, so that proper provision may be made for the segregation and detention of prisoners and those charged with crimes. And the work of the circuit courts should be speeded up, by increasing the number of judges if necessary, so that persons arrested and detained may not be kept at public expense for weeks and months and so that continuations and delays of various kinds and all the other matters that now clog the ways of justice may no longer serve to bring the law and the courts into ill repute.

In the counties surveyed the jails ranged all the way from old structures badly in need of repairs to relatively modern fire-proof buildings. The races and sexes were separately kept in every case, but some of the jails were inadequately equipped with cells, toilets, and baths. The inadequacy of such buildings is in keeping with and no doubts helps to produce the atmosphere one finds about them. Its effect can hardly be said to be elevating.

Various methods of handling jails were found. Allowances for dieting prisoners ranged all the way from forty cents each per day to seventy-five cents. No effort has been made to discover how much it costs to give prisoners a sufficient amount of substantial and well-prepared food per day. No doubt it costs more per prisoner to feed two or three than ten or a dozen, and the number in any jail varies from time to time. However, there is probably no good reason why the allowance for food per day should range from forty to seventy-five cents.

The law allows the jailor a small turnkey fee when a prisoner is admitted or discharged, but he rarely collects it.

The sheriff may be directly in charge of the jail, as in Fairfield County. There the county has built a home for the jailor. It is joined to the jail by a covered passage. The sheriff and his wife purchase the food and a federal prisoner prepares it for the inmates of the jail. In Laurens County the appropriation bill names the jailor and specifies his other duties, which are to act as special deputy and bookkeeper to the sheriff. In the other counties surveyed the jail was in charge of a deputy named by the sheriff himself. None of the jailors hesitated to take the writer to inspect their jails, though one stated that the jail was in bad shape. When the writer called on the morning that was set for making the visit, the deputy found that other duties demanded his attention. However, he readily gave the writer a note to the man who was actually in charge of the jail, a federal "trusty." The latter apparently took considerable pride in pointing out the defects of the building. Not infrequently he referred to himself in apologetic terms, which however carried with them a poorly disguised tone of pride. A large room equipped with a number of steel cages for unruly prisoners was occupied by a few Negroes. Then there were two small rooms for white prisoners, one for males and the other for females. Only the former of these was occupied at the time. The "trusty," evidently spent nearly all his time with the other white prisoners, all of whom were federal prisoners. When he conducted the writer into the presence of these, there was a moment's curiosity on their part about the visitor, who was he? what was he doing? some "uplifter" perhaps? and then back to cigarette smoking with which they mixed profanity and veiled references to other days and deeds. All in all, they presented an air of superior boredom, for they were federal prisoners, and in the game they were playing these vacations in the county jails were necessary but rarely serious in their results.

Chaingangs. Doubtless jails and chaingangs can never be dispensed with. But if the management of the former rarely reflects credit upon local governments, even less may be said for the management of the latter. Chaingangs are maintained in thirty-four counties of the state. Where municipalities do not operate chaingangs, they are authorized to place convicts on the county chaingangs for the time sentenced, and the county authorities are authorized to exchange labor with the town authorities by placing county convicts on the public works of the town for the same number of days that town convicts work for the county. They were found in all six of the counties surveyed. In Darlington County the chaingang was managed in a very superior manner. Here was a permanent camp, enclosed, equipped with cages, water, toilets, and dining shed. Trucks carried the prisoners to work in the early morning and back to the camp at night. Vegetables were grown for the use of the prisoners on ten or more acres of land belonging to the camp. The men were well-fed at low cost and kept at regular work when not ill. In the other counties the management was less commendable. There were no permanent camps. Tents and cages were moved from place to place in accordance with the road working or road construction program. In some cases the gangs were divided into two or three sections encamped in as many different places. In all cases except one supplies were purchased by the county supervisor or county board. In the single exception the superintendent of the chaingang did the purchasing. Salaries of the superintendents ranged from $75 to $150 per month. In Aiken County with its chaingang divided into three sections the salaries of superintendents amounted to $5,400 per year.

The temporary camps were located as a rule on a flat, sandy, well-drained spot near a stream of water or perhaps a well. Satisfactory guards were very difficult to obtain; they gave trouble occasionally by excessive drinking. Occasional reports were heard of the ill-treatment of prisoners, but in the counties surveyed harsh treatment was undoubtedly the exception and not the rule. Counties which do not support chaingangs hire their prisoners to other counties. For these they may receive from twenty-five to fifty cents per day per prisoner. Fairfield County has an agreement with Chester County to take the prisoners of the latter at twenty-five cents per day, while Williamsburg County has a similar agreement with Berkeley County, except that the hire is fifty cents per day.

Poor homes and farms. Thirty-four counties of the state maintain poor homes and farms. Only three of the six counties surveyed were among this number. In the performance of no other function perhaps do the counties of the state lag so far behind. The care of the poor in many of the counties is not above the level of that of colonial days. The poor homes visited consisted in each instance of a group of little, old cottages, arranged for the most part more or less closely together on the county poor farm. There were no modern buildings and no modern conveniences. Some of the cottages were in bad repair.

Various methods of managing these homes were found. In Colleton County the county supervisor has general charge and makes all purchases for the home and farm. He purchases from local merchants on bid. The man in direct charge of the home is a "trusty," who was convicted of manslaughter. He is paid little or nothing for such duties as he performs, but his wife and children get food and clothing. However commendable the motive that led to the arrangement, the arrangement itself can not be commended. The Aiken County home does not differ materially from that of Colleton, except in its management. It is in charge of a superintendent who is paid $75 per month. The Laurens County home is in charge of a superintendent, who is paid $1,200 per year, while his wife receives $300 per year for the duties she performs. The superintendent purchases all supplies for the home by any method he may choose.

The following table shows the disbursements of six counties for the year 1929 for the poor and poor homes and farms. Three of the counties did not operate poor homes and farms.

DISBURSEMENTS FOR POOR RELIEF, 1929
Six Counties

County	Number of Inmates Reported in Poor Home	Disbursements
Fairfield	None	$1,445.65
Darlington	None	4,384.30
Williamsburg	None	2,065.79
Colleton	10-15	2,939.90
Aiken	30-40	8,611.30
Laurens	No estimate	4,083.13

Out-relief. Methods of providing out-relief are primitive. The amount that may be granted to an applicant ranges from $2.00 to $5.00 or more per month. In some counties the amount is fixed at a certain sum and there is no variation no matter what the needs of the applicant may be. In Williamsburg County the applicant gets $2.00 per month, no more, no less, regardless of race or condition. In Darlington County a white applicant may get $5.00, while a Negro may get only $3.00 per month. In a few counties the applicant may receive more than $5.00 per month, but as a rule the sum granted is small. The county board or the county supervisor usually grants the aid on application and with the advice of those who are familiar with the applicant and his conditions. When the appropriation is exhausted, applications are filed and placed on the list for out-relief when any of those on the existing list are removed by death or otherwise. In Williamsburg County the local merchants supply the poor whose applications have been approved by the proper authorities to the extent of $2.00 per month, and then at the end of the year they file their claims against the county.

Little headway has been made so far by the counties of the state in the matter of organized public welfare activities. Greenville County undoubtedly leads the state with its Charities and Corrections Commission. This commission has charge of the maintenance of the county jail and the county poor home and of the expenditure of the funds for the hospitalization of charity patients. The counties of the state might well follow the example of certain Virginia counties in setting up district homes for the more adequate care of their poor citizens.

CONSERVATION AND DEVELOPMENT SERVICES

Farm and home demonstration work. Under the present law of the state every county has both a farm and a home demonstration agent. In a few counties there will be found an assistant farm demonstration agent also. The assistant may be employed for the purpose of working with the Negro farmers. Charleston and perhaps a few other counties have home demonstration agents for work among the Negro homes. The counties no longer support the demonstration work, except to pay assistant agents in part and to pay stenographers, traveling expenses, and office rent, and to encourage club work in some cases. The agents are selected by the state authorities directing the coöperative extension work in agriculture and home economics in the state, but they must meet the approval of the respective county legislative delegations. Thus the state has taken over in the interest of a continuous policy the work of developing the farms and farm homes in all the counties. This policy is in keeping with the present tendencies of the states to take over more and more of those functions which were formerly administered at least in part by the counties. It has many things to commend it. On the other hand, it is possible that this development coming as it does in the interest of efficiency or because of indifference or incapacity on the part of local units to handle such functions intelligently bodes little good for the future of democracy. Those who cannot keep the machinery of local government out of the hands of corrupt or incompetent or unintelligent individuals can scarcely be expected long to exercise more wisdom and intelligence in the selection of state and national officials.

Game and fish protection. The protection of the wild life of the state, confined in the main to game and fish, is likewise the work of the state and not that of the counties. But each county has one or more game wardens. As a rule the game warden is appointed by the governor of the state on the recommendation of the county legislative delegation, but there are exceptions. In a number of counties he is nominated in the primary just as the county auditor is and then recommended and appointed.

These officials are paid in full by the state. The salary is usually $1,800 each. Numerous areas of the coastal section might be converted into game and fish preserves. As such they would become a permanent source of pleasure to a growing number of sport lovers and of increasing income to the state and the counties.

PART III

CONSTRUCTIVE SUGGESTIONS

CHAPTER VI

CONSTRUCTIVE SUGGESTIONS

Though county government was the last of the political institutions to receive the attention of political scientists, it is now an object of scrutiny emanating from many sources. The efforts of those who about two decades ago began to call attention to the fact that there had been but little improvement in county government since colonial days are now producing results. In that small group of rural sociologists, political scientists, and others, no name is entitled to a higher place than that of Dr. E. C. Branson, University of North Carolina. He was the pioneer in the field in the South. And today practically every southern state is giving some thought to the problems of county government, but the movement is not confined to any one section of the country. Some form of agitation affecting county government is to be found in no less than half the states of the Union.

Yet in every state where the county is an important unit of local government there are serious problems that demand attention. Why have these problems arisen? There are many answers to that question, but perhaps they may be included in the fact that governmental institutions at best are scarcely able to keep pace with the demands of a constantly changing civilization; at worst, they lag far behind. Rural institutions change very slowly, for rural people are generally conservative. County government is for the most part rural government. However, despite its resistance to change one may see in its history evidences of the influence of the political cycle through which at least the older American states are about to pass. In colonial days the people learned to fear an executive. The colonial governors were identified with a foreign tyrant. The colonial legislatures led in the struggle for freedom from the mother country. As a result, when independence was secured, they were given large powers. They were as a rule predominant in the affairs of the first American states. These bodies failed signally to measure up to expectations. Limitations were placed upon their powers, and the faith that had reposed in them was placed more directly in the people. But the people proved that they themselves were scarcely better endowed with wisdom than the legislatures. The present time finds a movement toward centralization in the state again, but this time in the once-feared executives rather than in the legislatures. The county government is beginning to feel also the influence of business organizations and practices. In fact, the significant developments in local government in America have been attributed in the main to a desire for efficiency.[1]

The present tendencies are not to be condemned because the desire for efficiency may be in part responsible for them. Neither are they a threat to democracy. They indicate dissatisfaction with results so far achieved; they challenge our interpretation of democracy and demand that in the future political faith shall be grounded on more knowledge. No type of government operates automatically. There is no authority in human affairs which rules wisely and with even-handed justice, while citizenship takes its ease or pursues with vigor immediate and selfish ends. General participation in civic affairs on the part of the citizenship from the standpoint of enlightened self-interest, to borrow from Dr. Branson, is the foundation of a truly democratic government. Lack of such participation is responsible for the present condition of county government and county affairs. Its importance remains yet to be generally understood. From this standpoint the problems of county government are everywhere very much the same.

In the preceding chapters the development of county government in the state has been briefly traced. Its present structure has been portrayed as well as the manner in which it functions. The structure is characterized by an almost total lack of uniformity and an extreme decentralization of power, notwithstanding the fact that it is almost wholly within the hands of the state legislature. That it has functioned fairly well, relatively speaking, despite its structural defects, is perhaps the most striking fact to be found in connection with it. The means and methods by which it may be improved are no longer open to question. They have already been worked out and in some instances put into actual and satisfactory operation.

In the first place, the county, generally speaking, needs to be

---

[1] G. Montagu Harris, *Local Government in Many Lands*, p. 272.

enlarged. Columbia, the capital of the state, is probably as easily reached today by the average citizen of the state as was his county-seat town in 1900. The automobile and good roads have multiplied the radius of his activities eight or ten times, and the state is in effect no larger today than one of the larger counties thirty-five years ago. Furthermore, one set of county officials with some additional clerical help can serve a population of 200,000 or 300,000 or more just as well as one of 9,000 or 13,000. The annual salary bill of one complete set of county officials is no inconsiderable sum. The county needs to be larger in order to contain more wealth. If it is so poor that a large per cent of its revenue is absorbed in the payment of salaries, there is not enough left for roads, schools, health, and public welfare, and unless the state provides grants-in-aid in liberal amounts the county drops behind.

A second need and a more important one is the reorganization of the county government. Reorganization is necessary in order that the government may be simplified and that the principles of uniformity and unity may be introduced. It needs to have a responsible head. Direct lines of responsibility should be fixed throughout its structure. In some matters at least it should be subject to effective state supervision and control in the interest of the people of the state as a whole. The times demand efficiency and economy, and these can not be had in the fullest measure under the present system. All duplications of government over particular areas within the county should be reduced to a minimum. No subdivision of the county should be incorporated for purposes that may be attained just as well otherwise. We shall consider first the problem of county consolidation.

COUNTY CONSOLIDATIONS

Agitation for consolidation of counties is becoming widespread in the South, though the movement is by no means confined to that section. The great burden of taxation is forcing the issue. It is frequently pointed out that 1,503 of the 3,064 counties in the United States are to be found in the South. All southern states have too many counties, though South Carolina is much better situated in that respect than North Carolina or Georgia, her nearest neighbors. Nevertheless, there are too many counties in the state, and a program of consolidation should be carried out as rapidly as possible. Despite high tax rates, the counties almost without exception must borrow in anticipation of tax collections. Because of accumulations of delinquent taxes and of failure to keep expenditures within appropriations county debt is in some instances being increased for operating purposes. This is in addition to debts incurred for permanent improvements.

Because of the enormous and ever increasing cost of government it is necessary that the highest efficiency and economy be attained in governmental function. According to the Report of the National Industrial Conference Board the total cost of government in the United States for the fiscal year 1927 was $12,292,500,000. Of this vast sum, $6,454,400,000 represented the cost of local government. In other words, the cost of local governments, counties, and their subdivisions and municipalities, is fifty-three per cent of the total, as shown in the following table.

COST OF GOVERNMENT IN THE UNITED STATES
FOR THE FISCAL YEAR 1927[2]

Government	Amount	Per Cent
Federal	$ 4,069,000,000	33
State	1,769,100,000	14
Local	6,454,400,000	53
Total	$12,292,500,000	100

The increase in the per capita cost of government in the nation for a fourteen-year period closing with 1927 is shown in the next table.

INCREASE IN PER CAPITA COST OF GOVERNMENT
FOURTEEN-YEAR PERIOD

	Year		Per Cent
Government	1913	1927	Increase
Federal	$ 7.17	$ 34.30	378.3
State	3.97	13.96	251.6
Local	19.10	54.41	184.8
Total	$30.24	$102.67[3]	

Because of the decrease in the value of the dollar, the increase in per capita cost appears to be greater than it really is. However, the per capita cost in 1927 in 1913-dollars was $75.10, or approximately a 150 per cent increase in fourteen years. The ratio of increase in the cost of local government during the period is less than that of state or federal government, but it represents an enor-

[2] Op. cit., p. 13.
[3] Op. cit., p. 2.

mous increase. The figures for the cost of county government alone are not available.

According to the report of the comptroller general of the state for the year 1930, the actual cost of operating the state government, including all departments and institutions, was $7,707,941.61. But the total disbursements of the state for the same period were $54,279,343.16. Of this sum, $9,039,710.42 was distributed to the counties. The total disbursements of the counties for the period were $46,462,128.14. County disbursements slightly exceeded those of the state, despite the fact that the state was in the midst of its road building program. The per capita disbursements of the counties for the year 1930 were $26.81. The total tax levy in the state for county and school purposes for 1930 was $19,145,-455.42, which represented a per capita levy of $11.05. Table VII shows the per capita taxable property of the counties for 1930, and the per capita disbursements for all county purposes. A table showing the true per capita wealth and income would have been of more value. However, the table serves to indicate that the cost of county government in the state is excessive. It has been estimated that forty per cent of the revenues of local governments are wasted. If the statement be true, the taxpayer can well afford to urge county consolidation and the reorganization of county government, so that his taxes may be reduced or the quality of the services provided by his government may be greatly improved.

The problem of the consolidation of counties is one of sufficient importance to merit a carefully prepared program to be used as a guide in so far as possible. The new county ought not to be a purely artificial and arbitrary political area. It should approximate as nearly as possible a natural area of local self-government, while it is also an administrative district of the state. It must be built upon two factors, namely, population and wealth. It should be sufficiently elastic to be adjustable to changes made advisable by shifts in population and by improved means and methods of transportation and communication. On the other hand, it should be rigid enough to resist changes which may be sought for purely political purposes. It should be organized not only with an eye to the best aggregation of population and wealth for efficient and economical administration, but also as a nursery in the school of democracy. It should be so organized as to develop, in so far as

TABLE VII

PER CAPITA TAXABLE PROPERTY AND TOTAL COUNTY
DISBURSEMENTS

County	Per Capita Taxable Property 1930	Per Capita County Disbursements 1930	Percentage of Per Capita Taxable Property
Abbeville........	$211.60	$33.77	15.9
Aiken...........	248.00	30.45	12.2
Allendale.......	197.50	17.02	8.6
Anderson.......	248.48	26.88	10.8
Bamberg........	181.34	15.74	8.6
Barnwell........	205.58	23.32	11.3
Beaufort........	184.37	15.28	8.3
Berkeley........	177.13	23.53	13.3
Calhoun........	179.50	13.83	7.7
Charleston......	367.98	15.96	4.3
Cherokee.......	288.62	25.41	8.8
Chester.........	331.06	24.75	7.4
Chesterfield.....	149.60	17.30	11.6
Clarendon......	116.21	12.78	10.9
Colleton........	190.39	33.28	17.5
Darlington......	221.13	22.84	10.3
Dillon..........	194.89	24.19	12.4
Dorchester......	161.70	32.88	20.3
Edgefield.......	193.22	27.45	14.2
Fairfield........	340.36	24.75	7.3
Florence........	196.02	22.72	11.6
Georgetown.....	188.86	25.57	13.5
Greenville......	280.06	31.93	11.4
Greenwood......	277.20	26.31	9.5
Hampton........	213.57	19.78	9.3
Horry..........	111.12	26.38	23.7
Jasper..........	343.41	21.22	6.2
Kershaw........	235.73	32.31	13.7
Lancaster.......	193.45	42.07	21.7
Laurens........	221.78	37.70	17.0
Lee............	180.42	15.43	8.6
Lexington.......	214.27	24.57	11.5
Marion.........	175.39	10.63	6.1
Marlboro........	195.95	26.49	13.5
McCormick.....	200.03	54.26	27.1
Newberry.......	289.76	34.93	12.1
Oconee.........	185.07	33.30	18.0
Orangeburg.....	184.85	19.10	10.3
Pickens.........	238.51	41.09	17.2
Richland........	344.92	26.19	7.6
Saluda..........	153.80	23.12	15.0
Spartanburg.....	321.21	41.33	12.9
Sumter.........	183.90	19.04	10.4
Union..........	270.90	43.61	16.1
Williamsburg.....	148.87	18.98	12.8
York..........	250.78	26.10	10.4
State..........	$239.75	$26.81	11.2

is possible, interest and participation in local civic affairs by an increasing number of its citizens.

How may this be done? The answer is that it can not be done at once, nor perhaps ever completely. But it seems possible to take some steps in the direction of such an end. Natural barriers such as streams and mountains play a part in delimiting counties and communities, though their part grows less as improved means of transportation come into use. Next to the influence of topographical features in the shaping of natural areas is that of satisfactory trade relations. It is doubtful whether the small town is fully aware of the vital importance of such relations to its own existence. Such relationships make the most satisfactory basis upon which to develop coöperation in other and equally important fields, such as the establishment of schools, churches, libraries, health and welfare services, and other agencies and services of social and civic consequence. The state is covered with a network of over-lapping trade areas with their trade centers ranging all the way from the cross-roads village to the largest cities. If these areas were charted, they would serve as a basis upon which to study county consolidation. These areas are now in process of rapid change, but as the state's program of development nears completion the change will become less marked. An equally important factor to be considered in any program of county consolidation is the new consolidated school. The program of school consolidation is not complete, but nevertheless if it is carefully worked out it would be of great value. The highways and the highway program make the third important factor to be taken into consideration. A chart of the trade areas of the state, a map showing the location of the consolidated schools and the probable locations of future consolidations, and a map of the highway system and the future highway program, would provide one with the material for a basis upon which to work out a program for the reconstruction of county areas. The rural communities of the future are likely to be centered around the consolidated school. If it is located in the open country, the small store and the filling station soon appear nearby. The church should and will probably follow later. A village may gradually develop. If the school is located in a large village or small town, a greater number of services may be had within its vicinity. A large number of these communities or potential communities will be found to be within the trade area of a large town or city. Such a center immediately suggests itself for the county seat, but of course not every such center can become a county seat. The area of the state will not automatically divide itself into county units of the desired size with sharp distinctions between them. It would still be necessary to fix arbitrary boundaries in many instances. Nevertheless, such an approach to the problem of county consolidation seems to be the best possible one.

It is probable, however, that county consolidation will not wait upon any plan or program. It will come by the simple expedient of making one county out of two or more existing ones, when the citizens become convinced that such action will reduce their tax burdens. There are no constitutional barriers in the way of such consolidation. The legislature may provide for consolidation after the issue has been passed upon favorably by the people of each county concerned in an election held for the purpose.[4] Such consolidations have been made in other states. The first of these was made in the state of Tennessee. In 1919 James County, a small, poor county, was consolidated with the adjoining county of Hamilton. The city of Chattanooga is the county seat of the latter. The consolidation appears to have proved most satisfactory in every respect. The cost of one set of county officials has been eliminated. The former county of James has better roads and schools than before the consolidation, while its taxes have been reduced. The first year after the consolidation its tax rate dropped from $2.50 per hundred to $1.28. Some time later the county of Meigs, which also adjoins Hamilton, sought consolidation with the latter, but it has not yet been effected. At the time the tax rate in Meigs was $4.00 per hundred, while that of Hamilton was $1.40 per hundred.

Following this first consolidation many plans and programs have been brought forward for state-wide consolidation of counties.

The most radical of these advocated the reduction of the number of counties in the state to eleven with areas of approximately four thousand square miles each. Recently the State Tax Committee has recommended that thirty-four counties be consolidated with adjacent ones in the next ten years.

4 South Carolina Constitution of 1895, Art. VII, sec. 10.

The second consolidation was effected in Georgia. In 1931 Fulton and Campbell counties were consolidated. It is reported that DeKalb County is now seeking consolidation with the enlarged Fulton, while the grand jury of Crawford County has recommended that it be consolidated with the county of Bibb.

No other consolidations have actually taken place, but agitation is wide-spread and additional consolidations may be expected to be consummated in these and other states in the future. A program of county consolidation has been presented to the governor of North Carolina advocating the reduction of the one hundred counties in that state to eighty-eight. Reduction in the number of counties is being advocated also in the states of Mississippi, Alabama, Florida, and Virginia among others. In 1928 Governor Alfred E. Smith of New York proposed the reduction of the sixty-two counties in that state to twelve.

The program of county consolidation in the state should aim at the elimination of those counties having the least resources in population and wealth, for as a rule it is in these that tax burdens are highest. If such is not the case, it may be due to the absence of certain services or to the general low standards of the services provided. It is doubtful if counties with less than $10,000,000 of taxables, even under the present low valuation, have sufficient wealth upon which to operate on an economical basis. The elimination of all counties with less than such a sum of taxables would reduce the number of counties in the state by sixteen or more. Twenty-five or thirty counties would serve the state just as well as forty-six. The greater number of consolidations would of necessity have to be made in the coastal plain and along the Savannah River, for generally speaking it is in these areas that population is sparse and industries as a rule few and small. But the interests and influence of the consolidated areas, wherever located, in the affairs of the state government need not be sacrificed nor diminished. Each consolidated county may be given representation in the General Assembly equal to that of the old counties out of which it was created.

THE REORGANIZATION OF THE COUNTY GOVERNMENT

The problem of the reorganization of the county government is a greater one than that of the consolidation of the counties, but if county government is to be improved to any great degree the problem must be solved. A radical change in the organization seems to be absolutely necessary. County government by legislative delegations is a tradition in the state from which it will be very difficult for many reasons to break away. Nevertheless, it is quite clear that the price must be paid, if the people of the state really want responsible, economical, and efficient county government.

Under the present system there is no single official or board to which all other county officials are responsible. Thus there is no local control over county affairs as a whole. Neither is there any effective state control over them. The qualified electors may refuse to re-elect an official, but that sort of control is of little real value. It does not provide accurate records, if he has not kept them, nor does it replace wasted or stolen public funds. While his term of office lasts the voters have no control over him, and there is no competent person whose business it is to see whether or not he is performing his duties. It is possible therefore for him to be neglecting his duties or wasting the public funds, while nothing is done about it. County government needs machinery by which its affairs can be and are constantly checked and by which county officials may be called to immediate account when the public welfare demands it. To compare the county government organization as it exists with that of a progressive and successful private corporation should be sufficient to convince anyone that it is inadequate for the duties it must perform. And the importance of the county as a business organization can be appreciated when it is pointed out that for the fiscal year 1929-30 expenditures averaged slightly more than one million dollars per county.

As has already been stated, the administration of county affairs from the first has been centralized in a manner in the state. But this control is vested in the legislature, whereas it should be vested in the executive department, if effective state control is desired. The result is that the General Assembly does not enact general laws for the benefit of all the counties. Instead there are forty-six miniature legislatures passing many local laws for their respective counties by virtue of the courtesies which they extend to each other in the meetings of the General Assembly. Thus it turns out that the county legislative delegations are largely responsible for the administration of county affairs, though they are not held responsible. The county delegation does not pass the laws; the laws are passed by the General Assembly of which it is but a small part. But it has other ways of escape from responsibility. The state has had no experience with any other method of county administration, while the creation of new officials and boards and the distribution of small jobs as widely as possible tend to obscure and to justify the resulting waste, since it seems to inure to the personal gain of an increasing number of citizens. In other words, the present plan seems to be democratic.

Now if the state proposes to administer county affairs effectively, it can doubtless do so through the executive department, but not through the legislature. The legislature should turn its attention away from the enactment of local legislation to the creation of an effective administrative organization operating under general laws. That is, it should set up a state department for handling each department of county affairs, if one does not already exist. The department heads should be appointed by the governor of the state and should be responsible to him for the administration of their own departments. All employees in these departments should perhaps be chosen by competitive examinations and should be placed under civil service regulations. Thus the state could administer both state and county affairs through a body of trained, non-political officials. However, the legislature could not set up such an organization without some changes in the state constitution.

There is a growing tendency in the direction of such state administration. Several states have assumed more effective control over county fiscal affairs, while one has gone to much greater lengths. Recently North Carolina has taken over all county roads to be administered by a reorganized state highway department. The public schools of the state have also been taken over. No other state has advanced so far in this direction. And while the success of the experiment remains to be seen, the probabilities are that state administration in general will prove much superior from the standpoints of economy and efficiency. Whether the states generally will eventually take over the administration of county affairs can not now be foreseen. But whatever the future course of events may be, there is no intention here to urge the adoption of such a system. The only point to be made is that state control over county affairs in order to be effective must be administrative rather than purely legislative; that is, the executive department must control county affairs, must have the authority and the power to direct county officials, and to remove them and bring them to justice through the courts when that needs to be done. Direct legislative control has resulted, as can readily be seen, in the creation of an ever increasing variety of fragmentary and disconnected local administrative machinery. Therefore, such control has not been and obviously can not be effective. Furthermore, the legislature is in session only a few months each year. The legislators give the remainder of their time to private affairs. A more important fact, however, is that legislators are chosen to pass laws, that is, to lay down general policies of administration. Their business is not administration. It is this failure to distinguish between legislative and administrative functions that is in part responsible for the present county government organization and the consequent chaos in county affairs. So much for state administration of county affairs. Such administration on the plan outlined would replace all county officials with state officials. Our purpose, however, is to consider the reorganization of county government from the standpoint of county administration.

The position taken here is that there is a place for the county in our system of government, a place not merely as an administrative district of the state, but rather as a unit of the largest possible measure of self-government. But it seems needless to add that local self-government must be more economical and more efficient, if it expects to survive. No pretensions to virtues which are supposed to be inherent in democracy, if accompanied with the present waste, can enable it to survive for long the pressure of present tax burdens. County government must be reorganized in the interest of efficiency and economy. Whatever measure of self-government it retains will be in the interest of democracy, but that doubtless will depend more upon results achieved than upon any vague faith.

In the reorganization of the county government it is necessary that certain principles should be observed. It is difficult to discover any sound reason why county government should not be uniform throughout the state. It may be necessary for some counties to have a larger organization than others, or possibly to be given some additional powers. Nevertheless, the government may have and should have a basic uniformity. But the application of this principle will be more far-reaching in its effects than at first appears. It means, in fact, no less than that the county legislative delegations shall be largely barred from control over county affairs, except as the latter are controlled by general laws. The enactment of local laws must be reduced to a minimum. The application of the principle should result in greater efficiency and economy in the county and certainly in economy of time in the state legislature. The latter spends much time each year in the enactment of numerous local laws, changing the number of members of some board or the manner of their selection, abolishing an old office or creating a new one, or attending to some other equally unimportant matter. Such a change would fix the arena of local politics in the county rather than as now in the shifting conferences of the legislative delegation.

In the next place, county government is a whole, and it should be treated as such. It should have unity. At the head of it should be placed a single individual or board wholly responsible for it. It should be divided into a number of departments, the heads of which are appointed by the governing official or body of the county, and direct lines of responsibility should be fixed down through each department. Only thus can responsibility be definitely placed and better results secured. Centralization of authority must replace decentralization. A county board of commissioners can not be held responsible for county affairs if all county officials including themselves are elected by popular vote. Under such conditions the officials will be concerned mainly in keeping in favor with the voters, whatever the board may desire. The voters may be influenced more by the officer's apparent friendliness and sympathy with the problems of the individual citizen than by his competency for the work demanded of him. These qualities with popular appeal are much to be desired in public officials, but they may be used, and in some instances have been used, as a cloak to cover up inefficiency and even crookedness in public office. Public officials will perform their duties when they understand that not to do so will result in their dismissal. The governing body must then have the power to appoint and to dismiss county officials.

Thus we come to the application of the principle of the short ballot. If it is charged that the short ballot is not democratic, the answer is that the charge does not rest upon a foundation of fact. County government should exist for the purpose of doing certain things for the citizens, things which they can not do so well for themselves individually. The chief interest of the citizens lies in how well these things are done rather than in who does them. The citizens can select a competent board to direct county affairs and they can hold that board responsible. The board in order to be efficient must select trained men to administer the affairs of the county under their direction. There is no other way by which county government may be efficient and at the same time directly responsible to the people.

The use of trained men in the administration of county affairs is not new. For years county boards have been employing trained engineers, trained health officials, and trained teachers and trained demonstration agents. Results should be equally satisfactory in the employment of trained police forces, trained public welfare officials, trained accountants, trained tax assessing officials, and other trained finance officials. The change would have to be made gradually for lack of well-trained men for some departments, but it would benefit both officials and citizens. The citizens would benefit from the high standards of public service, while those who aspired to public office could secure training for the work they wished to do and then perhaps look forward to a life's career in the public service. As a result, county government would come to be looked upon as a business rather than as a game of politics in which the end always justifies the means.

In the reorganization of county government the problem of overlapping governmental organizations within the county should receive careful consideration. Such organizations frequently result in duplications of structure or function that are not necessary. No county in the state is now faced, nor is it likely to be soon, with the problems of a metropolitan area. However, four counties in the state contain cities of considerable size. Where the majority of the population is in the city, it might be profitable to consider the extension of the city limits to coincide with those of the county, even though to do so would include large areas of rural territory. A reorganized city government should then take the place of the present city and county governments. Under a new charter provision could be made for the protection of the interests of other municipalities within the area and for the creation of both urban and rural municipalities in the future with certain powers of self-government.

A rural municipality is an incorporated rural area with certain powers of self-government. It may include hamlets, villages, or small towns. In North Carolina a law was passed in 1919 authorizing the establishment of such municipalities under the designation of incorporated rural communities. Such municipalities are to be found in the United States and Canada, but the number is not large. In some instances they have been created by a special act of the state legislature. An instance is that of Plainsboro Township, New Jersey, incorporated in 1919.[5] Such municipalities offer rural people excellent machinery for working out some of their problems together, but few of them have been established because perhaps the need for them is not yet realized. In the event numerous and important municipalities might develop within the area the charter should provide perhaps for a large governing body for the city with representation from each municipality. A charter of such a nature was presented to the voters of Alameda County, California, in 1922. Recently the city of Pittsburg and vicinity have been considering a somewhat similar charter, while San Francisco has adopted one of the same nature as the first step in the city's proposed absorption of San Mateo County.

Under such a plan the city would not be faced periodically with the problem of annexation of territory, nor with those other problems that so frequently arise on account of the suburban areas.

Each of the remaining counties should have the opportunity to adopt a charter very similar to that suggested for the city-county. Provision should be made in it for the protection of the interests of such municipalities as already exist as well as for the creation of urban-rural municipalities in the future with certain powers of self-government. These municipalities, whether in a county or a city-county, should have their governing boards. These boards should have power to fix the local tax rates, to determine the services which the municipality should provide additional to or

[5] Theodore B. Manny, *Rural Municipalities*, pp. 195-205.

supplementary to those provided by the county or city-county, and to determine the policy and program of local development within certain limits. But the construction of streets and walks, the extension of water and sewer systems, and other local work should be under the direction of the county or city-county department of public works. The officials of this department might be considered employees of the municipality for such purposes. Under this plan the county would be a unit with one governing board, providing certain uniform services to the whole area, while the municipalities should provide additional and supplemental services and exercise certain control over them. Certain functions, however, could be performed for both the municipalities and the county or city-county by one set of officials. For instance, one set of tax assessing and tax collecting officials would be sufficient for the whole area. Municipal funds could be left in the custody of the county or city-county treasurer and disbursed by him at the direction of the governing bodies of the municipalities. One general court and one set of law enforcing officials under a responsible head would be better for the whole area. Criminals operate without regard to rural or urban territory. There is no reason why law enforcing officials should not operate with like freedom.

It would be necessary for the county or city-county to be zoned for purposes of taxation. Zone one would include the whole county upon which a uniform rate would be levied. But each municipality, whether urban or rural, might consist of one or more additional zones, depending upon whether the services provided were limited to given areas or extended to the whole of the municipality. This problem appears to present no great difficulty.

Finally, the county is but a part of a larger whole, the state. Whatever powers it exercises are given to it by the state. The exact working relationship between the two in any given case is not always easy to determine, and it is constantly changing. But in this instance all three departments of the state government have authority to exercise control over county affairs, but none of them has the power. How much control the state should exercise over departments of county government is a problem by no means definitely settled, but there is a growing conviction that it must exercise a large measure of control over county fiscal affairs. Such control should enable county government to be more economical and should help to bring about more uniformity in the cost of county government throughout the state. In this field, state control has made considerable advances in a few instances. The movement will doubtless gain momentum and advances will be made much more rapidly in the future.

It is upon the basis of the foregoing principles that the suggestions which follow have been made.

PROPOSED ORGANIZATION AND RECOMMENDATIONS

Changes in the state organization. In order that the reorganization of county government may be more effective it is necessary that there be some reorganization of the state government. It is suggested therefore that section twenty-four of Article IV of the state constitution be so amended as to provide for the appointment of the secretary of state, the comptroller general, the attorney general, the treasurer, the adjutant and inspector general, and the superintendent of education by the governor of the state. This change is similar to that proposed in the model state constitution prepared by the National Municipal League. A few states have taken steps in the direction of such a change. The governor is nominally the head of the executive department. He should be in fact. The executive department is responsible for the actual administration of state affairs, and it should be given the power to administer effectively. Since the governor is elected by popular vote every four years and is not eligible for reëlection, there is little foundation for fear that he will abuse his power. Certain statutory changes seem to be needed along with this reorganization, and the following are suggested.

1. That the comptroller general of the state be given powers similar to those conferred on the North Carolina Local Government Commission established in 1931. He should have the power to prepare a uniform system of accounts for county officials and to require their adoption as rapidly as possible; to supervise, inspect, and audit county and municipal records; to supervise all county borrowing; to market all county bonds and notes; to require the preparation and filing with him of county and municipal budgets before their adoption; to supervise the custody and investment of the sinking funds of counties and their subdivisions.

The comptroller general has some authority over county auditors and treasurers at present, but he does not have the power to make that authority effective.

2. That a state bureau of personnel be created with a director to be appointed by the governor. This bureau should be charged with setting up qualifications for those who should enter the various departments of the public service both county and state. It should keep a list of eligibles at all times. These persons should be chosen by competitive examination, and perhaps with certain exceptions be placed under civil service regulations.

Persons eligible for teaching and administrative work in the public schools should be certified to the director of the bureau of personnel by the state department of education, while the director of coöperative extension work in agriculture and home economics should furnish the bureau with a list of those eligible for farm and home demonstration agents.

3. That a state bureau of purchasing be established to make all purchases for state departments and institutions and to place its facilities at the service of county purchasing agents.

Fifteen states have adopted centralized purchasing,[6] but no state purchasing agency buys everything needed by the entire state government. However, if we except perishable foodstuffs, it seems that all other purchases should be made by the purchasing agency. Special provision could be made for emergencies.

4. That a department of public safety be created to be in charge of a commissioner to be appointed by the governor of the state. The enforcement of the law should be taken over by the state. The heterogeneous aggregation of state and local law enforcing officials should be replaced as rapidly as possible by a single body of trained men operating under the direction of one authority.

5. That the state department of public welfare be revived with a commissioner to be appointed by the governor.

Constitutional changes affecting the county organization. In the reorganization of the county government it would be necessary first of all to make some changes in the state constitution. It might be wise to fix numerous details of the organization so that they would not be subject to legislative change. Constitutions as a rule should be elastic. But since the General Assembly of the state is accustomed to giving so much time to the details of county government, it may be that nothing short of fixed constitutional provisions would keep it from returning to its old habits. As

[6] Russell Forbes, *Governmental Purchasing*, pp. 37-39.

between two evils, constitutional provisions seem preferable. Therefore, the following recommendations are made:

1. That the constitution of the state be so amended as to provide for a county board, consisting of five members, for each county, to be elected by popular vote from the county at large. This board may be called the county board of commissioners or the county board of directors, if the latter is preferred. Both terms are in use in the counties. The board should be solely responsible for the administration of county affairs. The terms of the board members should overlap, so that not more than three members would be elected at any one time after the first election. This provision would enable the county to change its administrative policies, while profiting by the services of two members who are already familiar with county affairs.

2. That the provisions of the constitution requiring that the judge of probate, the clerk of the circuit courts, the sheriff, and the coroner be elected by popular vote be abolished. Instead of these provisions an amendment should be adopted vesting the appointment of all county officials in the county board, except that the board may delegate administrative authority to a county manager. The important administrative officials should be appointed from lists of eligibles furnished by the state bureau of personnel.

It is important that provision be made for the employment of a county manager, whether explicitly so called or not. The nation, the states, the cities, one and all, need administrative headship. It is equally important in case of the county. No business organization of any consequence operates without an executive head representing a board of directors. County government has long been headless. The need is for a business expert, elected by the board of county commissioners or supervisors and clothed with delegated powers as an administrator to act between sessions of the executive authority of the county—elected and dismissed by this overhead authority for proper cause.

The county needs an administrator who is clothed with authority to carry out the will of his board and who is accessible at all times. In the smaller counties the manager might also act as head of the department of finance or of public works. In the large counties heavier duties might make such an arrangement impossible. In every case the manager should be chosen by the county board and specific administrative authority should be delegated to him by the board. He is responsible to the board alone. The board has power to call him to account at any time. The board meets regularly once or twice each month, and it may have special meetings. But the manager is on the job at all times. He must be an expert in his field. His expert knowledge of county government must be at the service of the county board as it formulates general policies of county administration, but it is equally important that he be on the ground at all times to consult with, advise, supervise, and direct county affairs in general.

Numerous cities have found it advantageous to employ city managers. It is a detail of representative democracy. The county would doubtless profit by following the example of more than 500 cities in the United States. County managers have been chosen by two New Jersey counties, and so-called county managers have been employed in certain North Carolina and Virginia counties, with good results in some instances. But in no case was the manager a manager in fact. So far, the county manager has not had a fair trial. However, a new county manager plan goes into effect in Arlington County, Virginia, in 1932. Under this plan a few constitutional county officers are still to be elected by popular vote. Nevertheless, it is believed that the Virginia county is leading the way to a type of county administration that will find wide acceptance before another decade is past.

3. That an additional amendment be adopted combining the duties of the judge of probate with those of the clerk of the circuit courts, and providing for the appointment of the latter official by the circuit judge from a list of eligibles.

Perhaps there should be included in this amendment also a provision for the appointment of a small number of magistrates in each county by the circuit court clerk from a list of those qualified for the work.

4. That an amendment to the constitution be adopted providing for the consolidation of county and city governments of any county, or of any departments of those governments, when it is in the public interest to do so.

There are instances of such consolidations. Three departments of the governments of the city of Wilmington and the County of New Hanover, North Carolina, have been consolidated. In case there is only one city in a county and both cover the same area there could be no reason for two sets of officials. In other cases the problem is a difficult one. In view of the fact that counties will probably be larger in the future and that each may contain a number of municipalities and organized rural communities the constitution might well carry a provision authorizing counties under certain conditions to adopt a charter providing for federated county government. This might take the form of some of the plans that have been already mentioned. A unitary plan might be acceptable later. The terms of the constitutional provision should be elastic, however, in order that the counties might be enabled to take advantage of better plans that may be developed.

5. That the constitution be amended so that the General Assembly may not be able to attach special provisions to general laws. This would require merely the elimination of the proviso in item XII of section thirty-four of Article II of the constitution.

Statutory provisions affecting the general organization of the county government. It is suggested that the General Assembly enact general laws affecting the county government organization as follows:

1. That county administration be divided into five general divisions: the department of finance, the department of public works, the department of education, the department of health, and the department of public welfare.
2. That counties be authorized, where it seems economical and wise to do so, to establish joint departments of health and public welfare, and county-group hospitals and homes for aged and infirm citizens, and jails.

Statutory provisions affecting the department of finance. The department of finance is the heart of the county government. If it is not well organized and administered on sound principles, the whole county organization finds itself in confusion. It is recommended that the General Assembly enact general laws governing the finance departments as follows:

1. That the county board of commissioners of each county be required to appoint a county accountant from a list of eligibles furnished by the state bureau of personnel, and that the duties of this official shall be those of county accountant, clerk to the county board, and county purchasing agent.

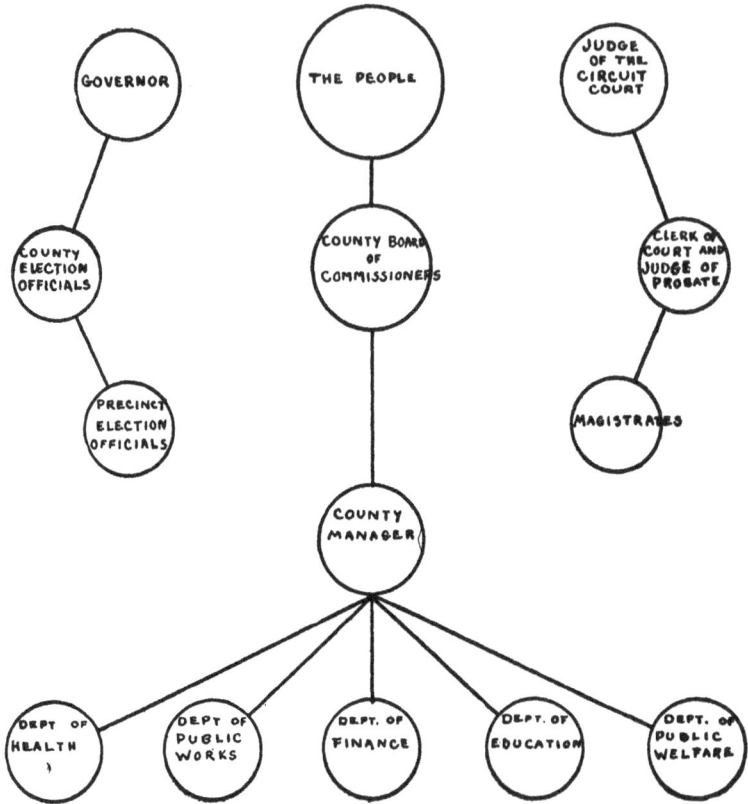

DIAGRAM III

A Plan Suggested for Reorganized County Government

Law enforcing officials are not included in the diagram. They should be state officials and therefore appointed and directed by the state. However, if they are to be chosen locally, it is suggested that a sixth department be added. This department should be called the department of Public Safety and the sheriff should be the head of it. He shall be appointed by the county manager.

The county accountant would thus be the head of the department of finance. In the smaller counties he might be county manager also, if one is employed. As county accountant, he would be familiar with all departments and with all financial details of county affairs; as clerk to the county board, he would be in constant touch with the governing body of the county. He would thus be enabled to keep the board informed concerning the details of county finances, while through the board he would become familiar with the policies of the administration. Each county now has a clerk to the county board or to the county supervisor. In Aiken County he is also virtually the county purchasing agent. The same may be true of other counties. Under the present organization the county board hires the clerk. This recommendation merely gives him additional duties and requires that he be a trained accountant.

2. That after the installation of the uniform system of accounting, as required by the comptroller general, all accounting for general purposes, schools, roads, and subdivisions other than municipalities be placed under the supervision of the county accountant.

Such a requirement would make one official responsible for the bookkeeping that is now done in the offices of the county supervisor, the county superintendent of schools, the treasurer, and the auditor. Modern bookkeeping methods and devices, not now in general use, could be installed and used economically in many counties, and clerks and bookkeepers who have alternate periods of strenuous work and idleness could be kept busily engaged at all times. The number of clerks could probably be reduced. The change should result in well-kept records and in some economies.

3. That the present county auditor be retained, but given the title of county tax supervisor, for that is really what he is at present. He should be appointed from a list of eligibles and should be authorized to name his own assistants and to direct them. Because of the close relations existing between his duties and those of the register of mesne conveyances, it is suggested that the duties of the latter official be transferred from the clerk of the circuit court to the new tax supervisor. Thus the tax supervisor would have no excuse for not keeping track of transfers of property.

Freeing the tax supervisor from direct political pressure and giving him authority to appoint his own assistants should result, at least, in the prompt handling of tax listing and assessing. It would also eliminate a large number of district and county officials. The tax supervisor would be on the job all the time. As the state bureau of personnel became able to furnish the county boards with lists of persons trained in the technique of tax assessment, more equitable assessments should result. The county board of commissioners should be given the powers of a county board of equalization and review.

4. That the county treasurer be retained, except that he be appointed by the county board from a list of eligibles, as in the case of other county officials. To the duties he now performs should be added those of the delinquent tax collector. The county sinking fund commissions should be abolished and their duties conferred on the treasurer subject to the supervision of the comptroller general.

Tax executions under the present plan are issued by the treasurer, who is the tax collector of the county, to the delinquent tax collector. By a slight change in the form the execution could be issued as well by the county accountant to the treasurer. This change would leave the collection of all taxes entirely in the hands of one official. No sheriff would be called upon to collect delinquent taxes, while numerous special delinquent tax collectors and a few delinquent tax commissions could be dispensed with. The salaries paid the county treasurers are sufficient to justify their collecting the delinquent taxes without additional compensation, except necessary expenses.

5. That the county treasurer be required to furnish a corporate surety bond not less in amount than the average daily balance of funds in his custody. The premium on this bond should be paid out of the county treasury.
6. That depositories be required to furnish corporate surety bonds or to pledge approved securities equal at all times to the amount of public funds deposited in them.

To these recommendations let us add those having to do with state control over county affairs. Some of them have already been given.

7. That the comptroller general be given power to require that comprehensive budgets be prepared and filed with him for approval before their adoption by the respective county boards and before the fixing by them of the county tax levies.
8. That he be vested with power to require county accountants to file with him true statements showing the entire debt of the county and its subdivisions other than the municipalities.
9. That he be vested with power to correct any failure in county budgets to keep appropriations within revenue or to make due provision for meeting all legal liabilities and obligations.

10. That he be given power to require all counties and their subdivisions to file applications with him when they desire to borrow money on note or bond issue and to approve or reject these applications after thorough investigation of the purpose for which the debt is to be incurred and the financial condition of the county or district concerned. He should have power to market all debt offerings of the counties and to attend to the payment of interest on all county and district bonds and the principal of such bonds on maturity. His power should enable him also to require that all bonds issued in the future shall be serial bonds with annual payments beginning not later than two years after issue.

11. That he be given power to supervise, inspect, and audit the records and accounts of the counties and their subdivisions.

12. That he require a detailed annual report from each county accountant to take the place of the annual settlement sheet now in use. He should be required by law to publish an annual financial report of all counties.

13. That the governor of the state be given power to remove any county officer guilty of malfeasance in office or of knowingly violating the provisions of the law regulating the manner of the discharge of his duties.

The county accountant would be the head of the department of finance, which would consist of at least three principal divisions. All employees in the department, except those already named, should be selected by the county accountant.

Statutory provisions affecting the department of public works. Jurisdiction over county highways, public buildings, and other public property is vested in the county board of commissioners. The actual administration of the highways and the care of public property with certain other details should be placed in the department of public works. The following recommendations are made with reference to it:

1. That the county board of commissioners appoint a county engineer from a list of eligibles, to be the head of the department of public works. As such, he shall have charge of the construction and maintenance of the county highways and bridges and shall have the care of public buildings and other public property. He should be given power to appoint his assistants.

2. That the county engineer be authorized to employ the county chaingang, where it exists, subject to the general regulations and inspection of the county superintendent of public welfare.

3. That all district road boards and township road supervisors be abolished.

4. That the county engineer be required to prepare and file an annual budget with the county accountant.

5. That all road fund accounts and other accounts of the department of public works be kept under the direction of the county accountant.

6. That the capitation road tax be abolished or made uniform throughout the state.

7. That the county purchasing agent make purchases of all highway materials and equipment through the state purchasing bureau.

The state highway department and the county departments of public works should be closely related. It would be well for the former to be authorized to prepare uniform specifications for various classes of roads and types of construction and to require their use by the county engineers. The state highway department should also prepare contracts, and be ready at all times to give counsel in highway problems.

Constitutional Changes affecting the department of education. The constitution limits the size of school districts. In a few counties these limitations have been removed by constitutional amendments. It is recommended that they be removed throughout the state. It should be completed as rapidly as possible by piece-meal methods, if necessary. However, it seems that it might be done by the adoption of one amendment.

Statutory provisions affecting the department of education. There is some division of opinion as to the best method of selecting county boards of education. Education is the most important business of the county. To elect the county board of education by popular vote might be best. However, the board of education at present is appointed and plays a minor part in educational affairs of the county, while the county superintendent is elected by the people. The following suggestions call for some radical changes.

1. That the county board of commissioners appoint the county board of education. This board should consist of three members appointed for overlapping terms.

2. That the county board of education be vested with authority to appoint the county superintendent of schools from a list of eligibles furnished by the state bureau of personnel.

3. That the county board of education and the county superintendent of schools be authorized to appoint advisory boards of district trustees consisting of three members for each district. At

least two of these trustees should be required to sign vouchers issued to teachers.

4. That the county board of education and the county superintendent of schools be vested with authority to create, abolish, change, or consolidate school districts with the approval of a majority of the people affected.

5. That all special charter school districts other than those of the larger cities be abolished, and that all tax levies for the support of a minimum term of eight months be made on a county-wide basis. District levies should be continued where district obligations have already been incurred and where these can not be taken over on an equitable basis by the county, and also where districts may wish to maintain schools for terms longer than eight months.

6. That all school accounting be done under the direction of the county accountant.

7. That the county superintendent of schools and the county board of education prepare a school budget each year and file it with the county accountant. This and other departmental budgets are to be included in the consolidated county budget to be submitted to the comptroller general for his approval.

8. That the county superintendent of schools plot on maps of the county the transportation routes, locations of schools, number of pupils and distances to be hauled. The actual transportation of pupils however should be under the supervision of the county superintendent of public welfare.

9. That the supervisor of rural elementary schools be chosen by the county board of education from a list of eligibles, and that she be required to work under the direction of the county superintendent of schools.

10. That the school board be required to establish a county library and to select a librarian from an approved list, who shall work in coöperation with the superintendent of schools. The county library should supplement the school libraries. It should have sub-stations in all consolidated schools and at such other points as will serve best to bring it within reach of all the people of the county.

A uniform system of school accounts would necessarily be included in those forms devised by the comptroller general and required to be installed and kept by the county accountants.

The establishment of a county library as an essential part of every county department of education, and the development of the conception of the school as an institution for the education of all the people, not merely the children, are two matters that can not be over-emphasized. The law authorizes any county, township, or municipality to establish a library and levy not exceeding two mills for its support.[7] A few county libraries are to be found in the state already. Laurens County has recently established one on a small scale. County libraries attempting to reach all of the rural people are to be found here and there in perhaps every southern state. Those in Guilford and a few other North Carolina counties are noteworthy. Rosenwald demonstration libraries are to be found in several southern states. They are showing the way to provide library service to all the people. A noteworthy example is the Coahoma County, Mississippi, library. However, grants have been made to Charleston and Richland counties and demonstration libraries may be already in operation in these counties. As a rule however the importance of the library as a center in each county where "The best that has been thought and said" and where reliable up-to-date information may be had has not been realized.

Statutory provisions affecting the department of health. Health departments are already in existence in several counties in the state. They are needed in every county. The field of public health services is undoubtedly an expanding one. The following provisions concerning the department of health are suggested:

1. That all counties be required either singly or jointly to establish departments of public health. The department should be operated under the direction of a health officer appointed by the county board of commissioners from a list of eligibles.
2. That the county board of commissioners appoint an advisory health board to assist the county health officer.
3. That the office of county physician be abolished.
4. That physicians be required to report all cases of pellagra, tuberculosis, and venereal disease to the health officer.
5. That the health officer file an annual budget with the county accountant.
6. That where two or more counties form a health district with one health officer in charge each county be required to employ a full-time county nurse.

The department of public welfare. Organized public welfare can hardly be said to exist in the state. The state board of public welfare created some years ago has had no funds appropriated for its use since 1926. Greenville County with its Charities and Corrections Commission stands well in advance of the counties in the

[7] Code, 1922, Vol. 3, sec. 4480.

state in this field. Organized public welfare activities are needed throughout the state. Methods of distributing poor relief and of managing poor homes and farms have probably not changed since colonial days. More attention should be given to delinquent youth and to enforcing the compulsory school law. Organized public welfare service is a necessary complementary service to that of public health. It is recommended that laws be enacted establishing public welfare departments as follows:

1. That the counties of the state be required either singly or jointly to establish departments of public welfare. Each department should be in charge of a superintendent of public welfare chosen by the county board of commissioners from a list of eligibles. If the department is a joint department, the superintendent may be chosen by the county boards concerned acting jointly.

2. That the county board of commissioners be required to appoint an advisory board of public welfare.

3. That the counties be authorized to establish county-group or district homes equipped with modern conveniences for the care of their aged and infirm citizens, and that these homes be operated under the general supervision of the county superintendents of public welfare.

The first district home and farm in the United States was established in Virginia. It was authorized by an act passed in 1918. In 1926 and in 1928 four district homes were established. The largest of these districts comprised six counties. These district homes replaced old county homes which lacked every modern convenience. They have resulted in savings for the counties, though that was not the sole reason for their establishment.

4. That the operation of the county jail be placed under the supervision of the county superintendent of public welfare. The counties should be authorized to build county-group jails where it is economical to do so.

5. That the county chaingang, unless taken over by the state, be placed under the supervision of the county superintendent of public welfare, except that the prisoners shall be employed by the county engineer.

6. That the county superintendent of public welfare be authorized to distribute all out-relief.

7. That the county board of commissioners appoint a school attendance officer to work under the direction of the county superintendent of public welfare and in coöperation with the county superintendent of schools. This officer should be chosen from a

list of eligibles and be given the following duties: to keep the school census up-to-date with the help of the teachers and administrative officials of the schools, to enforce the compulsory school laws, and to supervise the transportation of school children.

8. That the superintendent of public welfare be required to exercise supervision over paroled persons, to administer mothers' aid where provided, and to assist the unemployed in getting work.

9. That the supervision of public parks and playgrounds be delegated to the county superintendent of public welfare.

10. That the superintendent of public welfare be required to file a budget annually with the county accountant.

Persons trained for the various phases of public welfare work are not very numerous. The state superintendent of public welfare should be authorized to certify a list of eligibles to the director of the bureau of personnel.

Additional recommendations. Certain other county problems may be treated briefly. The salaries of the county home and farm demonstration agents are no longer paid out of county funds. These officials are in fact state agents, but it is recommended that they be appointed by the county board of commissioners from lists of eligibles. No change in the election machinery of the counties is suggested other than that it seems probable that one set of county election commissioners and of precinct election managers would be sufficient. Such a change would reduce the election officials by half. The county board of commissioners should hire the county legal advisor, and he should be advisor to the county manager also where the latter is employed.

When we come to the problems of law enforcement and the courts and certain problems of conservation, the way ahead is more difficult. A complicated system of courts should never be created. The supreme court, the circuit courts, and the magistrate courts in each county make a simple system of courts. Two serious criticisms may be made of the system. The provision of the constitution authorizing the supreme court to call the circuit judges to its assistance when constitutional questions are involved seems to suggest that the resulting decisions of the court may be based upon political rather than upon legal considerations. For that reason the provision in the constitution should be stricken out. The other criticism is that no qualifications are required for the office of magistrate.

Some county courts have been created. These courts are inferior to the circuit courts, though they may appeal directly to the supreme court. There seems no urgent necessity for the creation of such courts. It may be that the courts in every case should be state courts, and that the punishment of crime could be more easily attained and all the ends of justice could be better served by replacing the county and even the municipal courts with circuit courts. Such a change would probably require more circuits and certainly more judges. The tendency, however, is to create more inferior courts, and perhaps as counties become less numerous there may be a place for one general county court in each county.

In some counties in the state the sheriff is no longer the important officer he once was. Perhaps the office as it exists now should be abolished and the title transferred to some other county office. Otherwise, there is such a long tradition behind the office that it will be more difficult to abolish than that of the coroner, which still persists despite the fact that it has long outlasted its usefulness. Besides the sheriff, there is a remarkable variety of law enforcing officials in the state. The governor directs his state constables; the state highway department directs the state highway patrol; the sheriff and the deputies and special deputies, the rural police, and the special constables and magistrates' constables in general direct themselves. Then there are the municipal police forces and the county game wardens.

The main business of all these officials is the prevention of crime and the enforcement of the law. This is the work of the state. Therefore, one can suggest few strong reasons why all the work of all these officials, except possibly the execution of the civil processes of the courts, should not be done by one organized and disciplined body of state police chosen and directed by a state commissioner of public safety appointed by the governor of the state. This body might be organized along the lines of the Pennsylvania state constabulary and equipped with horses, motorcycles, and automobiles. The horses could be used in patrolling the remote and isolated rural areas, the motorcycles and automobiles elsewhere. A force of perhaps three hundred men carefully chosen for the work and carefully trained would be far more effective than the much larger force now employed, and its cost would probably be no greater than that of the present system. Thus law enforcement would be far removed from the pressure of local politics.

To work out such a system of police and to include in it the work of the sheriff and other local law enforcing officials would require some pioneer work. No state has so far attempted such a thing. Many problems would have to be solved, but the attempt should be made. Undoubtedly such a system would result in better law enforcement and therefore in better attitudes on the part of the citizen toward law enforcing officials, and to law and order in general. No one can doubt the need for such a change in attitudes.

In conclusion. County government as outlined in this chapter is in distinct contrast to the present organization. Exactly such county government is nowhere in operation at this time, but almost every year finds a step taken towards it by some county. There can be no doubt that these suggestions point the way in general to a solution of some of the problems of county government in the state. Despite its resistance to change, county government is slowly being reorganized. The central problem of reorganization is the creation of the best possible machinery for the administration of county affairs with a minimum of legislation. The new organization must be relatively simple, it must have a responsible head, and it must function economically and efficiently. As a unit, it must be responsible to the people, that is, it must be democratic. The people should through their governing board lay down the general policies of administration. Trained public servants should be hired to do the work. High qualifications for public offices will doubtless place them beyond the reach of some who aspire to them. Upon careful consideration that will be seen to be an advantage. Training for the public service and the promise to capable men and women of life careers in it can do much for its improvement and its elevation in public esteem. If the county does not wish to yield all its important functions to the state, it is well that it take thought for its future.

BIBLIOGRAPHY

BOOKS AND PAMPHLETS

Acts and Joint Resolutions of the General Assembly of South Carolina, 1922-30, 9 Vols.

Annual Report of the South Carolina State Highway Department For the Fiscal Year Ending December 31, 1929.

Archdale, John. *A New Description of South Carolina.* London: J. Wyat, 1707.

Bemis, Edward W. "Local Government in the South and Southwest," *Johns Hopkins University Studies,* Vol. XI. Baltimore: 1893.

Blachly, Frederick F., and Oatman, Miriam E. *Government of Oklahoma.* Oklahoma City, Oklahoma: Harlow Publishing Company, 1924.

Blakely, Roy G. "State Income Taxation," *Publication No. 31, League of Minnesota Municipalities.* Minneapolis: 1930.

Boucher, C. S. "The Ante-bellum Attitude of South Carolina Towards Manufacturing and Agriculture," *Washington University Studies,* Vol. 3, Part 2. St. Louis: 1916.

—— "Sectionalism, Representation, and the Electoral Question in Ante-bellum South Carolina," *Washington University Studies,* Vol. 4, Part 2. St. Louis: 1916.

Branson, E. C., and Others. "County Government and County Affairs in North Carolina," *The North Carolina Club Yearbook, 1917-1918.* Chapel Hill, N. C.: The University of North Carolina, 1918.

—— *Syllabus of Home County Studies.* Chapel Hill, N. C.: The University of North Carolina, 1914.

Brookings Institution. *Report on a Survey of the Organization and Administration of County Government in North Carolina.* Washington, D. C.: 1930.

Buck, A. E. *Public Budgeting.* New York: Harper, 1929.

Carroll, B. R. *Historical Collections.* 2 vols. New York: Harper, 1836.

Channing, Edward. "Town and County Government in the English Colonies of North America," *Johns Hopkins University Studies,* Second Series. Baltimore: 1884.

Childs, Richard S. "Rural Municipalities of Tomorrow," *Proceedings of the Fifth National Country Life Conference.* New York: 1922.

Cole, G. D. H. *The Future of Local Government.* London and New York: Cassell & Co., Ltd., 1921.

Committee on County Government of the National Municipal League. *A Model County Manager Law.*

Compton, R. T. "Fiscal Problems of Rural Decline," *Special Report No. 2 of the New York State Tax Commission.* Albany, N. Y.: J. B. Lyon Co., 1929.

Crane, V. W. *The Southern Frontier.* Durham, N. C.: Duke University Press, 1928.

Dodd, Walter F. *State Government.* New York: Century, 1923.

Fairlie, John A. *Local Government in Counties, Towns, and Villages.* New York: Century, 1923.

Fairlie, John A., and Kneier, Chas. M. *County Government and Administration.* New York: Century, 1930.

Fiske, John. *Civil Government in the United States.* Boston: Houghton, 1890.

Forbes, Russell. *Governmental Purchasing.* New York: Harper, 1929.

Gaines, Elizabeth V. *County Government in Virginia.* Richmond, Virginia: Virginia League of Women Voters, 1919.

Galpin, Chas. J. *Rural Social Problems.* New York: Century, 1924.

Gee, Wilson, and Corson, J. J. *A Statistical Study of Virginia.* University, Virginia: The Institute for Research in Social Sciences, 1927.

General School Law of South Carolina inclusive of the Year 1929.

Gregg, Alexander. *History of Old Cheraws.* Columbia, S. C.: The State Co., 1905.

Green, Fletcher M. *The Constitutional Development of The South Atlantic States, 1776-1860.* Chapel Hill, N. C.: The University of North Carolina Press, 1930.

Harris, G. Montagu. *Local Government in Many Lands.* Westminster: P. S. King and Son, Ltd., 1926.

Hayes, A. W. *Rural Community Organization.* Chicago: University of Chicago Press, 1921.

Henry, H. M. *The Police Control of The Slave In South Carolina.* Emory, Virginia: 1914.

Hewatt, Alexander. *An Historical Account of the Rise and Progress of The Colonies of South Carolina and Georgia.* London: Donaldson, 1779.

Houston, David F. "A Critical Study of Nullification in South Carolina," *Harvard Historical Studies,* Vol. 3. New York: Longmans, 1896.

Howard, George E. "An Introduction to The Local Constitutional History of the United States," *Johns Hopkins University Studies in Historical and Political Science.* Baltimore, 1889.

James, Herman G. *Local Government in the United States.* New York: Appleton, 1921.

———— *County Government in Texas.* Austin: University of Texas, 1917.

Kendrick, M. Slade. "The Collection of General Property Taxes on Farm Property in the United States with Emphasis on New York," *Bulletin No. 469, Cornell University Agricultural Experiment Station.* Ithaca, New York: 1928.

Kennedy, R. M. "Public Libraries, A Need of South Carolina," *Bulletin No. 37, The University of South Carolina.* Columbia, S. C.: 1914.

BIBLIOGRAPHY 211

Kilpatrick, Wylie. *Problems in Contemporary County Government.* University, Virginia: The Institute for Research in the Social Sciences, 1930.

Kirkpatrick, E. L., and Others. "Rural Organizations and the Farm Family," *Research Bulletin 96, Agricultural Experiment Station of the University of Wisconsin.* Madison, Wisconsin: 1929.

Knight, Edgar W. "Reconstruction and Education in South Carolina." Reprint from articles in *South Atlantic Quarterly,* October, 1919, and January, 1920.

Landrum, J. B. O. *Colonial and Revolutionary History of Upper South Carolina.* Greenville, S. C.: Shannon & Co., 1897.

Laski, Harold J. *The Foundations of Sovereignty and Other Essays.* New York: Harcourt, 1921.

Lawson, John. *The History of Carolina.* London: W. Taylor, 1714.

League of Minnesota Municipalities. *Minnesota Yearbook.* Minneapolis: 1930.

Long, Harriet C. *County Library Service.* Chicago: American Library Association, 1925.

Manny, Theodore B. *Rural Municipalities.* New York: Century, 1930.

Mathewson, A. M. *The County Unit System of Connecticut.* New Haven: The Whaples-Bullis Co., 1917.

Maxey, Chester C. *County Administration* (In Delaware). New York: Macmillan, 1919.

McCrady, Edward. *South Carolina in the Revolution.* 2 Vols. New York: Macmillan, 1901.

———*South Carolina Under the Proprietary Government.* New York: Macmillan, 1897.

———*South Carolina Under the Royal Government.* New York: Macmillan, 1889.

Meriwether, Colyer. *History of Higher Education in South Carolina with Sketch of the Free School System.* Washington, D. C.: Government Printing Office, 1889.

Mills, Robert. *Statistics of South Carolina.* Charleston, S. C.: Hurlburt & Lloyd. 1826.

Muller, Helen M. (compiler) "County Manager Government." *The Reference Shelf, Vol. 6, No. 8.* New York: The H. W. Wilson Co., 1930.

Munro, William B. *The Government of the United States, National, State, and Local.* (Revised Edition) New York: Macmillan, 1925.

New York Bureau of Municipal Research, *County Government in Virginia.* 1927.

North Carolina Senate Bill No. 162. *A Bill to be Entitled an Act to Create a Local Government Commission and a Director of Local Government, and to Prescribe the Powers and Duties of Such Commission and Director.*

Odum, H. W., and Willard, D. W. *Systems of Public Welfare.* Chapel Hill, N. C.: The University of North Carolina Press, 1925.

Odum, H. W. *Public Welfare and Social Work.* Chapel Hill, N. C.:
The University of North Carolina Press, 1926.

Odum, H. W., and Others. "Attainable Standards in Municipal Problems," *The University of North Carolina Extension Bulletin.*
Chapel Hill, N. C.: 1921.

Patterson, Caleb P. *American Government.* New York: Heath, 1929.

Porter, Kirk H. *County and Township Government in the United
States.* New York: Macmillan, 1922.

Ramage, B. J. "Local Government and Free Schools in South Carolina," *Johns Hopkins University Studies in Historical and Political
Science,* First Series. Baltimore: 1883.

Ramsay, David. *The History of South Carolina from British Province
to Independent State.* 2 Vols. Charleston, S. C.: D. Longworth,
1809.

Raum, G. B. *The Existing Conflict between Republican Government
and Southern Oligarchy.* New York: Chas. M. Green Printing Co.,
1884.

*Report of the Commission on Simplification and Economy of State and
Local Government to the General Assembly of Virginia, 1924.*

*Report of the Comptroller-General of South Carolina for the Fiscal
Year 1930.*

Report of the (N. C.) County Government Commission, 1930.

*Report of the Joint Special Committee on Revenue and Taxation Ap-
pointed by the (S. C.) General Assembly 1920 Session, 1921.*

Reynolds, John S. *Reconstruction in South Carolina.* Columbia, S. C.:
The State Co., 1905.

Rivers, W. J. *A Sketch of the History of South Carolina to the Close
of the Proprietary Government.* Charleston, S. C.: McCarter & Co.,
1856.

Salley, A. S., Jr. "The Origin of Carolina," *Bulletin No. 8 of the
South Carolina Historical Commission.* Columbia, S. C.: The State
Co., 1926.

Shambaugh, Benj. F. (Editor) "County Government and Administration in Iowa," *Applied History Series,* Vol. IV. Iowa City,
Iowa: State Historical Society of Iowa, 1925.

Simkins, Francis B. *The Tillman Movement in South Carolina.* Durham, N. C.: Duke University Press, 1926.

*Sixty-First Annual Report of the State Superintendent of Education
of South Carolina.* 1929.

Smith, W. Roy. *South Carolina as a Royal Province.* New York:
Macmillan, 1903.

Smith, Bruce. *The State Police.* New York: Macmillan, 1925.

Snowden, Yates. *History of South Carolina.* Vols. I and II. Chicago
and New York: The Lewis Publishing Co., 1920.

Spencer, D. E. "Local Government in Wisconsin," *Johns Hopkins
University Studies in Historical and Political Science,* Vol. VIII.
Baltimore: 1890.

South Carolina, a Handbook Prepared by the Department of Agriculture, Commerce and Industries, and Clemson College, 1927.

South Carolina Code, 1922, 3 Vols.

South Carolina Income Tax Act of 1926 with 1930 Amendments.

South Carolina Statutes, 1670-1838. 6 Vols.

South Carolina Tax Commission, Fifteenth Annual Report, 1929.

South Carolina Tax Commission, *Guide for the Assessment of Automobiles and Trucks.* 1930.

State Department of Agriculture, Commerce and Industries, *The South Carolina Yearbook.* 1929.

Stene, Edwin O. "State Supervision of Local Finance in Minnesota," *Publication No. 30, The League of Minnesota Municipalities.* Minneapolis: 1930.

Stevens, E. A. *County Commissioners and the Powers and Duties of Commissioners Courts.* Austin, Texas: Van Boeckman-Jones Co., 1923.

"Survey of Laurens County (S. C.) Public Schools," *The Report of the Survey Commission.* February, 1928.

Third Biennial Report of the Department of Conservation and Development of North Carolina, 1929-30.

Thomas, J. P., Jr. *The Formation of Judicial and Political Subdivisions of South Carolina.* Columbia, S. C.: Bryan Printing Co., 1890.

Thompson, Henry T. *The Establishment of the Public School System in South Carolina.* Columbia, S. C.: Bryan Printing Co., 1927.

Thorpe, F. N. *Federal and State Constitutions,* Vol. 6, pp. 3241-3355. Washington, D. C.: Government Printing Office, 1909.

United States Department of Agriculture, Bureau of Public Roads, *Local Roads* and *State Highway Systems.*

United States Department of Commerce, Bureau of Census. *Census of South Carolina Manufactures, 1929; South Carolina Farm Census, 1930.*

University of North Carolina. Department of Rural Social Economics. Numerous files of newspaper clippings, pamphlets, and current material on county government.

University of North Carolina Institute for Research in Social Science. County government and County Affairs in each of sixty North Carolina counties by Paul W. Wager and others. County Government and County Affairs in Neshoba, Covington, Lafayette, and Washington counties, Mississippi, by Edward A. Terry and Columbus Andrews. County Government and County Affairs in Fairfield, Darlington, Williamsburg, Colleton, Aiken, and Laurens counties, South Carolina, by Columbus Andrews.

Van Deusen, J. G. *Economic Bases of Disunion in South Carolina.* New York: Columbia University Press, 1928.

Wager, Paul W. *County Government in North Carolina.* Chapel Hill, N. C.: The University of North Carolina Press, 1928.

Wager, Paul W. "Problems of County Government," an Address at the Third Annual Session of the Institute of Public Affairs and International Relations, July, 1929. Bulletin of the University of Georgia, Athens, Georgia.

Wallace, David D. *The South Carolina Constitution of 1895.* Bulletin No. 197, The University of South Carolina, Columbia, S. C., 1927.

White, Albert B. *The Making of the English Constitution.* New York: Putnam, 1908.

White, H. A. *The Making of South Carolina.* New York: Silver, Burdett & Co., 1906.

Whyte, W. E. *Local Government in Scotland.* Edinburgh: Wm. Hodge & Co., 1925.

Whitney, Edson L. "Government of the Colony of South Carolina," *Johns Hopkins University Studies,* Vol. XIII. Baltimore, 1895.

Willoughby, W. F. *The Government of Modern States.* New York: Century, 1924.

AMERICAN CITY

Chamberlain, N. "The Greatest Need of Local Government," August, 1925.

Peel, A. J. "Some Problems of County Accounting," June, 1924.

Riser, L. A. "Effectiveness of County Health Departments," November, 1920.

Sikes, George C. "Advantages of City and County Consolidation," September, 1919.

Willis, P. L. "City-County Consolidation in Montana," February, 1923.

NATIONAL MUNICIPAL REVIEW

Anderson, William. "How England Has Solved Some Familiar County Problems," July, 1918.

Barth, Harry A. "County Government in The Southwest," March, 1925.

Branson, E. C. "County Government in North Carolina," September, 1921.

Campion, Alfred H. "San Francisco Approves Plan for Consolidation with San Mateo County," May, 1931.

Childs, Richard S. "County Affairs," April, 1921.

—— "Westchester County (N. Y.) Plans a New Government," June, 1925.

Corson, John J., 3rd. "The Year 1930 in The History of Virginia Counties," April, 1931.

Dodds, H. W. "A County Manager Charter in Maryland," August, 1920.

Fair, Eugene. "The Missouri County Board—Its Personnel and Procedure," November, 1925.

Fleisher, John. "Nassau County (N. Y.) Plans A New Government," July, 1919.

Goodrich, R. M. "The County Board in Minnesota," December, 1924.
Hatten, C. Roy. "The Movement for County Government Reform in Michigan," November, 1920.
Hatton, A. R. "The Butte-Silver Bow County Consolidated Charter," June, 1923.
Moses, Robert. "Home Rule for Two New York Counties," January, 1922, and November, 1922.
Nanry, William H. "San Francisco Adopts a New Charter," May, 1931.
Parks, Wade R. "County Government in Montana," March, 1919.
Reed, Henry E. "County Government in Oregon—A Growing Problem," February, 1921.
Reed, Thos. H. "Dual Government for Metropolitan Regions," February, 1927.
Reid, Hugh. "Arlington County Adopts the Manager Plan," March, 1931.
Sikes, George C. "Consolidation Problems in California," March, 1918.
Studensky, Paul. "Federated Government for Pittsburgh and Vicinity," September, 1926.
Wager, Paul W., and Jones, Howard P. "Signs of Progress in County Government," August, 1930.
Whitnall, G. G. "City and County Consolidation for Los Angeles," January, 1921.

PUBLIC MANAGEMENT

Kneier, Chas. M. "The County Manager Plan," February, 1930.
Parkman, Henry. "Personnel Management in Massachusetts Counties," February, 1931.
Wager, Paul W. "The Future of the Small Town and Rural Areas," April, 1931.
——— "The Case for the County Manager," March, 1930.

THE ANNALS

Barth, Harry A. "The Trend in County Revenues," May, 1924.
Fairlie, John A. "Reorganization in Counties and Townships," May, 1924.
Harley, Herbert. "An Efficient County Court System," September, 1917.

REVIEW OF REVIEWS

Howell, E. B. "New Plan for Government of Counties," June, 1923.
Severance, M. F. "County Units of Minnesota," July, 1922.

RURAL AMERICA

Corson, John J., 3rd. "Whither the American County Almshouse," June, 1931.
Kirsch, Mary M. "Consolidation of Counties," March, 1931.

THE AMERICAN POLITICAL SCIENCE REVIEW

Bromage, Arthur W. "The Crisis in County Government in Michigan," February, 1931, pp. 135-146.

THE PROGRESSIVE FARMER

Allred, C. E. "County Consolidation," Kentucky-Tennessee Edition, July, 1931.

ADDENDUM

SUGGESTED CHANGES IN
COUNTY GOVERNMENT AND COUNTY AFFAIRS
IN SOUTH CAROLINA

By M. A. WRIGHT, Attorney-at-Law
Conway, S. C.
December 12, 1931

ACKNOWLEDGMENT

The Committee on Government of the South Carolina Council wishes to acknowledge its indebtedness for assistance in the preparation of this report on County Government in South Carolina to Dr. E. C. Branson, Dr. S. H. Hobbs and Mr. Columbus Andrews of the University of North Carolina, and Professor S. M. Derrick of the University of South Carolina. A great deal of the material contained in the report is based on Mr. Andrews's studies of County Government in South Carolina; on Dr. D. D. Wallace's bulletin on the South Carolina Constitution of 1895, issued by the University of South Carolina; on Dr. Wylie Kilpatrick's Problems in Contemporary County Government issued by the University of Virginia, and on the Brookings Institution's report on a Survey of the Organization and Administration of County Government in North Carolina.

The committee wishes to record its grateful acknowledgment of the assistance derived from these sources.

M. A. WRIGHT, *Chairman.*

INTRODUCTION

This committee is charged with the duty of making a study of state, county and municipal governments in South Carolina, and with offering suggestions for improvements in existing systems. It early reached the conclusion that a proper starting point was the county. Since the county government comes into closer touch and contact with the people than the State government, its inefficiency produces evil results which are more widely and keenly felt by those who give it support.

Further, until recent years but little study and attention have been given to county government. Frequent innovations have been introduced in state governments as the result of investigations conducted in that field. Cities have carried on experiments designed to improve the type of government of municipalities. A great amount of research has been accomplished by competent investigators in both state and city governments; courses of study in those subjects have been given for many years in colleges and universities. But until recently there has been no indication of any intelligent interest in the equally vital question of county government. Until 1917 it is said that there was no course in county government in any American college or university.

The result of this lack of interest has been immediately reflected in the type of government with which counties have been afflicted. A prominent authority is responsible for the statement that "There is not at the present moment a single county in the United States which has anything approaching a really good organization." Dr. Charles A. Beard has declared: "The county methods of transacting business generally are assailed as obsolete, crude and extravagant where not actually and wilfully corrupt." Dr. C. C. Maxey's investigation led him to conclude that "County administration is disintegrated, indirect, over-elaborate, unduly expensive, and largely removed from popular scrutiny and control." There is nothing in the situation in South Carolina which indicates that this state is exempt from these general indictments.

The total actual expenditures of the counties of South Carolina for the year 1930 were approximately $26,000,000. Recent investigations into the subject have led to the deliberate conclusion that 40 per cent of the revenues of county governments are wasted. Therefore, solely on the basis of reducing expenditures or of securing value received from use of the county's revenue, it is imperative that serious consideration be given to the existing systems.

It is realized, of course, that no system is self-operating, and that all depend for their success on the constant and intelligent interest of those who live under them. No magic formula has yet been devised by which this interest may be produced or maintained. But it would seem that a step in that direction might be taken if the plan of county government should be so fashioned that the voter would know whom to praise or to blame for its administration. There would not be the same feeling of futility in casting a ballot if the voter knew that his vote would have some theoretical effect at least in improving the government which he supports.

The County as an Agency of the State

A great deal of the difficulty of administration of county government is due to the theory underlying the creation of counties. That theory, as the successive constitutions of the State make clear, is that the counties are mere agencies of the State government. Municipalities secure their charters and are given extremely broad powers in determination of matters of purely local concern. Their powers, within their spheres, are comparable to the powers of the state itself in its own larger sphere. On the other hand, the county must go to the legislature, composed of representatives of the entire State, for authority to create or discontinue an office or agency of the county, to raise or lower the salary of any officer or employee, to bridge a stream, to erect a county hospital, or even to build a fence around the courthouse—matters of not the remotest concern to persons living outside of the limits of the county. To be sure, under the system in vogue, through legislative courtesy the General Assembly usually acts as the local delegation may determine. But decisions on all of these and a multitude of other relatively trivial matters must be reached in Columbia, to which point only a few persons having some interest in the questions involved may go to make their wishes and influence felt.

If all matters of purely local concern could be determined at the courthouse, several beneficial results would accrue: (a) the efforts of the General Assembly could be devoted to the matters of state-wide importance, with consequent saving of time and larger opportunity for study; (b) the delegation would not be so subject to influence and suggestion from those having a direct interest in the questions involved without having that influence and suggestion offset by the expressed interest of those whose concern is not so personal or acute, and (c) a closer approach would be made toward making the government of the county more directly responsive to the will of its inhabitants.

A larger measure of autonomy is essential to the perfection of county government. The county must be given something of the same power and authority within its borders as are exercised by cities. Only by this means can anything approaching county consciousness be created and county pride stimulated. This does not mean that the advantages which accrue through supervision of certain county activities by state agencies should be lost, but rather that this supervision should be extended over independent autonomous units rather than, as at present, over what are in effect merely other agencies of the state.

Through this new conception of the function of the county it may be hoped that initiative in conducting well considered experiments in county government may be encouraged. The results of such successful experiment in one county would be immediately available to all others.

While it is desirable to afford the individual counties this opportunity to conduct experiments in the management of their own affairs, it does not follow that there should not remain some basic uniformity in county governments. The judiciary system, the school system, the highway system, the public health system, law enforcement and fiscal affairs are fields in which there is necessarily an inter-relation between the counties and the State. State supervision is and will continue to be necessary in these and perhaps other fields. To have county governments furnish clear reports of their activities to the State government is essential for purposes of comparing methods pursued and results achieved by each county with the others. No government is better than its bookkeeping. Uniformity to a certain extent in the systems of county government is essential for the preparation and preservation of records by some central agency. The legislative delegations of the forty-six counties under the present plan have authority, which is generally exercised, to create forty-six separate and distinct systems of county government entirely dissimilar each to the other. While a certain measure of elasticity is desirable, there can be no effective supervision or coördination of the affairs of counties which are conducted according to forty-six separate plans.

THE COUNTY'S OFFICIAL PERSONNEL

In the natural and commendable zeal for democracy which underlay the formation of counties, the people were determined to reserve for themselves the power of naming at the ballot box all of their public servants. While, with the variety of systems prevailing, there is some diversity in the offices filled at the polls, it may be said that the typical county in South Carolina elects the following officers: State senator, members of the house of representatives, county superintendent of education, clerk of court, register of mesne conveyance, master in equity, treasurer, sheriff, road supervisor, coroner, and probate judge. In the cases of certain of these officers, appointment is made by the governor, but the practice is to appoint those who are chosen by the electorate. In addition, some counties elect the members of the county board of commissioners and rural policemen.

Each officer elected by the people feels responsibility only to the people. Hence, county government lacks anything approaching a head or a major executive. There has grown up a decentralization of authority which renders it in most instances impossible to fix any measure of responsibility on any one official for the conduct of county affairs. The situation is analagous to the election by a corporation's forty thousand stockholders of all its officers and employees. Corporations have long since found it necessary for the stockholders to elect a board of directors who, in turn, select and remove their own agents as circumstances dictate. No corporation would long survive which permitted its zeal for the hollow name of democracy to lead its stockholders into filling all of its offices and choosing the heads of departments. That county government has survived on such a basis is due only to the fact that the resources of the people are constantly called upon to pay for their errors in judgment.

In no city in the state do the voters elect the chiefs of police and fire departments, the superintendent of parks and playgrounds, the city clerk and other subordinate officials of the city government. They elect the mayor and council, or the commission, as the case may be, and leave to such group the selection of the agents through which it will act. There has been no feeling that such a method deprived the voters of any substantial right, no assailing the plan on the ground of its alleged lack of democracy. Yet the course followed by the counties in the election by the voters of the sheriff, clerk of court, treasurer and all other officials is rigidly adhered to in the face of abundant evidence of the inefficiency of the system.

If the county government may be said to have anything approaching a head, that head is the legislative delegation, which itself is divided into members of the house of representatives on the one hand and the senator with the veto power on the other. In most of the counties the county board of commissioners is appointed by the governor on the recommendation of the legislative delegation. The business of the legislative delegation, as the name implies, is purely legislative. The business of the county board of commissioners is purely administrative. We have, therefore, a situation in most of the counties in which an administrative body derives its authority from and is responsible to a legislative body. The principle of separation of legislative and executive duties is also one of the frequent expressions of the people's desire for democracy. But the anomaly implicit in that situation has received but scant consideration.

ACTUAL HEAD NEEDED

But the county should have an actual and not merely a nominal head. That head should be chosen by the people and be responsible to them for the administration of all county affairs outside of the realm of the legislative delegation's activities in regard to state affairs, and excepting also auditing and election matters. Since the general law makes provision for creation of the county board of commissioners and since its present functions are more nearly related to the functions of an executive head of the government, it would seem that the county board of commissioners should be chosen by the people and should be actually responsible for the administrative affairs of the county. With the exceptions above stated, the county board of commissioners should be given authority to choose all officers of the county.

AUDITOR

The auditor should be appointed by the comptroller-general. He should act in effect as a check on the operations of the county board of commissioners; his records afford some opportunity to determine whether or not the county is operating within its income and whether or not the expenditures proposed by the county board of commissioners are justified by the revenues. He should not, therefore, be chosen by them. The suggestion is made that the auditor be appointed by the comptroller-general, since his relations are largely with that office and since he should be one having technical qualifications as a bookkeeper, on the merits of which the electorate cannot be expected intelligently to pass.

ELECTION OFFICIALS

Since the county board of commissioners and the legislative delegation, under the plan contemplated, would be the only elective officers chosen at the polls, the board and the delegation should have nothing to do with the appointment of those who conduct the election. Such officials should be entirely free of any responsibility to or interference by the county board of commissioners or the legislative delegation. The entire election machinery should, so far as possible, be free of political control. Since the governor is also an elective official, there are objections to his too close association with such machinery. It is suggested, therefore, that the county board of registrars and the county election commissioners should be appointed by the state board of canvassers, and that the county election commissioners should continue to appoint the precinct election managers.

EDUCATIONAL SUPERVISION

The county board of education should be appointed by the county board of commissioners, and should be charged with the duty of recommending the county superintendent of education for appointment by the state board. In that choice the county board of education should not be limited to residents of the county but should possess the same freedom of selection as is enjoyed by school trustees in selecting a superintendent of schools. The county unit system in the management of fiscal school affairs should be adopted by all counties in the state, leaving to the local trustees the supervision of operation of local schools.

BOARD AND SUBORDINATES

All officers chosen by the county board of commissioners should have authority to choose and remove their own assistants and clerical help. The board of county commissioners should have the right, as city councils now have, to discharge any of its own appointees at any time for reasons satisfactory to it, doing so immediately or after rule to show cause. Under the present method there is no provision for discharging an unsatisfactory county official during his term of office except upon some violation of law or improper conduct on his part, permitting the governor to exercise a prerogative which is greatly limited by statutory provisions and decisions of the court.

The county board of commissioners should consist of three or five members whose terms expire on successive years. This would insure some continuity of policy and not cause the hiatus in county affairs attendant upon a complete change in executive control.

The plan herein outlined vests the county board of commissioners with authority as to the internal concerns of the county comparable to the authority enjoyed by a town or city council. It should be given power to determine the county's budget; to prescribe regulations governing subordinate officials, and to pass the necessary enactments to protect the public health, safety and welfare, where such enactments are not in conflict with the general state law or the constitution. Its power of enactment should not extend to incorporated towns or cities.

Incidentally, the function of collection of taxes is not logically a part of the duties of the sheriff, and in very few counties is properly discharged by him. This function should be discharged through other agents determined by the county board.

COUNTY MANAGER

Provision should be made for the optional appointment by the county board of commissioners of a county manager who would be solely responsible to the board. If this plan is followed, the county manager should have the full power of appointment and removal of officers herein suggested for the county board of commissioners. The board should be left free to choose its manager from beyond the limits of the county if it should so desire, and should have as to the county manager the right of removal whenever in its judgment that right should be exercised. It is believed that there are many advantages in the employment of a county manager, but it is at the same time felt that for the present such employment should be optional with the county board.

PLAN IN DETAIL

Since several officers of the county in many instances have duties relating to the same or similar matters, it is felt that such officers may with profit be considered as constituting departments of the government. At present there is no meeting of such officers for interchange of ideas or information. Conferences held every six months or oftener, as desired, between all officials constituting a department, may reasonably be expected to improve the public service. The chairman of the county board of commissioners should be ex-officio the head of each department. The practical application of this idea is illustrated below:

The Department of Finance would consist of:

The auditor, who would perform his present duties;

The township or district boards of assessors, appointed by the auditors;

The county board of equalization composed of the chairmen of the local boards of assessors;

The treasurer, whose duties would consist of the collection of taxes, the custody and disbursement of county funds; and

The delinquent tax collector.

The Department of Justice would consist of:

The clerk of court, who would also act as register of mesne conveyance and probate judge;

The magistrates, who should be greatly diminished in numbers and appointed by the judge of the circuit from names suggested by the county board of commissioners;

The master in equity, who would discharge his present functions, or whose office may be consolidated with such other office as the county board of commissioners may determine;

Proposed System of County Government for South Carolina

The county attorney, who would act as legal adviser to the county officers;

The sheriff;

The jailer, rural policemen and deputies, appointed by the sheriff. In the event of the establishment of a state police system there would be no need of county police or deputies; and

The constables, who would be appointed by the magistrates.

The coroner's office should be abolished and its duties imposed on the magistrate resident at the county seat.

The Department of Education would consist of:

The county board of education;

The county superintendent, appointed by the State Board on the recommendation of the county board; and

School district trustees, appointed by the county board of education.

The Department of Health would consist of:

A board of health, composed of three persons named by the county board of commissioners, and acting without compensation in an advisory capacity to the county health unit; and

The county health doctor and nurse or nurses, appointed by the state board of health, subject to the approval of the county board of health.

The Department of Highways and Public Works would consist of:

The supervisor, who would have general supervision over roads and public buildings and other property;

The foreman of the chaingang and superintendent of the poorhouse and farm, appointed by the supervisor; and

The county engineer, where his services are needed.

The maintenance of county road forces is necessary until such time as all public roads are embraced within the state highway system. On the basis of efficiency and economy of operation, the plan of having all public roads as a part of the state highway system is worthy of serious legislative consideration.

A great number of serious objections exist to the maintenance of chaingangs, and their early discontinuance by sending all prisoners to the state penitentiary, it is hoped, may be accomplished. Similarly, jails, except for the incarceration of those awaiting trial, have no economic justification. Due to overhead expense district poor homes or farms jointly maintained by several counties would be preferable to the present system.

The Department of Agriculture would consist of:

Three persons, named by the county board of commissioners, who would act without compensation in an advisory capacity to the farm and home demonstration forces of the county; and

The farm and home demonstration agents to be appointed by the extension department of Clemson College, and Winthrop College, respectively.

The board of agriculture would be charged with the duty of initiating means by which the agricultural interests of the county, including forestry, may be fostered.

The Department of Public Welfare would consist of:

Three persons, named by the county board of commissioners, and serving without compensation, who would exercise investigatory and advisory functions as to administration of the penal and charitable institutions of the county.

The Department of Audit would consist of:

A competent bookkeeper or auditor, who would also act as clerk to the county board of commissioners and as purchasing agent for the county. In connection with the discharge of the latter function he would, prior to purchase, submit the county's requirements to the state purchasing agent herein contemplated. He would be further required to keep the county board of commissioners constantly advised as to the fiscal affairs of the county and should upon request furnish such information to the grand jury or solicitor.

The compensation of all officials should be fixed by the county board of commissioners of each county. The term of office, subject to the right of removal, should be fixed by a general legislative act, applicable to all counties.

ADVANTAGES OF PLAN

Among advantages flowing from the proposed arrangement would be the following:

(1) It would make authority and responsibility coexistent in the same body.

(2) By reducing the number of offices filled at the polls, it would focus the attention of the people on government rather than on politics.

(3) It would permit the legislative delegation to devote its full time and energy to the solution of matters of state-wide importance.

(4) It would make possible the filling of county offices on the basis of merit rather than on the basis of political acumen.

(5) By the power of removal it would afford the incentive for proper discharge of duties by subordinate officers which comes from knowledge that their conduct is being supervised by those having authority to make substitution if the management of their respective offices is not satisfactory.

(6) It would attract into the public service men who are undeniably competent but who have no flair for politics.

(7) It would afford an opportunity for county planning which is impossible under the present system of divided responsibility.

FEE SYSTEM

All officers and employees of the county should be paid fixed and definite salaries. The fee system which prevails in a large number of counties results in great disparity of compensation for the performance of identical duties. It causes the officers and employees of the county to feel that their first duty is to those who pay the largest fees to their offices rather than to the county as a whole. It results in the neglect of performance of duties paying no fees or smaller fees in the interest of performing promptly those duties which result in payment of larger fees. A county officer should feel that he is the servant of all the people of the county rather than of those merely who make use of his office, and that all of the duties of his office are equally entitled to prompt and faithful discharge.

STATE POLICE SYSTEM

Though it is beyond the scope of this report, the committee takes occasion to point out that the enforcement of law is a matter of state-wide rather than local concern. Criminals violate not the law of the county but the law of the state. Hence the law enforcement officers, apart from those of municipalities, should function as parts of a coördinated state system. The committee feels that a state police system is essential to the efficient enforcement of law in South Carolina. The experience of other states abundantly justifies this conclusion.

THE COUNTY'S FINANCES

The system of county finances involves the return and assessment of property for taxation, the determination of the tax rate, the collection of taxes, the custody and disbursement of public funds, and the issue and retirement of the county's notes and bonds.

The officials directly or indirectly involved in the exercise of fiscal functions are the county auditor, the county treasurer, the township or district boards of assessors, the county board of equalization, the delinquent tax collector or sheriff, the sinking fund commission and the county board of commissioners. Their functions are well understood.

RESULTS OF SYSTEM

That the system is by no means a perfect one is indicated by the facts that there is great disparity in the assessed valuation of property between districts and between counties; that the amount of delinquent tax executions steadily grows; that larger numbers of executions are returned nulla bona; that the operating deficits of counties have steadily grown; that sinking funds have been applied to other purposes than those for which they were created; that thousands of dollars have been lost to the taxpayers through defalcations; and that other thousands have been lost through deposit in banks without requiring security for the protection of public funds.

Of course, as every student of the question has pointed out, so long as both the state and county impose taxes on tangible property, equity in assessment for taxation may not be expected. While it is beyond the scope of this report, it may be reëmphasized that a proper fiscal system for the state as a whole contemplates the withdrawal of the State from taxation of tangible property, leaving to each county the determination of values and the rate of tax to be imposed on such property. Under such an arrangement no county will be concerned with or affected by the assessments or levies of any other county, except as throwing light on the adequacy and equity of its own assessments and levies. Until that plan is adopted, however, any system having to do with the fiscal affairs of the county must be predicated on the dual interest of the state and county in the county's discharge of fiscal functions.

Indeed, in this field, recent events have demonstrated that the necessity is for more rather than less supervision on the part of state agencies. This fact makes it practically impossible to delimit this report to purely county fiscal affairs.

County Bond Issues

At present there is no limit in issue of bonds aside from that of the relationship of the issues to assessed valuations as stated in the constitution. There are a great many other factors worthy of consideration aside from the ratio of issues to taxable wealth, viz: whether or not the issue is for a permanent improvement; if so, the reasonably expected length of service of the improvement; the capacity of the population to retire the issue without the infliction of an onerous tax rate; whether or not the issue is for a legitimate county purpose; the term, rate of interest and method of retirement.

The answer to these and similar questions requires the possession of more than ordinary technical information. It requires the close study of those having access to the experiences of communities similarly situated. It is likely that but few counties in South Carolina now have within the public service those capable of reaching intelligent decisions as to all of these matters.

The benefit of such judgment should be afforded by the state through some established agency qualified to act. It is, therefore, suggested that the question of issue of all county bonds should first be submitted to the State Tax Commission for approval or disapproval by it, and that its decision should be final. The commission should have the power to give its approval conditioned on modification by it of any of the details of the proposed issue. It should act only after public hearing open to opponents and proponents of the proposed issue.

It is further recommended that all county bonds should be of the serial type. A great deal of the embarrassment now felt by certain counties in meeting their issues arises from the mishandling of sinking funds. The serial type of bond has the advantage of eliminating the sinking fund and with it, the sinking fund commission. It has the further definite advantage of charging each county with notice that it is required to make provision each year for the payment of interest and retirement of bonds as they mature.

COUNTY NOTES

What is said as to approval or rejection by the State Tax Commission of proposed issues of bonds is equally applicable to proposed issues of county notes. When the county board of commissioners proposes to issue county notes to meet current expenses or for other purposes the details of the proposed issue should be submitted to the State Tax Commission which should have the same right of approval, rejection or modification as herein suggested as to proposed bond issues. It is, of course, understood that, as to both bonds and notes, the approval by the State Tax Commission in no sense guarantees the issue on the part of the state or imposes any liability for payment on the state.

COUNTY PURCHASES

At present all purchases by counties are made individually and usually from local sources. This has resulted in depriving the counties of the benefits derivable from collective purchasing. It has further resulted in a great deal of political favoritism in making of purchases. It is recommended that the state should authorize the State Tax Commission, or a state purchasing commission, should one be established, to designate a purchasing agent for all of the counties, and that each county should submit its staple requirements to such agent. All purchases should be made through him in the absence of ability to secure an equally favorable or better price from other sources.

OFFICIAL AND DEPOSITORY BONDS

The bonds of all county officers charged with collection, custody or disbursement of funds should be fixed at adequate amounts, and should be approved as to form and sufficiency by the county board of commissioners and the state treasurer. All such bonds should be written by surety companies approved by the insurance commissioner of South Carolina.

All deposits of public funds in banks should be secured by proper bonds or collateral to be passed upon by the county board of commissioners and by the state treasurer. If at any time the deposit exceeds the amount of depository bond or collateral, the bank should be required to furnish additional security to cover the excess, or the excess withdrawn and deposited in such bank as will furnish security for the amount.

The county board of commissioners should require the county treasurer to furnish it with full information as to tax executions issued by him; and should require monthly reports from the delinquent tax collector showing the exact status of all such executions.

REPORTS TO BOARD

Each county board of commissioners should have as its clerk a skilled bookkeeper or auditor charged with the duty of making to the board monthly reports as to the financial status of each officer of the county having responsibility for handling county funds in any manner.

FISCAL YEAR

Since school financing is so large a part of the entire question of fiscal management, and since school terms usually end in May or June, the fiscal year should end on July 1. This should be done not only for the sake of the schools but of all the other departments.

CONSOLIDATION OF COUNTIES

The division of the state into counties was effected at a time when means of communication were undeveloped and travel from one point to another was accomplished with difficulty. Hence, the areas of local government were small. During the past few years, due to the advent of the automobile and a better system of roads, travel has been greatly facilitated. The reason for the division of the state into a large number of small governmental units no longer exists. No new counties should be created.

A material economy in the expense of local government could be effected by reducing the number of units. It is believed that a consolidation of several of the smaller and financially weaker counties could be effected with a reduction of overhead expense. When it is realized that thirty per cent of the expenditures of the average county goes to the payment of salaries, the merits of any plan looking toward elimination of salaries through consolidation of units will be immediately appreciated.

Authorities agree that the overhead expense in any county having an assessed valuation of less than $10,000,000 constitutes an excessive burden. Thirty-six South Carolina counties are in that classification, and of that number nineteen have assessed valuations of less than $5,000,000.

The situation is such in South Carolina as to justify the appointment of an official non-partisan board to examine in detail the question of consolidation and to make recommendations to the general assembly based on its findings.

CONSTITUTIONAL CONVENTION

It is the sense of this committee that the reorganization herein contemplated and recommended should be submitted to the General Assembly for immediate enactment into law so far as may be within the province of the General Assembly. Wherever constitutional amendments are necessary, steps should be taken to submit them to the electorate.

The necessity for reorganization of state and county government is so imperative and many provisions of the state constitution are so archaic that a convention for the formulation of a new constitution should be held.

INDEX

Accountant, county, appointment proposed, 197; duties of, 197-198, 199
Addendum, 217-235
Additional recommendations, 206-208
Administration of justice, 151-164
Administrators, appointment of, 154
Agricultural agent, see farm demonstration agent
Agriculture, county department of proposed, 229
Agriculture, United States department of, report of Bureau of Public Roads, 133
Aiken county, corporate surety bonds required of county depositories, 115; health unit of, 166-167; purchasing agent of, 126; road administration of, 138-139; road working organization of, 136; school budget of, 121; supply bill of, 40
Anderson county, supply bill of, 40; hospital of, 167
Annual settlement, see tax settlement
Appeals, from magistrate's courts and other inferior courts, 156; from the county court, 156; from mayor's decision to town council, 157; from decision of town council to court of general sessions, 157; from civil and criminal court of Charleston, 159; from the city court of Charleston, 159
Appointment, see particular official
Appropriations, see county budgets
Assessment of property, 93-105; assessment machinery, 93; compensation of local assessment officials, 93-94; tax listing and assessing, 94-96; methods and standards of valuation, 96-99; additional assessments, 104-105
Assessors, see boards of assessors
Attendance officer, 205-206
Attorney, county, 52
Attorney general, state, duties of relative to county affairs, 88

Auditor, county, appointment of, 37, 52; duties of, 53-54; proposed appointment of, 224; proposed duties of, 224; official bond of, 94
Audits, county, 129-130

Ballot, short, 190
Barnwell county, supply bill of, 40
Beard, Charles A., 219
Beaufort county, supply bill of, 40
Berkeley county, created in 1682, 5; supply bill of, 41
Boards of assessors, township and district, 55; appointment of, 37, 55; composition of, 55-56; duties of, 56-57; proposed appointment of, 226
Board of county commissioners, creation of, 21; selection of, 21, 46-47; composition of, 46; general law provides for, 37, 46; powers of, 21, 46-50; annual reports of 46; road powers of, 133, 134; proposed composition of, 195, 225; proposed duties of, 195, 225
Board of education, see county board of education
Board of equalization, see county board of equalization
Boards of health, creation of, 72; proposed appointment of, 204
Board of public welfare, proposed appointment of, 205
Board of registration, appointment of, 37, 71; duties of, 72
Bonds, county, 122; purposes of, 123; limits of, 122; proposed limits of, 232; proposed types of, 232. See also official bonds
Bookkeeping, county, 126-129; forms of prescribed by comptroller general, 127
Borrowing, county, practices of, 123
Boundaries, county, 77, 78
Branson, E. C., 81, 177, 178
Budgets, county, 120-122; school, 121-122

County government organization, 33-76

County government, proposed reorganization of, 185-208, 226-230; proposed statutory provisions affecting, 197; proposed divisions of, 197, 226-229; proposed constitutional changes affecting, 194

County-group homes, proposed provision for, 197

County-group hospitals, proposed provision for, 197

County-group jails, proposed provision for, 197

County health conservation and development officials, 72-73

County health boards and appointments, number of, 72; composition of, 72-73

County highway engineers, number of, 51; compensation of, 137; work of, 135, 137, 138; proposed appointment of, 201; proposed duties of, 201, 202

County hospitals, number of, 167; appropriations for, 167

County jails, number of, 168; condition of, 168; allowances for dieting prisoners of, 168; management of, 168, 169; proposed supervision of, 205

County judges, qualifications of, 71; election of, 71; appointment of, 155

County legislative delegations, composition of, 34; powers of, 34-46, 119, 133, 134, 172

County librarian, proposed selection of, 203; proposed duties of, 203

County library, proposed establishment of, 203

County manager, necessity for, 195, 196; proposed provisions for, 195, 225, 226

County notes, proposed control over issue of, 233

County officials, appointment of, 37, 38; six groups of, 73-75

County physicians, number of, 167; duties of, 52, 167, 168; compensation of, 167; proposed abolition of, 204

County poorhomes and farms, number of, 170; management of, 171

County purchasing, 124-126

County purchasing agent, proposed selection of, 197, 233

County school commissioner, election of, 22

County self government, benefits of, 220, 221

County solicitor, appointment of, 71

County superintendent of schools, election of, 61; qualifications of, 61; duties of, 61-62; proposed appointment of, 202, 224, 228

County supervisor, selection of, 37; number of, 38; general law provides for, 46; powers of, 47-50; the work of, 138, 139, 171

County tax supervisor, see tax supervisor

County supply bills, preparation of, 40

County treasurer, see treasurer

Court and law enforcement officials, 65-71

Court of common pleas, establishment of, 9

Court of general sessions, establishment of, 9

Court of probate, see probate court

Court, salaries and costs pertaining to, 163

Courts for the trial of slaves, the establishment of, 10

Courts in colonial period, establishment of, 9; administrative duties of, 11

Craven county, created in 1682, 5

Criminal jurisdiction, of court of general sessions, 160; of magistrates' courts, 67, 71; of county courts, 71, 155, 156; of municipal courts, 156, 157, 158, 159

Darlington county, rural police of, 39; purchasing policy of, 126; road working organization of, 135; road administration of, 137, 138; health unit of, 165

Debt, limitations of, 26, 122

Deeds, recording of, 66, 160

Delinquent tax collector, originally the sheriff, 58; appointment of, 59;

www.ingramcontent.com/pod-product-compliance
Lightning Source LLC
Chambersburg PA
CBHW021813270326
41932CB00007B/163